Workers Unite!

Workers Unite!

The International 150 Years Later

Edited by
Marcello Musto

Bloomsbury Academic
An imprint of Bloomsbury Publishing Inc

B L O O M S B U R Y
NEW YORK • LONDON • NEW DELHI • SYDNEY

Bloomsbury Academic
An imprint of Bloomsbury Publishing Inc

1385 Broadway	50 Bedford Square
New York	London
NY 10018	WC1B 3DP
USA	UK

www.bloomsbury.com

BLOOMSBURY and the Diana logo are trademarks of Bloomsbury Publishing Plc

First published 2014

© Marcello Musto, 2014

All rights reserved. No part of this publication may be reproduced or transmitted in any form or by any means, electronic or mechanical, including photocopying, recording, or any information storage or retrieval system, without prior permission in writing from the publishers.

No responsibility for loss caused to any individual or organization acting on or refraining from action as a result of the material in this publication can be accepted by Bloomsbury or the author.

Library of Congress Cataloging-in-Publication Data
Workers Unite!: The International 150 Years Later/edited by Marcello Musto.
pages cm
Includes bibliographical references and index.
ISBN 978-1-62892-244-8 (hardback) – ISBN 978-1-62892-243-1 (paperback)
1. International Workingmen's Association (1864-1877)
2. Labor movement–History–19th century. 3. Labor unions–History–19th century.
4. Communism–History–19th century. I. Musto, Marcello.

HX11.I5W67 2014
331.88'6–dc23

2014018650

ISBN: HB: 978-1-6289-2244-8
PB: 978-1-6289-2243-1
ePDF: 978-1-6289-2245-5
ePub: 978-1-6289-2246-2

Typeset by Deanta Global Publishing Services, Chennai, India

To my mother Lucia, who one May Day, when I was just a child, first showed me the workers and their red flags.

Contents

Preface *Marcello Musto* — xiii

Introduction *Marcello Musto* — 1

The International Working Men's Association: Addresses,
Resolutions, Interventions, Documents — 69

Part 1   The Inaugural Address

1   Karl Marx, *Inaugural Address of the International
    Working Men's Association* — 73

Part 2   The Political Program

2   Karl Marx, *[Resolutions of the Geneva Congress (1866)]* — 83
3   Various Authors, *[Resolutions of the Brussels Congress (1868)]* — 89

Part 3   Labour

4   Karl Marx, *[Inquiry on the Situation of the Working Classes]* — 97
5   François Dupleix – Ferdinand Quinet – Jean Marly – Adrien Schettel – Jean Henri de Beaumont, *[On Machinery and its Effects]* — 99
6   P. Eslens – Eugène Hins – Paul Robin, *[On Woman's Emancipation and Independence]* — 101
7   Karl Marx, *[The Influence of Machinery in the Hands of Capitalists]* — 103
8   Eugène Steens, *[The Effect of Machinery on the Situation of Workers]* — 105
9   Pierre Fluse, *[The Effect of Machinery on the Wages and Situation of Workers]* — 110

10	Eugène Tartaret, [For the Reduction of Working Hours]	113
11	V. Tinayre, [On Working Women's Equality and the Inclusion of Different Political Opinions]	116

Part 4 Trade Union and Strike

12	Karl Marx, [The Necessity and Limits of Trade Union Struggle]	119
13	Karl Marx, [Against Strike Breaking]	122
14	Various Authors, [Interference in Trades' Disputes]	124
15	César De Paepe, [Strikes, Unions, and the Affiliation of Unions with the International]	126
16	Karl Marx, The Belgian Massacre	130
17	Jean Louis Pindy, [Resolution on Resistance Funds]	132
18	Eugène Hins, [Resistance Societies as the Organization of the Future]	135
19	Robert Applegarth, [On the Resistance Societies]	136
20	Adhémar Schwitzguébel, [On Resistance Funds]	138
21	Alfred Herman, [Promoting Solidarity for Strikers]	141
22	Johann Philipp Becker, [International Trade Union Organization]	143

Part 5 Cooperative Movement and Credit

23	César De Paepe, [Credit and the Emancipation of the Working Class]	147
24	Ludwig Buechner – César De Paepe – André Murat – Louis Müller – R. L. Garbe, [On the Cooperative Movement]	148
25	Johann Georg Eccarius – Henri Louis Tolain, [Fourth Estate and Modern Production]	152
26	Various Authors, [The Question of Mutual Credit Among Workers]	153
27	Aimé Grinand, [Cooperative and Workers' Emancipation]	154
28	Eugène Hins, [Cooperative Associations as a Model of the Future Society]	156

Part 6 On Inheritance

29	Karl Marx, *[On Inheritance]*	159
30	Mikhail Bakunin, *[On Abolition of Inheritance]*	161
31	Karl Marx, *[On the Right of Inheritance]*	163

Part 7 Collective Ownership and the State

32	Jean Vasseur, *[Definition and Role of the State]*	169
33	César De Paepe, *[On the Collectivization of the Land]*	170
34	Karl Marx, *[On Landed Property]*	175
35	Mikhail Bakunin, *[On the Question of Landed Property]*	176
36	César De Paepe, *[On the Reorganization of Landed Property]*	178
37	Emile Aubry, *[On Workers Capacity to Administer Society]*	180
38	Karl Marx – Friedrich Engels – Paul Lafargue, *[Critique of Bakunin's Politics]*	182
39	César de Paepe, *[On the Organization of Public Services in the Society of Future]*	187
40	James Guillaume, *[On the Abolition of the State]*	192
41	César de Paepe, *[On the People's State (Volksstaat)]*	194
42	Various Authors, *[On Collective Ownership]*	199

Part 8 Education

43	The Bookbinders of Paris, *[On Free Education]*	203
44	Karl Marx, *[On Education in Modern Society]*	206
45	César De Paepe, *[On State Education]*	208

Part 9 The Commune of Paris

46	Karl Marx, *[On the Paris Commune]*	211

Part 10 Internationalism and Opposition to War

47	Various Authors, *[International Solidarity]*	227

48	Eugene Dupont – Johann Georg Eccarius – Peter Fox – Hermann Jung – Karl Marx, *[On the Necessity of an International Organization]*	228
49	César de Paepe, *[On the True Causes of War]*	229
50	César De Paepe, *[Strike Against War]*	230
51	Louis Henri Tolain, *[Against War]*	232
52	Hafner, *[The Real Causes of the War]*	233
53	Karl Marx, *[England, Metropolis of Capital]*	235
54	Karl Marx, *[First Address on the Franco-Prussian War]*	236
55	Karl Marx, *[Second Address on the Franco-Prussian War]*	240
56	Karl Marx, *[The Novelty of the International]*	242
57	Karl Marx, *[On the Importance of Having the International]*	244

Part 11   The Irish Question

58	Eugene Dupont, *[On the Fenian Question]*	247
59	Karl Marx, *[Ireland and the English Working Class]*	249
60	Friedrich Engels, *[Relations Between the Irish Sections and the British Federal Council]*	251

Part 12   Concerning the United States

61	Karl Marx, *To Abraham Lincoln, President of the United States of America*	255
62	Karl Marx, *Address from the International Working Men's Association to President Johnson*	257
63	Karl Marx, *Address to the National Labour Union of the United States*	259
64	Johann Georg Eccarius, *[Eliminating Nationalism from the Minds of Working Men]*	261

Part 13   Political Organization

65	Friedrich Engels – Karl Marx, *General Rules of the International Working Men's Association*	265

66	Johann Georg Eccarius – Karl Kaub – George Odger – George Wheeler – William Worley, *To the Working Men of Great Britain and Ireland*	269
67	Charles Perron – Pioley – Reymond – Vézinaud – Sameul Treboux, *[On the Deprivation of Political Liberties]*	271
68	Karl Marx, *[Against Secret Societies]*	273
69	Friedrich Engels, *[On the Importance of Political Struggle]*	274
70	Édouard Vaillant, *[On Working Class Politics]*	276
71	Karl Marx, *[On the Political Action of the Working Class]*	278
72	Karl Marx, *[On the Question of Abstentionism]*	280
73	Friedrich Engels, *[Apropos of Working-Class Political Action]*	281
74	Karl Marx – Friedrich Engels, *[On the Political Action of the Working Class and Other Matters]*	283
75	Karl Marx, Friedrich Engels, *[Against Sectarianism]*	287
76	James Guillaume, *[Anarchist politics]*	290
77	Paris Section, *[On the Importance of Having a Central Organization of the Working Class]*	291
78	Mikhail Bakunin – James Guillaume, *[The Destruction of Political Power]*	293
79	Friedrich Adolph Sorge, *[The Struggle With Bourgeois Society]*	296
80	Friedrich Adolph Sorge – Carl Speyer, *[Passing on the Torch]*	298

Appendix: Eugène Pottier, *The Internationale*	300
Bibliography	303
Index	308

The working class is either revolutionary or it is nothing.
Karl Marx to Johann Baptist von Schweitzer,
13 February 1865

The emancipation of the working classes must be conquered by the working classes themselves.
Karl Marx, General Rules of the
International Working Men's Association

Proletarians of all countries, unite!
Karl Marx, Inaugural Address of the
International Working Men's Association

Preface

The bequest of the International Working Men's Association may be divided into two categories: (1) the minutes and documents of the General Council in London and (2) the records of congresses of the organization and interventions made at its various gatherings. Of all this material, never translated into any language in its entirety, approximately 7,000 pages have been published in the various original editions.

In English, the first of the above collections of texts appeared in Moscow, edited by the Institute of Marxism-Leninism in the Soviet Union and under the imprint of Progress Publishers, in five volumes entitled *The General Council of the First International*, to mark the hundredth anniversary of the foundation of the International. The first volume (1963 – issued in 8,500 copies) comprises texts from the 1864–66 period; the second (1964 – 8,700 copies) texts from the years 1866–68; the third (1966 – 8,000 copies) texts from 1868 to 1870; the fourth (1967 – 3,500 copies) texts from 1870 to 1871; and the fifth (1968 – 4,000 copies) texts from 1871 to 1872. They were published after the Russian edition (1961–65), from which they reproduced explanatory notes and indexes, and were reprinted between 1973 and 1974, in editions of about 3,000 copies each.

These books, each roughly 500 pages in length, are not easy to read and are mainly intended for the use of scholars and specialists. More popular, and with a larger diffusion, is the volume of Marx's writings entitled *The First International and After*, first published in London by Penguin/New Left Review in 1974 (currently available by Verso). Being an anthology of texts by a single author, however, it tended to reinforce the impression that a highly complex collective history could be captured in the texts written by Marx alone. Moreover, the selection lacked important documents such as the resolutions of the Brussels Congress of 1868, one of the most significant events in the life of the organization.

As to the documents of the congresses of the International, they have never appeared in English. They have been published in French, in Switzerland, in two different publications of the Graduate Institute of International Studies, under the direction of Jacques Freymond. The first, *La première Internationale* (Geneva: Droz, 1962), appeared in two volumes (the first relating to the 1866–68 period, the second to 1869–72), edited by Henri Burgelin, Knut Langfeldt and Miklós Molnár. The second, with the same title but edited by Bert Andréas and Miklós Molnár, was also published in two volumes: *Les conflits au sein de l'Internationale, 1872–1873* and *Les congrès et les conférences de l'Internationale, 1873–1877* (Geneva: Institut Universitaire de Hautes Études Internationales, 1971). Both of these key works were naturally very bulky (1,000 pages for the 1962 collection, more than 1,500 pages for the one published in 1971), and so, as with the Moscow edition on the General Council – or even more so, given the rather poor knowledge of French in English-speaking countries – their reception was limited mainly to experts in the field. Furthermore, since Soviet orthodoxy operated with a false schema of perfect congruity between the life of the Association and the biography of Marx, it paid no special attention to congresses in which he did not participate in person – Geneva 1866, Lausanne 1867, Brussels 1868 and Basel 1869 – and refused to consider any after 1872 (the year in which he withdrew) as part of the history of the organization.

The only congress of the International translated into English was the one held in The Hague. Its proceedings were published in 1958 in Madison by the University of Wisconsin, in a volume edited by Hans Gerth with the title *The First International: Minutes of the Hague Congress of 1872*. Nearly 20 years later, the Institute of Marxism-Leninism published with Progress in Moscow a new and more complete edition of this last great gathering: *The Hague Congress of the First International*. The first volume, *Minutes and Documents*, appeared in 1976; the second, *Reports and Letters*, in 1978. Finally, a set of further materials covering the activity of the new General Council in New York was included in the *Annali dell'Istituto Giangiacomo Feltrinelli* (fourth volume of 1961, printed the following year), under the editorship of Samuel Bernstein and with the title *Papers of the General Council of the International Workingmen's Association. New York (1872–1876)*. These books helped to fill a number of gaps, but they were intended mainly for scholars of Marxism and left-wing political militants, who in those days were legions and knowledgeably debated such issues.

The present anthology is seeing the light of day in a very different context. Whereas the publications around the time of the centenary of the International appeared in the period of the greatest struggle against the capitalist system, the hundred and fiftieth anniversary of its foundation takes place in the midst of a deep crisis. The world of labour has suffered an epochal defeat. The barbarism against which it fought and won important victories has returned to become the reality of our times. Moreover, it is sunk in profound ideological subordination to the dominant system. The task today, then, is to build again on the ruins, and direct familiarity with the original theorizations of the workers' movement may help significantly to reverse the trend. Such is the first motivation for this book. Offering to a new and inexperienced generation, in the clear and accessible form of an anthology, the beginnings of the long path taken by those who sought to 'storm the heavens' and not to obtain mere palliatives to the existing reality, so that the legacy of the International may live again in the critique of the present day.

The choice of texts in this volume has a precise aim: to show the economic and political shape of future society that members of the International were seeking to achieve (see especially the sections: 'Political Programme', 'Cooperative Movement and Credit', 'The Right to Inheritance', 'State and Collective Ownership' and 'The Paris Commune'). It therefore seemed essential to include all the writings that outlined the alternative to the capitalist system, including reformist measures to be obtained *hic et nunc* (see especially 'Inaugural Address', 'Labour', 'Trade Unions and the Strike' and 'Education'). Other significant elements in the volume are texts analysing major issues of international politics (in 'Internationalism and Opposition to War', 'The Irish Question', and 'Concerning the United States'), as well as the fundamental – and perennial – discussion on political forms (in 'Political Organization'). Without denying Marx's indispensable contribution – he is the author or co-author of 30 of the 80 documents – the elaboration of all these themes was a collective process, as we can see here from the writings of more than 30 internationalists, many of them ordinary workers. The emphasis on debates about the shape of socialist society made it seem appropriate to omit documents concerning the origins and development of the various federations, which are mainly of historical interest, and as far as possible those regarding the conflict between communists and anarchists, which has been the object of many exhaustive studies.

It should also be pointed out that the selection covers only 'official' texts of the International (the only exception is document 56, in so far as it reproduces what may be seen as a kind of closing speech at the London Conference of 1871). For this reason, the anthology omits journalistic articles, extracts from published works, letters and participant reconstructions in later years of the life of the International. Many texts of this kind are easy enough to obtain, and they could have distracted the reader's attention from the debates that actually took place at the sessions of the General Council and the various congresses of the International. Rather, the conscious editorial preference, based on available editions of the texts of the International, has been to highlight salient points of the political-theoretical debate. The volume accordingly reproduces for the first time in English – 33 of the 80 were unpublished in that language – previously inaccessible materials, including the reports of working commissions (documents 5, 6, 10, 14, 24, 25 and 27), various documents of local sections (documents 8, 9, 20, 33, 36 and 43), two short interventions by Bakunin (documents 30 and 36) and the important resolutions of the Saint-Imier Congress (document 78).

The chosen texts are organized chronologically within themes. Each document is accompanied with a brief introductory note that identifies: its date of composition and/or publication (or delivery in the case of speeches); its context; key information about its author; and details of where the text in question was first published and/or the edition of the collection of International documents in which it appears in full. A number of abbreviations have been used to keep the notes to a manageable length. Thus, GC stands for *The General Council of the First International*; PI for *La première Internationale* and HAGUE for *The Hague Congress of the First International* – in each case followed by a Roman numeral for the volume and an ordinary numeral for the page from which the document is extracted. The letters IWMA and CG stand respectively for the International Working Men's Association and its General Council. Finally, L1867 replaces *Procès-verbaux du congrès de l'Association Internationale des Travailleurs réuni à Lausanne du 2 au 8 septembre 1867* (La

Chaux-de-Fonds: Voix de l'Avenir, 1867); B1868 is short for *Troisième congrès de l'Association Internationale des Travailleurs. Compte rendu officiel* (supplement to the paper *Le Peuple Belge*, 6–30 September 1868); B1869 for *Association Internationale des Travailleurs: Compte rendu du IVe Congrès international, tenu à Bâle, en septembre 1869* (Brussels: Désirée Brismée, 1869) and B1876 for *Association Internationale des Travailleurs. Compte rendu officiel du VIIIe Congrès général tenu à Berne du 26 au 30 octobre 1876* (Berne: Lang, 1876).

The titles of the texts different from the original, and provided by the editor, appear between square brackets, in each case with a mention of the official title in the introductory note. The symbol '[...]' has been used to indicate extracts from texts that are not reproduced in their entirety. Occasionally, editorial additions not present in the original version also appear between square brackets.

The volume ends with an appendix containing the text of the famous anthem *The Internationale*, first composed in French by Eugène Pottier to mark the Paris Commune, and a bibliography of the main publications on the International.

The writings of the International from French were translated by George Comninel (documents 76 and 78), Paul Sharkey/Christine Henderson (document 39), Victor Wallis (documents 6 and 10), Christine Henderson (documents 5, 8, 43, 45, 49, 50, 67, 70 and 79) and Patrick Camiller (documents 9, 15, 17, 18, 19, 20, 22, 23, 24, 25, 27, 28, 30, 32, 33, 35, 36, 40, 41, 42, 51 and 52), who also has, with his usual comradely commitment, translated the Preface and the Introduction from Italian. Babak Amini and Carlo Fanelli provided kind assistance during the preparatory editorial work. Finally, very special thanks are due to George (Wikipedia) Comninel for his help with the revision of the entire volume.

Marcello Musto,
Toronto, 21 March 2014

Introduction

Marcello Musto

I Opening steps

On 28 September 1864, St Martin's Hall in the very heart of London was packed to overflowing with some 2,000 workmen. They had come to attend a meeting called by English trade union leaders and a small group of workers from the Continent: the advance notices had spoken of a 'deputation organized by the workmen of Paris', which would 'deliver their reply to the Address of their English brethren, and submit a plan for a better understanding between the peoples'.[1] In fact, when a number of French and English workers' organizations had met in London a year earlier, in July 1863, to express solidarity with the Polish people against Tsarist occupation, they had also declared what they saw as the key objectives for the working-class movement. The preparatory *Address of English to French Workmen*, drafted by the prominent union leader George Odger (1813–77) and published in the bi-weekly *The Bee-Hive*, stated:

> A fraternity of peoples is highly necessary for the cause of labour, for we find that whenever we attempt to better our social condition by reducing the hours of toil, or by raising the price of labour, our employers threaten us with bringing over Frenchmen, Germans, Belgians and others to do our work at a reduced rate of wages; and we are sorry to say that this has been done, though not from any desire on the part of our continental brethren to injure us, but through a want of regular and systematic communication between the industrial classes of all countries. Our aim is to bring up the

---

[1] David Ryazanov, 'Zur Geschichte der Ersten Internationale.' *Marx-Engels Archiv* I (1925): 171.

wages of the ill-paid to as near a level as possible with that of those who are better remunerated, and not to allow our employers to play us off one against the other, and so drag us down to the lowest possible condition, suitable to their avaricious bargaining.²

The organizers of this initiative did not imagine – nor could they have foreseen – what it would lead to shortly afterwards. Their idea was to build an international forum where the main problems affecting workers could be examined and discussed, but this did not include the actual founding of an organization to coordinate the trade union and political action of the working class. Similarly, their ideology was initially permeated with general ethical-humanitarian elements, such as the importance of fraternity among peoples and world peace, rather than class conflict and clearly defined political objectives. Because of these limitations, the meeting at St Martin's Hall might have been just another of those vaguely democratic initiatives of the period with no real follow-through. But in reality it gave birth to the prototype of all organizations of the workers' movement, which both reformists and revolutionaries would subsequently take as their point of reference: the International Working Men's Association.³

It was soon arousing passions all over Europe. It made class solidarity a shared ideal and inspired large numbers of men and women to struggle for the most radical of goals: changing the world. Thus, on the occasion of the Third Congress of the International, held in Brussels in 1868, the leader writer of *The Times* accurately identified the scope of the project:

> It is not ... a mere improvement that is contemplated, but nothing less than a regeneration, and that not of one nation only, but of mankind. This is certainly the most extensive aim ever contemplated by any institution, with the exception, perhaps, of the Christian Church. To be brief, this is the programme of the International Workingmen's Association.⁴

---

² Ibid., p. 172.
³ Near the end of the life of the International when considering for approval the revised Statute of the organization, members of the GC raised the question of whether 'persons' should be substituted for 'men'. Friedrich Engels (1820–95) responded that 'it was generally understood that men was a generic term including both sexes', making the point that the association was and had been open to women and men, GC, V, p. 256.
⁴ Quoted in G. M. Stekloff, *History of the First International*. New York: Russell & Russell, 1968 [1928], p. ii.

Thanks to the International, the workers' movement was able to gain a clearer understanding of the mechanisms of the capitalist mode of production, to become more aware of its own strength, and to develop new and more advanced forms of struggle. The organization resonated far beyond the frontiers of Europe, generating hope that a different world was possible among the artisans of Buenos Aires, the early workers' associations in Calcutta, and even the labour groups in Australia and New Zealand that applied to join it.

Conversely, news of its founding inspired horror in the ruling classes. The idea that the workers too wanted to play an active role in history sent shivers down their spine, and many a government set its sights on eradicating the International and harried it with all the means at its disposal.

II The right man in the right place

The workers' organizations that founded the International were something of a motley. The central driving force was British trade unionism, whose leaders – nearly all reformist in their worldview – were mainly interested in economic questions; they fought to improve the workers' conditions, but without calling capitalism into question. Hence they conceived of the International as an instrument that might favour their objectives, by preventing the import of manpower from abroad in the event of strikes.

Another significant force in the organization was the mutualists, long dominant in France but strong also in Belgium and French-speaking Switzerland. In keeping with the theories of Pierre-Joseph Proudhon (1809–65), they were opposed to any working-class involvement in politics and to the strike as a weapon of struggle, as well as holding conservative positions on women's emancipation. Advocating a cooperative system along federalist lines, they maintained that it was possible to change capitalism by means of equal access to credit. In the end, therefore, they may be said to have constituted the right wing of the International.

Alongside these two components, which formed the numerical majority, there were others of a different hue again. The third in importance were the communists, grouped around the figure of Karl Marx (1818–83) and active in small circles with very limited influence – above all in a number of German and Swiss cities, and in London. They were anticapitalist: that is, they opposed the existing system of production and espoused the necessity of political action to overthrow it.

At the time of its founding, the ranks of the International also included elements that had nothing to do with the socialist tradition, such as certain groups of East European exiles inspired by vaguely democratic ideas. Among these were followers of Giuseppe Mazzini (1805–72), whose cross-class conception, mainly geared to national demands, considered the International useful for the issuing of general appeals for the liberation of oppressed peoples.[5]

The picture is further complicated by the fact that some groups of French, Belgian and Swiss workers who joined the International brought with them a variety of confused theories, some of a utopian inspiration; while the General Association of German Workers – the party led by followers of Ferdinand Lassalle (1825–64), which never affiliated to the International but orbited around it – was hostile to trade unionism and conceived of political action in rigidly national terms.

All these groups, with their complex web of cultures and political/trade union experiences, made their mark on the nascent International. It was an arduous task indeed to build a general framework and to keep such a broad organization together, if only on a federal basis. Besides, even after a common programme had been agreed upon, each tendency continued to exert a (sometimes centrifugal) influence in the local sections where it was in the majority.

To secure peaceful coexistence of all these currents in the same organization, around a programme so distant from the approaches with which each had started out, was Marx's great accomplishment. His political talents enabled

---

[5] There were even members of secret societies favouring republicanism and/or socialism, such as the Lodge of Philadelphia, among the early members. See Boris Nicolaevsky, *Secret Societies and the First International*, in Milorad Drachkovitch (ed.), *The Revolutionary Internationals, 1864-1943*. Stanford: Stanford University Press, 1966, pp. 36–56; Julian P. W. Archer, *The First International in France, 1864-1872*. Lanham, MD: University Press of America, 1997, pp. 33–5.

him to reconcile the seemingly irreconcilable, ensuring that the International did not swiftly follow the many previous workers' associations down the path to oblivion.[6] It was Marx who gave a clear purpose to the International, and Marx too who achieved a non-exclusionary, yet firmly class-based, political programme that won it a mass character beyond all sectarianism. The political soul of its General Council was always Marx: he drafted all its main resolutions and prepared all its congress reports (except the one for the Lausanne Congress in 1867, when he was totally occupied with the proofs for *Capital*). He was 'the right man in the right place',[7] as the German workers' leader Johann Georg Eccarius (1818–89) once put it.

Contrary to later fantasies that pictured Marx as the founder of the International, he was not even among the organizers of the meeting at St Martin's Hall. He sat 'in a non-speaking capacity on the platform',[8] he recalled in a letter to his friend Engels. Yet he immediately grasped the potential in the event and worked hard to ensure that the new organization successfully carried out its mission. Thanks to the prestige attaching to his name, at least in restricted circles, he was appointed to the 34-member standing committee,[9] where he soon gained sufficient trust to be given the task of writing the *Inaugural Address* and the *Provisional Statutes of the International*. In these fundamental texts, as in many others that followed, Marx drew on the best ideas of the various components of the International, while at the same time eliminating corporate inclinations and sectarian tones. He firmly linked economic and political struggle to each other, and made international thinking and international action an irreversible choice.[10]

It was mainly thanks to Marx's capacities that the International developed its function of political synthesis, unifying the various national contexts in

---

[6] Cf. Henry Collins and Chimen Abramsky, *Karl Marx and the British Labour Movement*. London: MacMillan, 1965, p. 34.
[7] Johann Georg Eccarius to Karl Marx, 12 October 1864, in *Marx-Engels-Gesamtausgabe*, vol. III/13. Berlin: Akademie, 2002, p. 11.
[8] Karl Marx to Friedrich Engels, 4 November 1864, in Karl Marx and Friedrich Engels, *Collected Works*, 50 vol., 1975–2005. Moscow: Progress Publishers [henceforth MECW], vol. 42, 1987, p. 16.
[9] At the founding meeting of the International, a Standing Committee was struck to organize the association. This became its Central Council, which subsequently became known as the General Council. Henceforth, these committees are identified simply as the General Council.
[10] See Gian Mario Bravo, *Marx e la Prima Internazionale*. Bari: Laterza, 1979, pp. 18–19.

a project of common struggle that recognized their significant autonomy, but not total independence, from the directive centre. The maintenance of unity was gruelling at times,[11] especially as Marx's anticapitalism was never the dominant political position within the organization. Over time, however, partly through his own tenacity, partly through occasional splits, Marx's thought became the hegemonic doctrine.[12] It was hard going, but the effort of political elaboration benefited considerably from the struggles of those years. The character of workers' mobilizations, the antisystemic challenge of the Paris Commune, the unprecedented task of holding together such a large and complex organization, the successive polemics with other tendencies in the workers' movement on various theoretical and political issues: all these impelled Marx to go beyond the limits of political economy alone, which had absorbed so much of his attention since the defeat of the 1848 revolution and the ebbing of the most progressive forces. He was also stimulated to develop and sometimes revise his ideas, to put old certainties up for discussion and ask himself new questions, and in particular to sharpen his critique of capitalism by drawing the broad outlines of a communist society. The orthodox Soviet view of Marx's role in the International, according to which he mechanically applied to the stage of history a political theory he had already forged in the confines of his study, is thus totally divorced from reality.[13]

III Membership and structure

During its lifetime and in subsequent decades, the International was depicted as a vast, financially powerful organization. The size of its membership was always overestimated, whether because of imperfect knowledge or because

---

[11] See Karl Marx to Friedrich Bolte, 23 November 1871, in MECW, vol. 44, p. 252, where he explained: 'the history of the International was a continual struggle on the part of the General Council against the sects and amateur experiments which attempted to assert themselves within the International itself against the genuine movement of the working class. This struggle was conducted at the Congresses, but far more in the private dealings of the General Council with the individual sections'.
[12] See Bravo, op. cit., p. 165.
[13] Cf. Maximilien Rubel, *Marx critique du marxisme*. Paris: Payot, 1974, p. 41: 'only the needs of mythology – if not mystification – could prompt them to see in this [political program] the consequence of "Marxism", that is, a fully realized doctrine, imposed from outside by an omniscient brain on an amorphous and inert mass of men in search of a social panacea'.

some of its leaders exaggerated the real situation or because opponents were looking for a pretext to justify a brutal crackdown. The public prosecutor who arraigned some of its French leaders in June 1870 stated that the organization had more than 800,000 members in Europe[14]; a year later, after the defeat of the Paris Commune, *The Times* put the total at 2½ million; and Oscar Testut (1840–unk.), the main person to study it in the conservative camp, predicted this would rise above 5 million.[15]

In reality, the membership figures were much lower. It has always been difficult to arrive at even approximate estimates, and that was true for its own leaders and those who studied it most closely.[16] But the present state of research allows the hypothesis that, at its peak in 1871–72, the tally reached more than 150,000: 50,000 in Britain, more than 30,000 in both France and Belgium, 6,000 in Switzerland, about 30,000 in Spain, about 25,000 in Italy, more than 10,000 in Germany (but mostly members of the Social Democratic Workers' Party), plus a few thousand each in a number of other European countries and 4,000 in the United States.[17]

In those times, when there was a dearth of effective working-class organizations apart from the English trade unions and the General Association of German Workers, such figures were certainly sizeable. It should also be borne in mind that, throughout its existence, the International was recognized as a legal organization only in Britain, Switzerland, Belgium and the United States. In other countries where it had a solid presence (France, Spain, Italy), it was on the margins of legality for a number of years, and its members were subjected to persecution. To join the International meant breaking the law in the 39 states of the German Confederation, and the few members in the Austro-Hungarian Empire were forced to operate in clandestine forms. However, the Association had a remarkable capacity to weld its components into a cohesive whole. Within a couple of years from its birth, it had succeeded in federating hundreds of workers' societies; from the end of 1868, thanks to propaganda

---

[14] See Oscar Testut, *L'Association internationale des travailleurs*. Lyon: Aime Vingtrinier, 1870, p. 310.
[15] *The Times*, 5 June 1871; Oscar Testut, *Le livre blue de l'Internationale*. Paris: Lachaud, 1871.
[16] On this issue, Marx declared at a meeting of the General Council on 20 December 1870: 'respecting the list of members, it would be not well to publish what the real strength was, as the outside public always thought the active members much more numerous than they really were', in GC, IV, p. 96.
[17] For more information, see the table on International membership in the Appendix.

conducted by followers of Mikhail Bakunin (1814–76), other societies were added in Spain, and after the Paris Commune sections sprang up also in Italy, Holland, Denmark and Portugal. The development of the International was doubtless uneven: while it was growing in some countries, elsewhere it was remaining level or falling back under the blows of repression. Yet a strong sense of belonging prevailed among those who joined the International for even a short time. When the cycle of struggles in which they had taken part came to an end, and adversity and personal hardship forced them to take a distance, they retained the bonds of class solidarity and responded as best they could to the call for a rally, the words of a poster or the unfurling of the red flag of struggle, in the name of an organization that had sustained them in their hour of need.[18]

Members of the International, however, comprised only a small part of the total workforce. In Paris they never numbered more than 10,000, and in other capital cities such as Rome, Vienna or Berlin they were rare birds indeed. Another aspect is the character of the workers who joined the International: it was supposed to be the organization of wage-labourers, but very few actually became members; the main influx came from construction workers in England, textile workers in Belgium and various types of artisans in France and Switzerland.

In Britain, with the sole exception of steelworkers, the International always had a sparse presence among the industrial proletariat.[19] Nowhere did the latter ever form a majority, at least after the expansion of the organization in Southern Europe. The other great limitation was the failure to draw in unskilled labour,[20] despite efforts in that direction beginning with the run-up to the first congress. The *Instructions for Delegates of the Provisional General Council. The Different Questions* are clear on this:

> Apart from their original purposes, they [trade unions] must now learn to act deliberately as organizing centres of the working class in the broad interest of its *complete emancipation*. They must aid every social and political

---

[18] See Julius Braunthal, *History of the International*. New York: Nelson, 1966 [1961], p. 116.
[19] See Collins and Abramsky, op. cit., p. 70; Jacques D'Hondt, 'Rapport de synthèse', in Colloque International sur La première Internationale, *La Première Internationale: l'institute, l'implantation, le rayonnement*. Paris: Éditions du Centre national de la recherche scientifique, 1968, p. 475.
[20] See Collins – Abramsky, op. cit., p. 289.

movement tending in that direction. Considering themselves and acting as the champions and representatives of the whole working class, they cannot fail to enlist the non-society men into their ranks. They must look carefully after the interests of the worst paid trades, such as the agricultural labourers, rendered powerless by exceptional circumstances. They must convince the world at large that their efforts, far from being narrow and selfish, aim at the emancipation of the downtrodden millions.[21]

In Britain too, however, unskilled workers did not stream into the International, the one exception being the diggers. The great majority of members there came from tailoring, clothing, shoemaking and cabinet-making – that is, from sectors of the working class that were then the best organized and the most class-conscious. In the end, the International remained an organization of employed workers; the jobless never became part of it. The provenance of its leaders reflected this, since all but a few had a background as artisans or brainworkers.

The resources of the International are similarly complicated. There was talk of fabulous wealth at its disposal,[22] but the truth is that its finances were chronically unstable. The membership fee for individuals was one shilling, while trade unions were supposed to contribute three pence for each of their members. In many countries, however, individual subscriptions were few and far between, and in Britain the contributions from trade unions were so unreliable and so often scaled down that the General Council had to face facts and leave them free to pay what they could. The sums collected were never higher than a few score pounds per annum,[23] barely enough to pay the general secretary's wage of four shillings a week and the rent for an office from which the organization was often threatened with eviction for arrears.

---

[21] From document 2, p. 87.
[22] In his diary, *Tägebuchblätter aus dem Jahre 1867 bis 1869*, Liepzig: von Hirzel, 1901, vol. VIII, p. 406, General Friedrich von Bernhardi reported 'from reliable sources' that a fund of more than £ 5,000,000 was deposited in London for the use of the International. See Braunthal, op. cit., p. 107.
[23] See Braunthal, op. cit., p. 108, who affirms that no complete statement of the General Council's annual income has been found among its papers. But a report by the treasurer, Cowell Stepney, has been found covering the income of the General Council from individual members' subscriptions for the first six years. The figures were: 1865 – £23; 1866 – £9 13s.; 1867 – £5 17s.; 1868 – £14 14s.; 1869 – £ 30 12s.; 1870 – 14£ 14s. The last financial report submitted by Engels to the Hague Congress for the year 1870–72 showed a deficit of more than £25 owed by the General Council to members of the General Council and others. Copies of some balance sheets of the International have been also published in Collins and Abramsky, op. cit., pp. 80–1.

In one of the key political-organizational documents of the International, Marx summarized its functions as follows: 'It is the business of the International Working Men's Association to combine and generalize the spontaneous movements of the working classes, but not to dictate or impose any doctrinary system whatever'.[24]

Despite the considerable autonomy granted to federations and local sections, the International always retained a locus of political leadership. Its General Council was the body that worked out a unifying synthesis of the various tendencies and issued guidelines for the organization as a whole. From October 1864 until August 1872 it met with great regularity, as many as 385 times. In the room filled with pipe and cigar smoke where the General Council held its sessions on Tuesday evening, its members debated a wide range of issues, such as: working conditions, the effects of new machinery, support for strikes, the role and importance of trade unions, the Irish question, various foreign policy matters, and, of course, how to build the society of the future. The General Council was also responsible for drafting the documents of the International: circulars, letters and resolutions for current purposes; special manifestos, addresses and appeals in particular circumstances.[25]

IV The formation of the International

The lack of synchrony between the key organizational junctures and the main political events in the life of the International makes it difficult to reconstruct its history in chronological sequence. In terms of organization, the principal stages were: (1) the birth of the International (1864–66), from its foundation to the First Congress (Geneva 1866); (2) the period of expansion (1866–70); (3) the revolutionary surge and the repression following the Paris Commune (1871–72); and (4) the split and crisis (1872–77). In terms of its theoretical

---

[24] From document 2, p. 85. See Karl Marx to Paul Lafargue, 19 April 1870, in MECW, vol. 43, p. 491: 'the General Council was not the Pope, that we allowed every section to have its own theoretical views of the real movement, always supposed that nothing directly opposite to our Rules was put forward.'

[25] See Georges Haupt, *L'Internazionale socialista dalla Comune a Lenin*. Torino: Einaudi, 1978, p. 78.

development, however, the principal stages were: (1) the initial debate among its various components and the laying of its own foundations (1864–65); (2) the struggle for hegemony between collectivists and mutualists (1866–69); and (3) the clash between centralists and autonomists (1870–77). The following paragraphs will cover both the organizational and theoretical aspects.

Britain was the first country where applications were made to join the International; the 4,000-member Operative Society of Bricklayers affiliated in February 1865, soon to be followed by associations of construction workers and shoemakers. In the first year of its existence, the General Council began serious activity to publicize the principles of the Association. This helped to broaden its horizon beyond purely economic questions, as we can see from the fact that it was among the organizations belonging to the (electoral) Reform League founded in February 1865.

In France, the International began to take shape in January 1865, when its first section was founded in Paris. Other major centres appeared shortly afterwards in Lyons and Caen. But it remained very limited in strength, unable to increase its base in the French capital, and during this period many other workers' organizations exceeded it in size; the Association had little ideological influence, and the relationship of forces as well as its own lack of political resolve made it impossible even to establish a national federation. Nevertheless, the French supporters of the International, who were mostly followers of Proudhon's mutualist theories, established themselves as the second largest group at the first conference of the organization, held in London between 25 and 29 September and attended by 30 delegates from England, France, Switzerland and Belgium, with a few representatives from Germany, Poland and Italy. Each of these provided information about the first steps taken by the International, especially at an organizational level. This conference decided to call the first general congress for the following year and laid down the main themes to be discussed there.

In the period between these two gatherings, the International continued to expand in Europe and established its first important nuclei in Belgium and French-speaking Switzerland. The Prussian Combination Laws, which prevented German political associations from having regular contacts with organizations in other countries, meant that the International was unable to open sections in what was then the German Confederation. The 5,000-members General Association of German Workers – the first workers' party in history, founded in 1863 and led by Lassalle's disciple Johann Baptist von Schweitzer (1833–75) – followed a line of ambivalent dialogue with Otto von Bismarck (1815–98) and showed little or no interest in the International during the early years of its existence; it was an indifference shared by Wilhelm Liebknecht (1826–90), despite his political proximity to Marx. Johann Philipp Becker (1809–86), one of the main leaders of the International in Switzerland, tried to find a way round these difficulties through the Geneva-based 'Group of German-speaking Sections', and for a long time he was the sole organizer of the early internationalist nuclei in the German Confederation.

These advances were greatly favoured by the diffusion of newspapers that either sympathized with the ideas of the International or were veritable organs of the General Council. Both categories contributed to the development of class consciousness and the rapid circulation of news concerning the activity of the International. Of those that appeared in the first few years of its existence, special mention should be made of the weekly *The Bee-Hive* and *The Miner and Workman's Advocate* (later *The Workman's Advocate* and then *The Commonwealth*), both published in London; the French-language weekly *Le Courrier International*, also published in London; *La Tribune du Peuple*, the official organ of the International in Belgium from August 1865; the *Journal de l'Association Internationale des Travailleurs*, the organ of the section in French-speaking Switzerland; *Le Courrier Français*, a Proudhonian weekly published in Paris; and Becker's *Der Vorbote* in Geneva.[26]

The activity of the General Council in London was decisive for the further strengthening of the International. In spring 1866, with its support for the strikers of the London Amalgamated Tailors, it played an active role for the first time in a workers' struggle, and following the success of the strike five societies of tailors, each numbering some 500 workers, decided to affiliate to the International. The positive outcome of other disputes attracted a number

---

[26] For a more complete appreciation of the many periodicals of the International or sympathetic see Giuseppe Del Bo (ed.), *Répertoire international des sources pour l'étude des mouvement sociaux aux XIXe et Xxe siècles. La Première Internationale*, vol. I: *Periodiqués 1864–1877*. Paris: Armand Colin, 1958.

of small unions, so that, by the time of its first congress, it already had 17 union affiliations with a total of more than 25,000 new members. The International was the first association to succeed in the far from simple task of enlisting trade union organizations into its ranks.[27]

Between 3 and 8 September 1866, the city of Geneva hosted the first congress of the International, with 60 delegates from Britain, France, Germany and Switzerland. By then the Association could point to a very favourable balance-sheet of the 2 years since its foundation, having rallied to its banner more than 100 trade unions and political organizations. Those taking part in the congress essentially divided into two blocs. The first, consisting of the British delegates, the few Germans and a majority of the Swiss, followed the directives of the General Council drawn up by Marx (who was not present in Geneva). The second, comprising the French delegates and some of the French-speaking Swiss, was made up of mutualists. At that time, in fact, moderate positions were prevalent in the International, and the mutualists, led by the Parisian Henri Tolain (1828–97), envisaged a society in which the worker would be at once producer, capitalist and consumer. They regarded the granting of free credit as a decisive measure for the transformation of society; considered women's labour to be objectionable from both an ethical and a social point of view; and opposed any interference by the state in work relations (including legislation to reduce the working day to 8 hours) on the grounds that it would threaten the private relationship between workers and employers and strengthen the system currently in force.

Basing themselves on resolutions prepared by Marx, the General Council leaders succeeded in marginalizing the numerically strong contingent of mutualists at the congress, and obtained votes in favour of state intervention. On the latter issue, in the section of the *Instructions for Delegates of the Provisional General Council* relating to 'Juvenile and children's labour (both sexes)', Marx had spelled things out clearly:

> This can only be effected by converting *social reason* into *social force*, and, under given circumstances, there exists no other method of doing so, than through *general laws*, enforced by the power of the state. In enforcing such laws, the working class do not fortify governmental power. On the contrary,

---

[27] Collins and Abramsky, op. cit., p. 65.

they transform that power, now used against them, into their own agency. They effect by a general act what they would vainly attempt by a multitude of isolated individual efforts.[28]

Thus, far from strengthening bourgeois society (as Proudhon and his followers wrongly believed), these reformist demands were an indispensable starting point for the emancipation of the working class.

Furthermore, the 'instructions' that Marx wrote for the Geneva congress underline the basic function of trade unions against which not only the mutualists but also certain followers of Robert Owen (1771–1858) in Britain and of Lassalle in Germany[29] had taken a stand:

> This activity of the Trades' Unions is not only legitimate, it is necessary. It cannot be dispensed with so long as the present system of production lasts. On the contrary, it must be generalized by the formation and the combination of Trades' Unions throughout all countries. On the other hand, unconsciously to themselves, the Trades' Unions were forming *centres of organization* of the working class, as the mediaeval municipalities and communes did for the middle class. If the Trades' Unions are required for the guerrilla fights between capital and labour, they are still more important as *organized agencies for superseding the very system of wages labour and capital rule*.

In the same document, Marx did not spare the existing unions his criticism. For they were

> too exclusively bent upon the local and immediate struggles with capital [and had] not yet fully understood their power of acting against the system of wage slavery itself. They therefore kept too much aloof from general social and political movements.[30]

He had argued exactly the same a year earlier, in an address to the General Council on 20 and 27 June, which was posthumously published as *Value, Price and Profit*:

---

[28] From document 2, p. 84.
[29] Ferdinad Lassalle advocated the concept of an 'iron law of wages', which held that efforts to increase wages were futile and a distraction for workers from the primary task of assuming political power in the State.
[30] From document 2, p. 86.

[T]he working class ought not to exaggerate to themselves the ultimate working of these everyday struggles. They ought not to forget that they are fighting with effects, but not with the causes of those effects; that they are retarding the downward movement, but not changing its direction; that they are applying palliatives, not curing the malady. They ought, therefore, not to be exclusively absorbed in these unavoidable guerrilla fights incessantly springing up from the never-ceasing encroachments of capital or changes of the market. They ought to understand that, with all the miseries it imposes upon them, the present system simultaneously engenders the material conditions and the social forms necessary for an economical reconstruction of society. Instead of the conservative motto, 'A fair day's wage for a fair day's work!' they ought to inscribe on their banner the revolutionary watchword, 'Abolition of the wages system!'[31]

V Growing strength

From late 1866 on, strikes intensified in many European countries. Organized by broad masses of workers, they helped to generate an awareness of their condition and formed the core of a new and important wave of struggles.

Although some governments of the time blamed the International for the unrest, most of the workers in question did not even know of its existence; the root cause of their protests was the dire working and living conditions they were forced to endure. The mobilizations did, however, usher in a period of contact and coordination with the International, which supported them with declarations and calls for solidarity, organized fund-raising for strikers, and helped to fight attempts by the bosses to weaken the workers' resistance.

It was because of its practical role in this period that workers began to recognize the International as an organization that defended their interests and, in some cases, asked to be affiliated to it.[32] The first major struggle to

---

[31] See document 12, p. 121. On the other hand, the need to differentiate between political and trade-union organization was always clear to Marx. In September 1869, he said in an interview with the German trade unionist Johann Hamann, published in the *Volksstaat*, n. 17 of the 27 November 1869: 'the trade unions should never be affiliated with or made dependent upon a political society if they are to fulfil the object for which they were formed. If this happens it means their death blow. The trade unions are the schools for Socialism.'

[32] See Jacques Freymond, 'Introduction', in PI, I, p. XI.

be won with its support was the Parisian bronze workers' strike of February–March 1867. Also successful in their outcome were the ironworkers' strike of February 1867 at Marchienne, the long dispute in the Provençal mineral basin between April 1867 and February 1868, and the Charleroi miners' strike and Geneva building workers' strike of spring 1868. The scenario was the same in each of these events: workers in other countries raised funds in support of the strikers and agreed not to accept work that would have turned them into industrial mercenaries, so that the bosses were forced to compromise on many of the strikers' demands. In the towns at the centre of the action, hundreds of new members were recruited to the International. As later observed in a report of the General Council: 'It is not the International Working Men's Association that pushes people into strikes, but strikes that push workers into the arms of the International Working Men's Association'.[33]

Thus, for all the difficulties bound up with the diversity of nationalities, languages and political cultures, the International managed to achieve unity and coordination across a wide range of organizations and spontaneous struggles. Its greatest merit was to demonstrate the absolute need for class solidarity and international cooperation, moving decisively beyond the partial character of the initial objectives and strategies.

From 1867 on, strengthened by success in achieving these goals, by increased membership and by a more efficient organization, the International made advances all over Continental Europe. It was its breakthrough year in France in particular, where the bronze workers' strike had the same knock-on effect that the London tailors' strike had produced in England. The number of members neared 1,000 in Paris and passed the 500 mark in Lyons and Vienne. Seven new sections were established, including one in Algiers on the southern shores of the Mediterranean (which, however, consisted only of French workers). Belgium too saw a rise in affiliations following the strikes, and as did Switzerland, where workers' leagues, cooperatives and political societies enthusiastically applied to join. The International now had 25 sections in Geneva alone, including the German-speaking one that served as a base for propaganda among the workers of the German Confederation.

---

[33] Various Authors, 'Report of the [French] General Council', 1 September 1869, in PI, II, p. 24.

But Britain was still the country where the International had its greatest presence. In the course of 1867, the affiliation of another dozen organizations took the membership to a good 50,000 – an impressive figure, if we bear in mind that it was reached in just 2 years, and that the total unionized workforce was then roughly 800,000.[34] Nowhere else did the membership of the International ever reach that level (in absolute terms, if not as a proportion of the population). In contrast to the progression of the 1864–67 period, however, the subsequent years in Britain were marked by a kind of stagnation. There were several reasons for this, but the main one was that, as we have seen, the International did not manage to break through into factory industry or the world of unskilled labour. The only exception in the latter was the United Excavators, which affiliated after the strike of August 1866, while the Malleable Ironworkers were among the rare few that signed up from the great factories of the North and the Midlands. The voice of the International did not reach either the coal and cotton industry or the engineering workers (who, because of their technical skills, never felt threatened by foreign competition). Those who joined the International in the greatest numbers were the construction workers. The 9,000-strong Amalgamated Society of Carpenters and Joiners, whose secretary Robert Applegarth (1834–1924) sat on the General Council, represented a fifth of the total membership; they were followed by the tailors, cobblers, cabinetmakers, binders, ribbon weavers, web weavers, saddlers and cigar makers – all trades unaltered by the Industrial Revolution. In January 1867, the London Trades Council decided to cooperate with the International but voted against affiliation; the episode brought it home to the General Council that it was unable to expand beyond its existing sphere of influence.

The growing institutionalization of the labour movement further contributed to this slowdown in the life of the International. The Reform Act, resulting from the battle first joined by the Reform League, expanded the franchise to more than a million British workers. The subsequent legalization of trade unions, which ended the risk of persecution and repression, allowed the Fourth Estate to become a real presence in society, with the result that the pragmatic rulers

---

[34] See Henri Collins, 'The International and the British Labour Movement: Origin of the International in England', in Colloque International sur La première Internationale, op. cit., p. 34.

of the country continued along the path of reform, and the labouring classes, so unlike their French counterparts, felt a growing sense of belonging as they pinned more of their hopes for the future on peaceful change.[35] The situation on the Continent was very different indeed. In the German Confederation, collective wage-bargaining was still virtually non-existent. In Belgium, strikes were repressed by the government almost as if they were acts of war, while in Switzerland they were still an anomaly that the established order found it difficult to tolerate. In France, it was declared that strikes would be legal in 1864, but the first labour unions still operated under severe restrictions.

This was the backdrop to the congress of 1867, where the International assembled with a new strength that had come from continuing broad-based expansion. Some bourgeois newspapers, including *The Times*, sent correspondents to follow its proceedings between 2 and 8 September. Again it was a Swiss city, Lausanne, which hosted the occasion, receiving 64 delegates[36] from six countries (with one each from Belgium and Italy). Marx was busy working on the proofs of *Capital* and absent from the General Council when preparatory documents were drafted, as well as from the congress itself.[37] The effects were certainly felt, as is evident in the congress's focus on bald reports of organizational growth in various countries and Proudhonian themes (such as the cooperative movement and alternative uses of credit) dear to the strongly represented mutualists.

Also discussed there was the question of war and militarism, at the request of the League for Peace and Freedom, whose inaugural congress was due to be held immediately afterwards. In the course of the debate, the delegate from Brussels, César de Paepe (1841–90), one of the most active and brilliant theoreticians of the International, formulated what later became the classical position of the workers' movement: that wars are inevitable in a capitalist system:

> If I had to express my sentiments to the Geneva [Peace] Congress, I would say: we want peace as much as you do, but we know that so long as there

---

[35] See Collins and Abramsky, op. cit., pp. 290–1.
[36] Although the rules called for one delegate for each 500 members, actual representation depended upon the ability of delegates to attend.
[37] Marx in fact continued not to attend Congresses, with the exception of the crucial The Hague Congress (1872).

exists what we call the principle of nationalities or patriotism, there will be war; so long as there are distinct classes, there will be war. War is not only the product of a monarch's ambition [...] the true cause of war is the interests of some capitalists; war is the result of the lack of equilibrium in the economic world, and the lack of equilibrium in the political world.[38]

Finally, there was a discussion of women's emancipation,[39] and the congress voted in favour of a report stating that 'the efforts of nations should aim at state ownership of the means of transport and circulation'.[40] This was the first collectivist declaration approved at a congress of the International. However, the mutualists remained totally opposed to the socialization of land ownership, and a deeper discussion of the issue was postponed until the next congress.

VI Defeat of the mutualists

Right from the earliest days of the International, Proudhon's ideas were hegemonic in France, French-speaking Switzerland, Wallonia and the city of Brussels. His disciples, particularly Tolain and Ernest Édouard Fribourg (unk.), succeeded in making a mark with their positions on the founding meeting in 1864, the London Conference of 1865, and the Geneva and Lausanne Congresses.

For 4 years the mutualists were the most moderate wing of the International. The British trade unions, which constituted the majority, did not share Marx's anticapitalism, but nor did they have the same pull on the policies of the organization that the followers of Proudhon were able to exercise.

Basing themselves on the theories of the French anarchist, the mutualists argued that the economic emancipation of the workers would be achieved through the founding of producer cooperatives and a central People's Bank. Resolutely hostile to state intervention in any field, they opposed socialization

---

[38] From document 49, p. 229. The position of De Paepe became later the standard view on war of the working class movement.
[39] See document 6, pp. 101–2.
[40] From document 32, p. 169.

of the land and the means of production as well as any use of the strike as a weapon. In 1868, for example, there were still many sections of the International that attached a negative, anti-economic value to this method of struggle. The *Report of the Liège Section on Strikes* was emblematic in this regard: 'The strike is a struggle. It therefore increases the bubbling of hatred between the people and the bourgeoisie, separating ever further two classes that should merge and unite with each other'.[41] The distance from the positions and theses of the General Council could scarcely have been greater.

Marx undoubtedly played a key role in the long struggle to reduce Proudhon's influence in the International. His ideas were fundamental to the theoretical development of its leaders, and he showed a remarkable capacity to assert them by winning every major conflict inside the organization. With regard to the cooperation, for example, in the 1866 *Instructions for the Delegates of the Provisional General Council. The Different Questions*, he had already declared that:

> To convert social production into one large and harmonious system of free and cooperative labour, *general social changes* are wanted, *changes of the general conditions of society*, never to be realized save by the transfer of the organized forces of society, viz., the state power, from capitalists and landlords to the producers themselves.
>
> Recommending to the workers "to embark in cooperative production rather than in cooperative stores. The latter touch but the surface of the present economical system, the former attacks its groundwork."[42]

The workers themselves, however, were already sidelining Proudhonian doctrines; it was above all the proliferation of strikes that convinced the mutualists of the error of their conceptions. Proletarian struggles showed both that the strike was necessary as an immediate means of improving conditions in the present and that it strengthened the class-consciousness essential for the construction of future society. It was real-life men and women who halted capitalist production to demand their rights and social justice, thereby shifting the balance of forces in the International and, more significantly, in society as

---

[41] Cassian Maréchal, 'Report of the Liège Section', PI, I, p. 268.
[42] From document 3, p. 85.

a whole. It was the Parisian bronze workers, the weavers of Rouen and Lyons, the coalminers of Saint-Étienne who – more forcefully than in any theoretical discussion – convinced the French leaders of the International of the need to socialize the land and industry. And it was the workers' movement that demonstrated, in opposition to Proudhon, that it was impossible to separate the social-economic question from the political question.[43]

The Brussels Congress, held between 6 and 13 September 1868 with the participation of ninety-nine delegates from France, Britain, Switzerland, Germany, Spain (1 delegate) and Belgium (fifty-five),[44] finally clipped the wings of the mutualists. The highpoint came when the assembly approved De Paepe's proposal on the socialization of the means of production – a decisive step forward in defining the economic basis of socialism, no longer simply in the writings of particular intellectuals but in the programme of a great transnational organization. As regards the mines and transport, the congress declared:

a. That the quarries, collieries, and other mines, as well as the railways, ought in a normal state of society to belong to the community represented by the state, a state itself subject to the laws of justice.
b. That the quarries, collieries, and other mines, and Railways, be let by the state, not to companies of capitalists as at present, but to companies of working men bound by contract to guarantee to society the rational and scientific working of the railways, etc., at a price as nearly as possible approximate to the working expense. The same contract ought to reserve to the state the right to verify the accounts of the companies, so as to present the possibility of any reconstitution of monopolies. A second contract ought to guarantee the mutual right of each member of the companies in respect to his fellow workmen.

As to landed property, it was agreed that:

that the economical development of modern society will create the social necessity of converting arable land into the common property of society, and of letting the soil on behalf of the state to agricultural companies under conditions analagous to those stated in regard to mines and railways.

---

[43] See Freymond, 'Introduction', in PI, I, p. XIV.
[44] Eugène Dupont (1831–81) represented a section from Naples, and the congress also saw the participation of Louis Auguste Blanqui (1805–81), as an observer.

And similar considerations were applied to the canals, roads and telegraphs:

> Considering that the roads and other means of communication require a common social direction, the Congress thinks they ought to remain the common property of society.

Finally, some interesting points were made about the environment:

> Considering that the abandonment of forests to private individuals causes the destruction of woods necessary for the conservation of springs, and, as a matter of course, of the good qualities of the soil, as well as the health and lives of the population, the Congress thinks that the forests ought to remain the property of society.[45]

In Brussels, then, the International made its first clear pronouncement on the socialization of the means of production by state authorities.[46] This marked an important victory for the General Council and the first appearance of socialist principles in the political programme of a major workers' organization.

In addition, the congress again discussed the question of war. A motion presented by Becker, which Marx later summarized in the published resolutions of the congress, stated:

> The workers alone have an evident logical interest in finally abolishing all war, both economic and political, individual and national, because in the end they always have to pay with their blood and their labour for the settling of accounts between the belligerents, regardless of whether they are on the winning or losing side.[47]

The workers were called upon to treat every war 'as a civil war'.[48] De Paepe also suggested the use of the general strike[49] – a proposal that Marx dismissed as 'nonsense',[50] but which actually tended to develop a class-consciousness capable of going beyond merely economic struggles.

---

[45] From document 3, pp. 91–2.
[46] This was possible thanks to the change in the Belgian sections, which moved to collectivism after their federal congress of July.
[47] PI, I, pp. 402–3.
[48] Ibid., p. 403.
[49] See document 50.
[50] Karl Marx to Friedrich Engels, 16 September 1868, in MECW, vol. 43, p. 101.

If the collectivist turn of the International began at the Brussels Congress, it was the Basel Congress held the next year from 5 to 12 September that consolidated it and eradicated Proudhonism even in its French homeland. This time there were 78 delegates at the congress, drawn not only from France, Switzerland, Germany, Britain and Belgium, but also, a clear sign of expansion, from Spain, Italy and Austria, plus a representative from the National Labor Union in the United States. The presence of the latter, as well as of Wilhelm Liebknecht (1826–1900) on behalf of one of the first organized working-class political forces (the Social Democratic Workers' Party of Germany, founded in Eisenach a few weeks earlier), helped to make the congress more solemn and to imbue it with hope. The catchment area of the association required to challenge the rule of capital was visibly enlarged, and the record of the proceedings as well as general reports on the activity of the congress transmitted the enthusiasm of the workers gathered there.

The resolutions of the Brussels Congress on landed property were reaffirmed, with 54 votes in favour, 4 against and 13 abstentions. Eleven of the French delegates – including Eugène Varlin (1838–71), later a prominent figure in the Paris Commune – even approved a new text which declared 'that society has the right to abolish individual ownership of the land and to make it part of the community'[51]; ten abstained and four (including Tolain) voted against. After Basel, the International in France was no longer mutualist.

The Basel Congress was also of interest because Mikhail Bakunin took part in the proceedings as a delegate. Having failed to win the leadership of the League for Peace and Freedom, he had founded the International Alliance for Socialist Democracy in September 1868 in Geneva, and in December this had applied to join the International. The General Council initially turned down the request, on the grounds that the International Alliance for Socialist Democracy continued to be affiliated to another parallel transnational structure, and that one of its objectives – 'the equalization of classes'[52] – was

---

[51] PI, II, p. 74.
[52] Mikhail Bakunin, 'Programme of the Alliance [International Alliance of Socialist Democracy]', in Arthur Lehning (ed.), *Michael Bakunin: Selected Writings*. London: Jonathan Cape, 1973, p. 174. The translation provided in this book is inaccurate and misleading. In *Fictitious Splits in the International*, Engels and Marx quoted directly from Bakunin's original document ('l'égalisation politique, économique et sociale des classes'), see document 75, p. 287.

radically different from a central pillar of the International, the abolition of classes. Shortly afterwards, however, the Alliance modified its programme and agreed to wind up its network of sections, many of which anyway existed only in Bakunin's imagination.[53] On 28 July 1869, the 104-member Geneva section was accordingly admitted to the International.[54] Marx knew Bakunin well enough, but he had underestimated the consequences of this step. For the influence of the famous Russian revolutionary rapidly increased in a number of Swiss, Spanish and French sections (as it did in Italian ones after the Paris Commune), and at the Basel Congress, thanks to his charisma and forceful style of argument, he already managed to affect the outcome of its deliberations. The vote on the right of inheritance, for example, was the first occasion on which the delegates rejected a proposal of the General Council.[55] Having finally defeated the mutualists and laid the spectre of Proudhon to rest, Marx now had to confront a much tougher rival, who formed a new tendency – collectivist anarchism – and sought to win control of the organization.

VII Development across Europe and opposition to the Franco-Prussian war

The late 1860s and early 1870s were a period rich in social conflicts. Many workers who took part in protest actions decided to make contact with the International, whose reputation was spreading ever wider, and despite its limited resources the General Council never failed to respond with appeals for solidarity to its European sections and the organization of fund-raising. This was the case in March 1869, for example, when 8,000 silk dyers and ribbon weavers in Basel asked for its support. The General Council could not send them more than £4 from its own funds, but it issued a circular that resulted in the collection of another £300 from a number of workers' groups in various countries. Even more significant was the struggle of Newcastle engineering workers to reduce the working day to 9 hours, when two emissaries of the

---

[53] See Edward Hallett Carr, *Michael Bakunin*. New York: Vintage, 1961 [1937], p. 392.
[54] According to Carr, op. cit, p. 374: 'the wooden horse had entered the Trojan citadel'.
[55] From document 31, p. 163.

General Council, James Cohn [Cohen] (unk.) and Eccarius, played a key role in stymying the bosses' attempt to introduce blackleg labour from the Continent. The success of this strike, a nationwide cause célèbre, served as a warning for the English capitalists, who from that time on gave up recruiting workers from across the Channel.[56]

The year 1869 witnessed significant expansion of the International all over Europe. Britain was an exception in this respect, however. The Trades Union Congress, meeting in Birmingham in August, recommended that all its member organizations should become part of the International. But the appeal fell on deaf ears, and the level of affiliation remained more or less the same as in 1867. While the union leaders fully backed Marx against the mutualists, they had little time for theoretical issues[57] and did not exactly glow with revolutionary ardour. This was the reason why Marx for a long time opposed the founding of a British federation of the International independent of the General Council.

In every European country where the International was reasonably strong, its members gave birth to new organizations completely autonomous from those already in existence, forming local sections and/or national federations as their number warranted. In Britain, however, the unions that made up the main force of the International naturally did not disband their own structures; besides, the London-based General Council fulfilled two functions at once, as world headquarters and as the leadership for Britain. In any case, the trade union affiliations kept some 50,000 workers in its orbit of influence, at a time when the International was making headway all across the Continent.

In France, the repressive policies of the Second Empire made 1868 a year of serious crisis for the International: all its sections disappeared, with the single exception of Rouen. The following year, however, saw a revival of the organization. Tolain ceased to be its figurehead in the aftermath of the Basel Congress, and new leaders such as Varlin, who had abandoned mutualist positions, came to the fore. The peak of expansion for the International came in 1870, but the real membership figures fell far short of the fantasies that some writers concocted and spread among the public. It should also be remembered that, despite its considerable growth, the organization never took root in 38

---

[56] See Braunthal, op. cit., p. 173.
[57] See Freymond, 'Introduction', in PI, I, p. XIX.

of the 90 *départements* that existed at the time in France. It is possible that the membership in Paris rose as high as 10,000, much of it affiliated to the International through cooperative societies, trade associations and resistance societies. Rigorous estimates would point to a figure of 3,000 each in Rouen and Lyons (where an uprising led to the proclamation of a People's Commune in September 1870 that was later drowned in blood) and to a little more than 4,000 in Marseilles. The national total can be estimated as more than 30,000.[58] Thus, although the International did not become a true mass organization in France, it certainly grew to a respectable size and aroused widespread interest, as we may gauge from the membership application that the Positivist Proletarians of Paris submitted to the General Council.[59] From 1870, even some disciples of Blanqui overcame their early reservations about an organization inspired by Proudhonian moderation and, witnessing the enthusiasm for it among workers, began to join it in their turn. Certainly much water had passed under the bridge since 1865, when the French sections of the International founded by Tolain and Fribourg[60] had been little more than glorified "study societies."[61] The guidelines for the organization in France now centred on the promotion of social conflict and political activity.

In Belgium, the period following the Brussels Congress of 1868 had been marked by the rise of syndicalism, a series of victorious strikes, and the affiliation of numerous workers' societies to the International. Membership peaked in the early 1870s at several tens of thousands, probably exceeding the number in the whole of France. It was here that the International achieved

---

[58] See Jacques Rougerie, 'Les sections française de l'Association Internationale des Travailleurs', in Colloque International sur La première Internationale, op. cit., p. 111, who spoke of 'some dozens of thousands'.

[59] See GC, III, p. 218. This request was declined because groups defined by their political tendency as such could not join the International. The decision became an official resolution the following year, at the London Conference of 1871, and it was approved by the delegates: 'the existing organizations of the International Working Men's Association will henceforth, in accordance with the letter and spirit of the general statutes, be obliged to be known and constituted simply and exclusively as branches, sections, etc. of the International Working Men's Association, with names of their respective localities attached; it will be forbidden for existing branches and societies to continue to be designated by the names of sects, that is, as mutualist, positivist, collectivist, or communist groups, etc.', in PI, II, p. 238.

[60] See Jacques Rougerie, 'L'A.I.T. et le mouvement ouvrier a Paris pendant les evenements de 1870–1871'. *International Review of Social History* XVII (1972) n. 1: 11–12. Both men subsequently abandoned the International and its ideas and Toulain was expelled from the organization, see document 25, footnote 23.

[61] Ernest Édouard Fribourg, *L'Association internationale des travailleurs*. Paris, 1871, p. 26.

both its highest numerical density in the general population and its greatest influence in society.

The positive evolution during this period was also apparent in Switzerland. In 1870 the total membership stood at 6,000 (out of a working population of roughly 700,000), including 2,000 in the 34 Geneva sections and another 800 in the Jura region. Not long afterwards, however, Bakunin's activity divided the organization into two groups of equal size. These confronted each other at the congress of the Romande Federation in April 1870, precisely on the question of whether the International Alliance for Socialist Democracy should be admitted to the Federation.[62] When it proved impossible to reconcile their positions, the proceedings continued in two parallel congresses, and a truce was agreed only after an intervention by the General Council. The group aligned with London was slightly smaller, yet retained the name Romande Federation, whereas the one linked to Bakunin had to adopt the name Jura Federation, even though its affiliation to the International was again recognized.

The leading lights in the former were Nikolai Utin (1845–83), who had founded in Geneva the first Russian section of the International,[63] and Johann Philipp Becker, who, despite his collaboration with Bakunin between summer 1868 and February 1870, had managed to prevent the Swiss organization from falling entirely into his hands. Anyway, the consolidation of the Jura Federation represented an important stage in the building of an anarcho-federalist current within the International. Its most prominent figure was the young James Guillaume (1844–1916), who played a key role in the dispute with London.

During this period, Bakunin's ideas began to spread in a number of cities, especially in Southern Europe, but the country where they took hold most rapidly was Spain. In fact, the International first developed in the Iberian peninsula through the activity of the Neapolitan anarchist Giuseppe Fanelli, who, at Bakunin's request, travelled to Barcelona and Madrid between October 1868 and spring 1869 to help found sections of the International and groups of the Alliance for Socialist Democracy (of which he was a member). His trip

---

[62] See Jacques Freymond (ed.), *Études et documents sur la Première Internationale en Suisse*. Genève: Droz, 1964, p. 295.
[63] See Woodford McLellan, *Revolutionary Exiles*. London: Frank Cass, 1979, pp. 83–107.

achieved its purpose. But his distribution of documents of both international organizations, often to the same people, was a prime example of the Bakuninite confusion and theoretical eclecticism of the time; the Spanish workers founded the International with the principles of the Alliance for Socialist Democracy. Still, Fanelli won over important cadres such as Anselmo Lorenzo (1841–1914), who had previously been exposed to Proudhon's texts translated into Spanish by the future Spanish president Francisco Pi y Margall (1824–1901). And adulterated though they were in various ways, the ideas of the International got through to a fledgling workers' movement eager to organize and engage in struggle. At the Basel Congress, the Spanish delegate Rafael Farga Pellicer (1840–90) could already point to the existence of several dozen sections.

In the North German Confederation, despite the existence of two political organizations of the workers' movement – the Lassallean General Association of German Workers and the Marxist Social Democratic Workers' Party of Germany – there was little enthusiasm for the International and few requests to affiliate to it. During its first 3 years, German militants virtually ignored its existence, fearing persecution at the hands of the authorities. But the picture changed somewhat after 1868, as the fame and successes of the International multiplied across Europe. From that point on, both of the rival parties aspired to represent its German wing. In the struggle against the Lassalleans – whose leader, Johann Baptist von Schweitzer (1833–75), never applied to affiliate their General Association – Liebknecht tried to play on the closeness of his organization to Marx's positions, but the affiliation of the Social Democratic Workers' Party of Germany to the International was more formal (or 'purely platonic',[64] as Engels put it) than real, with a minimal material and ideological commitment. Of its 10,000 or so members registered within a year of its foundation, only a few hundred joined the International on an individual basis (a procedure allowed under the Prussian Combination Laws).[65] The weak internationalism of the Germans therefore weighed more heavily than

---

[64] Friedrich Engels to Theodor Cuno, 7–8 May 1872, in MECW, vol. 44, p. 371.
[65] See Roger Morgan, *The German Social Democrats and the First International, 1864–1872*. New York: Cambridge University Press, 1965, p. 180, citing an assertion by Becker in the last issue of the *Verbote* that by the end of 1871 '58 [German-speaking] sections [of the International] had been founded (nearly half of them in Germany, the rest mainly in Switzerland), ten societies had joined in affiliated membership, and 385 individual members had been paying subscriptions'.

any legal aspects, and it declined still further in the second half of 1870 as the movement became more preoccupied with internal matters.[66]

There were two pieces of good news to make up for the German limitations. In May 1869, the first sections of the International were founded in the Netherlands, and they began to grow slowly in Amsterdam and Friesland. Soon afterwards, the International also began to pick up in Italy, where it had previously been present only in a handful of centres that had little or no relation with one another.

More significant still, at least symbolically and for the hopes it awakened, was the new mooring on the other side of the Atlantic, where immigrants who had arrived in recent years began to establish the first sections of the International in the United States. However, the organization suffered from two handicaps at birth that it would never overcome. Despite repeated exhortations from London, it was unable either to cut across the nationalist character of its various affiliated groups or to draw in workers born in the New World. When the German, French and Czech sections founded the Central Committee of the IWA for North America, in December 1870, it was unique in the history of the International in having only 'foreign-born' members. The most striking aspect of this anomaly was that the International in the United States never disposed of an English-language press organ.

Against this general background, marked by evident contradictions and uneven development between countries, the International made provisions for its fifth congress in September 1870. This was originally scheduled to be held in Paris, but repressive operations by the French government made the General Council opt instead for Mainz; Marx probably also thought that the greater number of German delegates close to his positions would help to stem the advance of the Bakuninists. But then the outbreak of the Franco-Prussian war, on 19 July 1870, left no choice but to call off the congress.

The conflict at the heart of Europe meant that the top priority now was to help the workers' movement express an independent position, far from the nationalist rhetoric of the time. In his *First Address on the Franco-Prussian War*, Marx called upon the French workers to drive out Louis Bonaparte (1808–73)

---

[66] Ibid., p. x.

and to obliterate the empire he had established 18 years earlier. The German workers, for their part, were supposed to prevent the defeat of Bonaparte from turning into an attack on the French people:

> [I]n contrast to old society, with its economical miseries and its political delirium, a new society is springing up, whose international rule will be *Peace*, because its national ruler will be everywhere the same – Labour! The pioneer of that new society is the International Working Men's Association.[67]

This text, in 30,000 copies (15,000 for Germany and 15,000 for France, printed in Geneva), was the first major foreign policy declaration of the International. One of the many who spoke enthusiastically in support of it was John Stuart Mill (1806–73): 'there was not one word in it that ought not to be there,' he wrote, and 'it could not have been done with fewer words'.[68]

The leaders of the Social Democratic Workers' Party, Wilhelm Liebknecht and August Bebel (1840–1913), were the only two members of parliament in the North German Confederation who refused to vote for the special war budget,[69] and sections of the International in France also sent messages of friendship and solidarity to the German workers. Yet the French defeat sealed the birth of a new and more potent age of nation-states in Europe, with all its accompanying chauvinism.

VIII The International and Paris Commune

After the German victory at Sedan and the capture of Bonaparte, a Third Republic was proclaimed in France on 4 September 1870. In January of the following year, a 4-month siege of Paris ended in the French acceptance of Bismarck's conditions; an ensuing armistice allowed the holding of elections and the appointment of Adolphe Thiers (1797–1877) as president of the republic, with the support of a huge Legitimist and Orleanist majority. In the capital, however, Progressive-Republican forces swept the board and there was

---

[67] From document 54, p. 239.
[68] John Stuart Mill, *The Collected Works of John Stuart Mill*, vol. XXXII. Toronto: University of Toronto Press, 1991, p. 244.
[69] The representatives of the Lassallean General Association of German Workers voted in favour.

widespread popular discontent. Faced with the prospect of a government that wanted to disarm the city and withhold any social reform, the Parisians turned against Thiers and on 18 March initiated the first great political event in the life of the workers' movement: the Paris Commune.

Although Bakunin had urged the workers to turn patriotic war into revolutionary war,[70] the General Council in London initially opted for silence. It charged Marx with the task of writing a text in the name of the International, but he delayed its publication for complicated, deeply held reasons. Well aware of the real relationship of forces on the ground as well as the weaknesses of the Paris Commune, he knew that it was doomed to defeat. He had even tried to warn the French working class back in September 1870, in his *Second Address on the Franco-Prussian War*:

> Any attempt at upsetting the new government in the present crisis, when the enemy is almost knocking at the doors of Paris, would be a desperate folly. The French workmen [...] must not allow themselves to be swayed by the national *souvenirs* of 1792 [...]. They have not to recapitulate the past, but to build up the future. Let them calmly and resolutely improve the opportunities of republican liberty, for the work of their own class organization. It will gift them with fresh herculean powers for the regeneration of France, and our common task – the emancipation of labour. Upon their energies and wisdom hinges the fate of the republic.[71]

A fervid declaration hailing the victory of the Paris Commune would have risked creating false expectations among workers throughout Europe, eventually becoming a source of demoralization and distrust. Marx therefore decided to postpone delivery and stayed away from meetings of the General Council for several weeks. His grim forebodings soon proved all too well founded, and on 28 May, little more than 2 months after its proclamation, the Paris Commune was drowned in blood. Two days later, he reappeared at the General Council with a manuscript entitled *The Civil War in France*; it was read and unanimously approved, then published over the names of all the General Council members. The document had a huge impact over the next few weeks,

---

[70] See Arthur Lehning, 'Introduction', in Idem. (ed.), *Bakunin – Archiv*, vol. VI: *Michel Bakounine sur la Guerre Franco-Allemande et la Révolution Sociale en France (1870–1871)*. Leiden: Brill, 1977, p. xvi.
[71] From document 57, p. 241.

greater than any other document of the workers' movement in the nineteenth century. Three English editions in quick succession won acclaim among the workers and caused uproar in bourgeois circles. It was also translated fully or partly into a dozen other languages, appearing in newspapers, magazines and booklets in various European countries and the United States.

Despite Marx's passionate defence, and despite the claims both of reactionary opponents and of dogmatic Marxists eager to glorify the International,[72] it is out of the question that the General Council actually pushed for the Parisian insurrection. Prominent figures in the organization did play a role – Leo Frankel (1844–96), for example, though Hungarian by origin, was placed in charge of work, industry and trade – but the leadership of the Paris Commune was in the hands of its radical Jacobin wing. Of the 85 representatives elected at the municipal elections of 26 March,[73] there were 15 moderates (the so-called 'parti des maires', a group of former mayors of the arrondissements) and four Radicals, who immediately resigned and never formed part of the Council of the Commune. Of the 66 remaining, 11 were without a clear political tendency, 14 came from the Committee of the National Guard, and 15 were radical-republicans and socialists; in addition there were 9 Blanquists and 17 members of the International.[74] Among the latter were Édouard Vaillant (1840–1915), Benoît Malon (1841–93), Auguste Serrailler (1840–72), Jean-Louis Pindy (1840–1917), Albert Theisz (1839–81), Charles Longuet (1839–1903) and the previously mentioned Varlin and Frankel. However, coming as they did from various political backgrounds and cultures, they did not constitute a monolithic group and often voted in different ways. This too favoured the hegemony of the Jacobin perspective of radical republicanism, which was reflected in the Montagnard-inspired decision in May (approved by two-thirds of the General Council, including the Blanquists) to create a Committee of Public Safety. Marx himself pointed out that 'the majority of the Commune was in no sense socialist, nor could it have been'.[75]

---

[72] See Georges Haupt, *Aspect of International Socialism 1871–1914*. Cambridge: Cambridge University Press, 1986, who warned against 'the reshaping of the reality of the Commune in order to make it conform to an image transfigured by ideology', p. 25.

[73] The seats were 92, but due to the multiple elections of some individuals the number of council members was reduced to 85.

[74] See Jacques Rougerie, *Paris libre 1871*. Paris: Seuil, 1971, p. 146; Pierre Milza, *L'année terrible*. Paris: Perrin 2009, p. 78.

[75] Karl Marx to Domela Nieuwenhuis, 22 February 1881, MECW, vol. 46, p. 66.

During the 'bloody week' (21–28 May) that followed the irruption of the horde from Versailles into Paris, some 10,000 Communards were killed in fighting or summarily executed; it was the bloodiest massacre in French history. Another 43,000 or more were taken prisoner, 13,500 of whom were subsequently sentenced to death, imprisonment, forced labour or deportation (many to the remote colony of New Caledonia). Another 7,000 managed to escape and take refuge in England, Belgium or Switzerland. The European conservative and liberal press completed the work of Thiers's soldiers, accusing the Communards of hideous crimes and trumpeting the victory of 'civilization' over the insolent workers' rebellion. From now on, the International was at the eye of the storm, held to blame for every act against the established order. 'When the great conflagration took place at Chicago,' Marx mused with bitter irony, 'the telegraph round the world announced it as the infernal deed of the International; and it is really wonderful that to its demoniacal agency has not been attributed the hurricane ravaging the West Indies'.[76]

Marx had to spend whole days answering press slanders about the International and himself: 'at this moment', he wrote, [he was] 'the best calumniated and the most menaced man of London'.[77] Meanwhile, governments all over Europe sharpened their instruments of repression, fearing that other uprisings might follow the one in Paris. Thiers immediately outlawed the International and asked the British prime minister William Ewart Gladstone (1809–98), to follow his example; it was the first diplomatic exchange relating to a workers' organization. Pope Pius IX (1792–1878) exerted similar pressure on the Swiss government, arguing that it would be a serious mistake to continue tolerating 'that International sect which would like to treat the whole of Europe as it treated Paris. Those gentlemen [...] are to be feared, because they work on behalf of the eternal enemies of God and mankind'.[78] Such language resulted in an agreement between France and Spain to extradite refugees from beyond the Pyrenees, and in repressive measures against the International in Belgium and Denmark. While London dragged its feet, unwilling to violate its principles of asylum, representatives of the German

---

[76] Karl Marx, *Report of the General Council to the Fifth Annual Congress of the International*, in GC, V, p. 461.
[77] Karl Marx to Ludwig Kugelmann, 18 June 1871, in MECW, vol. 44, p. 157.
[78] GC, V, p. 460.

and Austro-Hungarian governments met in Berlin in November 1872 and issued a joint statement on the 'social question':

1. that the tendencies of the International are in complete contrast with, and antagonistic to, the principles of the bourgeois society; they must therefore be vigorously repelled;
2. that the International constitutes a dangerous abuse of the freedom of assembly and, following its own practice and principle, state action against it must be international in scope and must therefore be based on the solidarity of all governments;
3. that even if some governments do not intend to pass a special law [against the International], as France has done, the ground should be cut from beneath the feet of the International Working Men's Association and its harmful activities.[79]

Lastly, Italy was not spared the onslaught. Most notably, Mazzini – who for a time had looked to the International with hope – considered that its principles had become those of 'denial of God, [...] the fatherland, [...] and all individual property'.[80]

Criticism of the Paris Commune even spread to sections of the workers' movement. Following the publication of *The Civil War in France*, both the trade union leader George Odger and the old Chartist Benjamin Lucraft (1809–97) resigned from the International, bending under the pressure of the hostile press campaign. However, no trade union withdrew its support for the organization – which suggests once again that the failure of the International to grow in Britain was due mainly to political apathy in the working class.[81]

Despite the bloody denouement in Paris and the wave of calumny and government repression elsewhere in Europe, the International grew stronger and more widely known in the wake of the Paris Commune. For the capitalists and the middle classes it represented a threat to the established order, but for the workers it fuelled hopes in a world without exploitation and injustice.[82]

---

[79] See Braunthal, op. cit., pp. 160–1.
[80] Giuseppe Mazzini, *L'Internazionale*, in Gian Mario Bravo, *La Prima Internazionale*, vol. II. Roma: Editori Riuniti, 1978, pp. 499–501.
[81] See Collins and Abramsky, op. cit., p. 222.
[82] See Haupt, *L'internazionale socialista dalla Comune a Lenin*, op. cit., p. 28.

Insurrectionary Paris fortified the workers' movement, impelling it to adopt more radical positions and to intensify its militancy. The experience showed that revolution was possible, that the goal could and should be to build a society utterly different from the capitalist order, but also that, in order to achieve this, the workers would have to create durable and well-organized forms of political association.[83]

This enormous vitality was apparent everywhere. Attendance at General Council meetings doubled, while newspapers linked to the International increased in both number and overall sales. Among those which made a serious contribution to the spread of socialist principles were: *L'Égalité* in Geneva, at first a Bakuninist paper, then – after a change of editor in 1870 – the main organ of the International in Switzerland; *Der Volksstaat* in Leipzig, the organ of the Social Democratic Workers' Party; *La Emancipación* in Madrid, the official paper of the Spanish Federation; *Il Gazzettino Rosa* in Milan, which went over to the International following the events in Paris; *Socialisten*, the first Danish workers' newssheet; and, probably the best of them all, *La Réforme Sociale* in Rouen.[84]

Finally, and most significantly, the International continued to expand in Belgium and Spain – where the level of workers' involvement had already been considerable before the Paris Commune – and experienced a real breakthrough in Italy. Many Mazzinians, disappointed with the positions taken by their erstwhile leader, joined forces with the organization and were soon among its principal local leaders. Even more important was the support of Giuseppe Garibaldi. Although he had only a vague idea of the Association whose headquarters were in London,[85] the 'hero of the two worlds' decided to throw his weight behind it and wrote a membership application that contained the famous sentence: 'The International is the sun of the future!'[86] Printed in dozens of workers' newssheets and papers, the letter was instrumental in persuading many of those who were wavering to join the organization.

---

[83] Ibid., pp. 93–5.
[84] See Georges Bourgin, Georges Duveau, Domenico De Marco, 'Préface', in Del Bo (ed.), op. cit., p. xv.
[85] See Nello Rosselli, *Mazzini e Bakunin*. Torino: Einaudi, 1927, pp. 323–4.
[86] Giuseppe Garibaldi to Giorgio Pallavicino, 14 November 1871, in Enrico Emilio Ximenes, *Epistolario di Giuseppe Garibaldi*, vol. I. Milano: Brigola 1885, p. 350.

The International also opened new sections in Portugal, where it was founded in October 1871, and in Denmark, in the same month, it began to link up most of the newly born trade unions in Copenhagen and Jutland. Another important development was the founding of Irish workers' sections in Britain, and the workers' leader John MacDonnell was appointed the General Council's corresponding secretary for Ireland. Unexpected requests for affiliation came from various other parts of the world: some English workers in Calcutta, labour groups in Victoria, Australia and Christchurch, New Zealand, and a number of artisans in Buenos Aires.

IX The London Conference of 1871

Two years had passed since the last congress of the International, but a new one could not be held under the prevailing circumstances. The General Council therefore decided to organize a conference in London; it took place between 17 and 23 September 1871, in the presence of 22 delegates[87] from Britain (Ireland too being represented for the first time), Belgium, Switzerland and Spain, plus the French exiles. Despite the efforts to make the event as representative as possible, it was in fact more in the way of an enlarged General Council meeting.

Marx had announced beforehand that the conference would be devoted 'exclusively to questions of organization and policy',[88] with theoretical discussions left to one side. He spelled this out at its first session:

> The General Council has convened a conference to agree with delegates from various countries the measures that need to be taken against the dangers facing the Association in a large number of countries, and to move towards a new organization corresponding to the needs of the situation. In the second place, to work out a response to the governments that are ceaselessly working to destroy the Association with every means at their disposal. And lastly to settle the Swiss dispute once and for all.[89]

---

[87] Actually the delegates who participated in the conference were only 19, since Cohen could not attend, while Eugène Dupont (1831–81) and Mac Donnell participated only in the first two sessions.
[88] Karl Marx, 15 August 1871, in GC, IV, p. 259.
[89] Karl Marx, 17 September 1871, in PI, II, p. 152.

Marx summoned all his energies for these priorities: to reorganize the International, to defend it from the offensive of hostile forces, and to check Bakunin's growing influence. By far the most active delegate at the conference, Marx took the floor as many as 102 times, blocked proposals that did not fit in with his plans, and won over those not yet convinced.[90] The gathering in London confirmed his stature within the organization, not only as the brains shaping its political line, but also as one of its most combative and capable militants.

The most important decision taken at the conference, for which it would be remembered later, was the approval of Vaillant's Resolution IX. The leader of the Blanquists – whose residual forces had joined the International after the end of the Paris Commune – proposed that the organization should be transformed into a centralized, disciplined party, under the leadership of the General Council. Despite some differences, particularly over the Blanquist position that a tightly organized nucleus of militants was sufficient for the revolution, Marx did not hesitate to form an alliance with Vaillant's group: not only to strengthen the opposition to Bakuninite anarchism within the International, but above all to create a broader consensus for the changes deemed necessary in the new phase of the class struggle. The resolution passed in London therefore stated,

> that against this collective power of the propertied classes the working class cannot act, as a class, except by constituting itself into a political party, distinct from, and opposed to, all old parties formed by the propertied classes; that this constitution of the working class into a political party is indispensable in order to ensure the triumph of the social revolution and its ultimate end – the abolition of classes; and that the combination of forces which the working class has already effected by its economic struggles ought at the same time to serve as a lever for its struggles against the political power of landlords and capitalists.

The conclusion was clear: 'the economic movement [of the working class] and its political action are indissolubly united.'[91]

---

[90] See Miklós Molnár, *Le déclin de la première internationale*. Genève: Droz, 1963, p. 127.
[91] From document 74, p. 285.

Whereas the Geneva Congress of 1866 established the importance of trade unions, the London Conference of 1871 shifted the focus to the other key instrument of the modern workers' movement: the political party. It should be stressed, however, that the understanding of this was much broader than that which developed in the twentieth century. Marx's conception should therefore be differentiated both from the Blanquists' – the two would openly clash later on – and from Lenin's, as adopted by communist organizations after the October Revolution.[92]

For Marx, the self-emancipation of the working class required a long and arduous process – the polar opposite of the theories and practices in Sergei Nechaev's (1847–82) *Catechism of a Revolutionary*, whose advocacy of secret societies was condemned by the delegates in London[93] but enthusiastically supported by Bakunin.

Only four delegates opposed Resolution IX at the London Conference, arguing for the need of having an 'abstensionist' position of not engaging in politics, but Marx's victory soon proved to be ephemeral. For the call to establish what amounted to political parties in every country and to confer broader powers on the General Council had grave repercussions in the internal life of the International; it was not ready to move so rapidly from a flexible to a politically uniform model of organization.[94]

The last decision taken in London was to set up a British Federal Council. Since, in Marx's view, the conditions for a revolution on the Continent had diminished with the defeat of the Paris Commune, it was no longer necessary to exercise close supervision over British initiatives.[95]

---

[92] In the early 1870s the working-class movement was organized as a political party only in Germany. Usage of the term 'party,' whether by the followers of Marx or of Bakunin, was therefore very confused. Even Marx used the term in a vague manner. For him, according to Rubel, op. cit., p. 183, 'the concept of party [...] corresponds to the concept of class'. It is useful to emphasize, finally, that the conflict which took place in the International between 1871 and 1872 did not focus on the construction of a political party (an expression uttered only twice at the London Conference and five times at the Congress of the Hague), but rather on the 'use [...] of the adjective "political"' (Haupt, *L'Internazionale socialista dalla Comune a Lenin*, op. cit., p. 84).

[93] See PI, II, p. 237, and Karl Marx, 'Declaration of the General Council on Nechayev's Misuse of the Name of the International Working Men's Association', in MECW, vol. 23, p. 23.

[94] See Jacques Freymond and Miklós Molnár, 'The Rise and Fall of the First International', in Milorad M. Drachkovitch (ed.), *The Revolutionary Internationals, 1864–1943*. Stanford: Stanford University Press, 1966, p. 27.

[95] See Collins and Abramsky, op. cit., p. 231. For a different opinion cf. Miklós Molnár, op. cit., p. 135.

Marx was convinced that virtually all the main federations and local sections would back the resolutions of the conference, but he soon had to think again. On 12 November, the Jura Federation called a congress of its own in the small commune of Sonvilier, and, although Bakunin was unable to attend, it officially launched the opposition within the International. In the *Circular to All Federations of the International Working Men's Association* issued at the end of the proceedings, Guillaume and the other participants accused the General Council of having introduced the 'authority principle' into the International and transformed its original structure into 'a hierarchical organization directed and governed by a committee'. The Swiss declared themselves 'against all directing authority, even should that authority be elected and endorsed by the workers', and insisted on 'retention of the principle of autonomy of the Sections', so that the General Council would become 'a simple correspondence and statistical bureau'.[96] Lastly, they called for a congress to be held as soon as possible.

Although the position of the Jura Federation was not unexpected, Marx was probably surprised when signs of restlessness and even rebellion against the political line of the General Council began to appear elsewhere. In a number of countries, the decisions taken in London were judged an unacceptable encroachment on local political autonomy. The Belgian Federation, which at the conference had aimed at mediation between the different sides, began to adopt a much more critical stance towards London, and the Dutch too later took their distance. In Southern Europe, where the reaction was even stronger, the opposition soon won considerable support. Indeed, the great majority of Iberian Internationalists came out against the General Council and endorsed Bakunin's ideas, partly, no doubt, because these were more in keeping with a region where the industrial proletariat had a presence only in the main cities, and where the workers' movement was still very weak and mainly concerned with economic demands. In Italy too, the results of the London Conference were seen in a negative light. Those who followed Mazzini gathered in Rome from 1 to 6 November 1871, in the General Congress of Italian Workers' Societies (the more moderate labour bloc), while most of the rest fell in with

---

[96] Various Authors, 'Circulaire du Congrès de Sonvilier', in PI, II, pp. 264–5.

Bakunin's positions. Those who met at Rimini between 4 and 6 August 1872 for the founding congress of the Italian Federation of the International took the most radical position against the General Council: they would not participate in the forthcoming congress of the International but proposed to hold an 'anti-authoritarian general congress'[97] in Neuchâtel, Switzerland. In fact, this would be the first act of the impending split.

The organization also saw a serious conflict explode on the other side of the Atlantic, albeit over different issues. In the course of 1871, the International had grown in a number of cities there, reaching a total of 50 sections with a combined membership of 2,700.[98] The figure increased further the next year (probably to around 4,000), but this was still only a tiny proportion of the American workforce of 2 million or more, and the organization was still unable to expand outside immigrant communities to draw in workers born in the United States. Internal strife also had a damaging effect, since the American Internationalists, largely based in New York, split into two in December 1871, each group claiming to be the legitimate representative of the International in the United States.

The first and initially the larger of the two, known as the Spring Street Council, proposed an alliance with the most liberal groups of American society; it could count on the support of Eccarius, the corresponding secretary for the General Council, and its most active branch was Section 12.[99] The second, with its headquarters at the Tenth Ward Hotel, maintained the orientation to the working class and had its most important figure in Friedrich Adolph Sorge (1828–1906). In March 1872, the General Council called for the holding of a unity congress in July, but the initiative failed and the split became official in May. The differences caused a haemorrhage of members from the International. The Tenth Ward Hotel group held its congress between 6 and 8 July 1872, giving birth to the North American Confederation with a membership of 950 spread among 22 sections (12 German, 4 French, 1 each Irish, Italian and Scandinavian, and only 3 English-speaking). Meanwhile, in

---

[97] Various Authors, *Risoluzione, programma e regolamento della federazione italiana dell'Associazione Internazionale dei Lavoratori*, in Gian Mario Bravo, *La Prima Internazionale*, op. cit., p. 787.

[98] A dozen of them, however, were not in touch with the Central Committee, see Samuel Bernstein, *The First International in America*. New York: Augustus M. Kelley, 1965, p. 65.

[99] The sections of the International in the United States were numbered.

May, some members of the Spring Street Council had attended the convention of the Equal Rights Party, which was standing Victoria Woodhull for the presidency of the United States; its lack of a class platform, with no more than general promises of regulation of working conditions and measures of job creation, persuaded some sections to abandon the Council, leaving it with only 1,500 members. After the birth of the American Confederation in July, the Council retained only 13 sections with a total of less than 500 members (mainly artisans and intellectuals), but these joined forces with the European federations challenging the line of the General Council.

The feuding across the Atlantic also harmed relations among members in London. John Hales (1839–unk), the secretary of the General Council from 1871 to 1872, took over Eccarius's position as US corresponding secretary, but followed the same policy. Very soon, both men's personal relations with Marx took a turn for the worse, and in Britain too the first internal conflicts began to emerge. Support for the General Council also came from the majority of the Swiss, from the French (now mostly Blanquists), the weak German forces, the recently constituted sections in Denmark, Ireland and Portugal, and the East European groups in Hungary and Bohemia. But they added up to much less than Marx had expected at the end of the London Conference.

The opposition to the General Council was varied in character and sometimes came from mainly personal motives; a strange alchemy held it together and made leadership of the International even more difficult. Still, beyond the fascination with Bakunin's theories in certain countries and Guillaume's capacity to unify the various oppositionists, the main factor militating against the resolution on 'Working-Class Political Action' was an environment unwilling to accept the qualitative step forward proposed by Marx. For all the accompanying claims of utility, the London turn was seen by many as crass interference; not only the group linked to Bakunin but most of the federations and local sections regarded the principle of autonomy and respect for the diverse realities making up the International as one of the cornerstones of the International. This miscalculation on Marx's part accelerated the crisis of the organization.[100]

---

[100] See Freymond and Molnár, op. cit., pp. 27–8.

X The Crisis of the International

The final battle came towards the end of summer 1872. After the terrible events of the previous 3 years – the Franco-Prussian war, the wave of repression following the Paris Commune, the numerous internal skirmishes – the International could at last meet again in congress. In the countries where it had recently sunk root, it was expanding through the enthusiastic efforts of union leaders and worker-activists suddenly fired by its slogans: it was in 1872 that the organization experienced its fastest growth in Italy, Denmark, Portugal and the Netherlands, at the very time when it was banned in France, Germany and the Austro-Hungarian Empire. Yet most of the membership remained unaware of the gravity of the conflicts that raged on within its leading group.[101]

The Fifth Congress of the International took place in The Hague between 2 and 7 September, attended by 65 delegates from a total of 14 countries. There were 18 French (including 4 Blanquists co-opted onto the General Council), 15 German, 7 Belgian, 5 British, 5 Spanish, 4 Swiss, 4 Dutch, 2 Austrian, and 1 each of Danish, Irish, Hungarian, Polish and Australian (W. E. Harcourt [unk.], from the Victoria section). The Frenchman Paul Lafargue was nominated by the Lisbon Federation (as well as the Madrid Federation). The Italian Internationalists failed to send their seven delegates, but even so it was certainly the most representative gathering in the history of the International.

The crucial importance of the event impelled Marx to attend in person,[102] accompanied by Engels. In fact, it was the only congress of the organization in which he took part. Neither De Paepe (perhaps aware that he would be unable to play the same mediating role as in London the previous year) nor Bakunin made it to the Dutch capital. But the 'autonomist' contingent, opposed to the decisions of the General Council, was present in strength, comprising all the delegates from Belgium, Spain and the Netherlands, a half of those from Switzerland, plus others from Britain, France and the United States: a total of 25 in all.

---

[101] See Haupt, *L'Internazionale socialista dalla Comune a Lenin*, op. cit., p. 88.
[102] See Karl Marx to Ludwig Kugelmann, 29 July 1872, in MECW, vol. 44, p. 413, where he noted this congress would be 'a matter of life and death for the International; and before I resign I want at least to protect it from disintegrating elements'.

By an irony of fate, the congress unfolded in Concordia Hall, although concord was little in evidence there; all the sessions were marked by irreducible antagonism between the two camps, resulting in debates that were far poorer than at the two previous congresses. This hostility was exacerbated by 3 days of sterile wrangling over the verification of credentials. The representation of the delegates was indeed completely skewed, not reflecting the true relationship of forces within the organization. In Germany, for instance, there were no sections of the International as such, while in France they had been driven underground and their mandates were highly debatable. Other representatives had been delegated as members of the General Council and did not express the will of any section.

Approval of the Hague Congress resolutions was possible only because of its distorted composition. Though spurious and, in many respects, only held together by the instrumentality of purpose, the coalition of delegates that was in the minority at the congress actually constituted the most numerous part of the International.[103]

The most important decision taken at The Hague was to incorporate Resolution IX of the 1871 London Conference into the statutes of the Association, as a new Article 7a. Whereas the *Provisional Statutes* of 1864 had stated that 'That the economical emancipation of the working classes is therefore the great end to which every political movement ought to be subordinate as a means',[104] this insertion mirrored the new relationship of forces within the organization. Political struggle was now the necessary instrument for the transformation of society since 'The lords of land and the lords of capital will always use their political privileges for the defence and perpetuation of their economical monopolies, and for the enslavement of labour. The conquest of political power has therefore become the great duty of the working class.'[105]

The International was now very different from how it had been at the time of its foundation: the radical–democratic components had walked out after being increasingly marginalized; the mutualists had been defeated and many converted; reformists no longer constituted the bulk of the organization

---

[103] See James Guillaume, *L'Internationale, Documents et Souvenirs (1864–1878)*, vol. II. New York: Burt Franklin, 1969 [1907], pp. 333–4; cf. Freymond, 'Introduction', in PI, I, p. 25.
[104] From document 65, p. 265.
[105] Ibid., p. 268.

(except in Britain); and anticapitalism had become the political line of the whole Association, as well as of recently formed tendencies such as the anarcho-collectivists. Moreover, although the years of the International had witnessed a degree of economic prosperity that in some cases made conditions less parlous, the workers understood that real change would come not through such palliatives but only through the end of human exploitation. They were also basing their struggles more and more on their own material needs, rather than on the initiatives of particular groups to which they belonged.

The wider picture, too, was radically different. The unification of Germany in 1871 confirmed the onset of a new age in which the nation-state would be the central form of political, legal and territorial identity; this placed a question mark over any supranational body that financed itself from membership dues in each individual country and required its members to surrender a sizeable share of their political leadership. At the same time, the growing differences between national movements and organizations made it extremely difficult for the General Council to produce a political synthesis capable of satisfying the demands of all. It is true that, right from the beginning, the International had been an agglomeration of trade unions and political associations far from easy to reconcile with one another, and that these had represented sensibilities and political tendencies more than organizations properly so called. By 1872, however, the various components of the Association – and workers' struggles, more generally – had become much more clearly defined and structured. The legalization of the British trade unions had officially made them part of national political life; the Belgian Federation of the International was a ramified organization, with a central leadership capable of making significant, and autonomous, contributions to theory; Germany had two workers' parties, the Social Democratic Workers' Party of Germany and the General Association of German Workers, each with representation in parliament; the French workers, from Lyons to Paris, had already tried 'storming the heavens'; and the Spanish Federation had expanded to the point where it was on the verge of becoming a mass organization. Similar changes had occurred in other countries.

The initial configuration of the International had thus become outmoded, just as its original mission had come to an end. The task was no longer to prepare for and organize Europe-wide support for strikes, nor to call congresses on the usefulness of trade unions or the need to socialize the land and the means of production. Such themes were now part of the collective heritage of the organization as a whole. After the Paris Commune, the real challenge for the workers' movement was a revolutionary one: How to organize in such a way as to end the capitalist mode of production and to overthrow the institutions of the bourgeois world? It was no longer a question of how to reform the existing society, but how to build a new one.[106] For this new advance in the class struggle, Marx thought it indispensable to build working-class political parties in each country. The document *To the Federal Council of the Spanish Region of the International Working Men's Association*, written by Engels in February 1871, was one of the most explicit statement of the General Council on this matter:

> Experience has shown everywhere that the best way to emancipate the workers from this domination of the old parties is to form in each country a proletarian party with a policy of its own, a policy which is manifestly different from that of the other parties, because it must express the conditions necessary for the emancipation of the working class. This policy may vary in details according to the specific circumstances of each country; but as the fundamental relations between labour and capital are the same everywhere and the political domination of the possessing classes over the exploited classes is an existing fact everywhere, the principles and aims of proletarian policy will be identical, at least in all western countries. [...] To give up fighting our adversaries in the political field would mean to abandon one of the most powerful weapons, particularly in the sphere of organization and propaganda.[107]

From this point on, therefore, the party was considered essential for the struggle of the proletariat: it had to be independent of all existing political forces and to be built, both programmatically and organizationally, in accordance with the national context. At the General Council session of 23 July 1872, Marx criticized not only the abstentionists (who had been attacking Resolution IX of the London Conference) but the equally dangerous position of 'the working classes of England and America', 'who let the middle classes use

---

[106] See Freymond, 'Introduction', in PI, I, p. X.
[107] From document 69, pp. 274–5.

them for political purposes'.[108] On the second point, he had already declared at the London Conference that 'politics must be adapted to the conditions of all countries',[109] and the following year, in a speech in Amsterdam immediately after the Hague Congress, he stressed:

> Someday the worker must seize political power in order to build up the new organization of labour; he must overthrow the old politics which sustain the old institutions, if he is not to lose Heaven on Earth, like the old Christians who neglected and despised politics. But we have not asserted that the ways to achieve that goal are everywhere the same. [...] We do not deny that there are countries [...] where the workers can attain their goal by peaceful means. This being the case, we must also recognize the fact that in most countries on the Continent the lever of our revolution must be force; it is force to which we must some day appeal in order to erect the rule of labour.[110]

Thus, although the workers' parties emerged in different forms in different countries, they should not subordinate themselves to national interests.[111] The struggle for socialism could not be confined in that way, and especially in the new historical context internationalism must continue to be the guiding beacon for the proletariat, as well as its vaccine against the deadly embrace of the state and the capitalist system.

During the Hague Congress, harsh polemics preceded a series of votes. Following the adoption of Article 7a, the goal of winning political power was inscribed in the statutes, and there was also an indication that a workers' party was the essential instrument for this. The subsequent decision to confer broader powers on the General Council – with 32 votes in favour, 6 against and 12 abstentions – made the situation even more intolerable for the minority, since the General Council now had the task of ensuring 'rigid observation of the principles and statutes and general rules of the International', and 'the right to suspend branches, sections, councils or federal committees and federations of the International until the next congress'.[112]

---

[108] Karl Marx, 23 July 1872, in GC, V, p. 263.
[109] Karl Marx, 20 September 1871, in PI, II, p. 195.
[110] Karl Marx, 'On The Hague Congress', in MECW, vol. 23, 1988, p. 255.
[111] See Haupt, *L'Internazionale socialista dalla Comune a Lenin*, op. cit., p. 100.
[112] PI, II, p. 374. The opposition had already advocated reducing the General Council's power at the Sonvilier Congress (see note 96), but Marx declared at The Hague: 'we would prefer to abolish the General Council rather than see it reduce to the role of letter box', PI, II, p. 354.

For the first time in the history of the International, its highest congress also approved (by 47 votes in favour and 9 abstentions) the General Council's decision to expel an organization: namely, the New York Section 12. Its motivation was as follows: 'The International Working Men's Association is based on the principle of the abolition of classes and cannot admit any bourgeois section'.[113] The expulsions of Bakunin (25 for, 6 against, 7 abstentions) and Guillaume (25 for, 9 against, 8 abstentions) also caused quite a stir, having been proposed by a commission of enquiry that described the Alliance for Socialist Democracy as 'a secret organization with statutes completely opposite to those of the International'.[114] However, the call to expel Adhemar Schwitzguébel (1844–95), one of the founders and most active members of the Jura Federation, was rejected (by a vote of 15 for, 17 against and 7 abstentions).[115] Finally, the congress authorized publication of a long report, *The Alliance for Socialist Democracy and the International Working Men's Association*, which traced the history of the organization led by Bakunin and analysed its public and secret activity country by country. Written by Engels, Lafargue and Marx, the document was published in French in July 1873.

The opposition at the congress was not uniform in its response to these attacks, some abstaining and others voting against. On the final day, however, a joint declaration read out by the worker Victor Dave (1845–1922) from the Hague section stated:

1. We the [...] supporters of the autonomy and federation of groups of working men shall continue our administrative relations with the General Council [...].

2. The federations which we represent will establish direct and permanent relations between themselves and all regularly branches of the Association. [...].

4. We call on all the federations and sections to prepare between now and the next general congress for the triumph within the International of the principles of federative autonomy as the basis of the organization of labour.[116]

---

[113] PI, II, p. 376.
[114] Ibid., p. 377.
[115] Ibid., p. 378. After this vote it was decided not to proceed with the other expulsions proposed by the commission.
[116] Various Author, ['Statement of the Minority'], in HAGUE, pp. 199–200.

This statement was more a tactical ploy, designed to avoid responsibility for a split that by then seemed inevitable, rather than a serious political undertaking to relaunch the organization. In this sense, it was similar to the proposals of the 'centralists' to augment the powers of the General Council, at a time when they were already planning a far more drastic alternative.

For, what took place in the morning session on 6 September – the most dramatic of the congress – was the final act of the International as it had been conceived and constructed over the years. Engels stood up to speak and, to the astonishment of those present, proposed that 'the seat of the General Council [should] be transferred to New York for the year 1872–1873, and that it should be formed by members of the American federal council'.[117] Thus, Marx and other 'founders' of the International would no longer be part of its central body, which would consist of people whose very names were unknown (Engels proposed 7, with the option to increase the total to a maximum of 15). The delegate Maltman Barry (1842–1909), a General Council member who supported Marx's positions, described better than anyone the reaction from the floor:

> Consternation and discomfiture stood plainly written on the faces of the party of dissension as [Engels] uttered the last words. [...] It was sometime before anyone rose to speak. It was a *coup d'état*, and each looked to his neighbour to break the spell.[118]

Engels argued that 'inter-group conflicts in London had reached such a pitch that [the General Council] had to be transferred elsewhere',[119] and that New York was the best choice in times of repression. But the Blanquists were violently opposed to the move, on the grounds that 'the International should first of all be the permanent insurrectionary organization of the proletariat'[120] and that 'when a party unites for struggle [...] its action is all the greater, the more its leadership committee is active, well armed and powerful'. Vaillant

---

[117] Friedrich Engels, 5 September 1872, in PI, II, p. 355.
[118] Maltman Barry, 'Report of the Fifth Annual General Congress of the International Working Men's Association, Held at The Hague, Holland, September 2–9, 1872', in Hans Gerth, *The First International: Minutes of The Hague Congress of 1872*. Madison: University of Wisconsin Press, 1958, pp. 279–80. This report does not appear in HAGUE.
[119] Friedrich Engels, 5 September 1872, in PI, II, p. 356.
[120] Édouard Vaillant, *Internationale et Révolution. A propos du Congrès de La Haye*, in PI, vol. III, p. 140.

and other followers of Blanqui present at The Hague thus felt betrayed when they saw 'the head' being shipped 'to the other side of the Atlantic [while] the armed body was fighting in [Europe]'.[121] Based on the assumption that 'the International had had an initiating role of economic struggle', they wanted it to play 'a similar role with respect to political struggle' and its transformation into an 'international workers' revolutionary party'.[122] Realizing that it would no longer be possible to exercise control over the General Council, they left the congress and, shortly afterwards, the International.

Many, even in the ranks of the majority, voted against the move to New York as tantamount to the end of the International as an operational structure. The decision, approved by only three votes (26 for, 23 against), eventually depended on 9 abstentions and the fact that some members of the minority were happy to see the General Council relocated far from their own centres of activity.

Another factor in the move was certainly Marx's view that it was better to give up the International than to see it end up as a sectarian organization in the hands of his opponents. The demise of the International, which would certainly follow the transfer of the General Council to New York, was infinitely preferable to a long and wasteful succession of fratricidal struggles.

Still, it is not convincing to argue – as many have done[123] – that the key reason for the decline of the International was the conflict between its two currents, or even between two men, Marx and Bakunin, however great their stature. Rather, it was the changes taking place in the world around it that rendered the International obsolete. The growth and transformation of the organizations of the workers' movement, the strengthening of the nation-state as a result of Italian and German unification, the expansion of the International in countries like Spain and Italy (where the economic and social conditions were very different from those in Britain or France), the drift towards even greater moderation in the British trade union movement, the repression following the Paris Commune: all these factors together made the original configuration of the International inappropriate to the new times.

---

[121] Ibid., p. 142.
[122] Ibid., p. 144.
[123] For a critical analysis of these positions see Miklós Molnár, 'Quelques remarques a propos de la crise de l'Internationale en 1872', in Colloque International sur La première Internationale, op. cit., p. 439.

Against this backdrop, with its prevalence of centrifugal trends, developments in the life of the International and its main protagonists naturally also played a role. The London Conference, for instance, was far from the saving event that Marx had hoped it would be; indeed, its rigid conduct significantly aggravated the internal crisis, by failing to take account of the prevailing moods or to display the foresight needed to avoid the strengthening of Bakunin and his group.[124] It proved a Pyrrhic victory for Marx – one which, in attempting to resolve internal conflicts, ended up accentuating them. It remains the case, however, that the decisions taken in London only speeded up a process that was already under way and impossible to reverse.

In addition to all these historical and organizational considerations, there were others of no lesser weight regarding the chief protagonist. As Marx had reminded delegates at a session of the London Conference in 1871, 'the work of the Council had become immense, obliged as it was to tackle both general questions and national questions'.[125] It was no longer the tiny organization of 1864 walking on an English and a French leg; it was now present in all European countries, each with its particular problems and characteristics. Not only was the organization everywhere wracked by internal conflicts, but the arrival of the Communard exiles in London, with new preoccupations and a variegated baggage of ideas, made it still more arduous for the General Council to perform its task of political synthesis.

Marx was sorely tried after 8 years of intense activity for the International.[126] Aware that the workers' forces were on the retreat following the defeat of the Paris Commune – the most important fact of the moment for him – he therefore resolved to devote the years ahead to the attempt to complete *Capital*. When he crossed the North Sea to the Netherlands, he must have felt that the battle awaiting him would be his last major one as a direct protagonist.

From the mute figure he had cut at that first meeting in St Martin's Hall in 1864, he had become recognized as the leader of the International not only

---

[124] Miklós Molnár, *Le Déclin de la Première Internationale*, op. cit., p. 144.
[125] Karl Marx, 22 September 1872, in PI, II, p. 217.
[126] Karl Marx to César De Paepe, 28 May 1872, MECW, vol. 44, p. 387: 'I can hardly wait for the next Congress. It will be the end of my slavery. After that I shall become a free man again; I shall accept no administrative functions any more, either for the General Council or for the British Federal Council'.

by congress delegates and the General Council but also by the wider public. Thus, although the International certainly owed a very great deal to Marx, it had also done much to change his life. Before its foundation, he had been known only in small circles of political activists. Later, and above all after the Paris Commune – as well as the publication of his magnum opus in 1867, of course – his fame spread among revolutionaries in many European countries, to the point where the press referred to him as the 'red terror doctor'. The responsibility deriving from his role in the International – which allowed him to experience up close so many economic and political struggles – was a further stimulus for his reflections on communism and profoundly enriched the whole of his anticapitalist theory.

XI Marx versus Bakunin

The battle between the two camps raged in the months following the Hague Congress, but only in a few cases did it centre on their existing theoretical and ideological differences. Marx often chose to caricature Bakunin's positions, painting him as an advocate of 'class equalization'[127] (based on the principles of the 1869 programme of the Alliance for Socialist Democracy) or of political abstentionism tout court. The Russian anarchist, for his part, who lacked the theoretical capacities of his adversary, preferred the terrain of personal accusations and insults. The only exception that set forth his positive ideas was the incomplete *Letter to La Liberté* (a Brussels paper) of early October 1872 – a text which, never sent, lay forgotten and was of no use to Bakunin's supporters in the constant round of skirmishes. The political position of the 'autonomists' emerges from it clearly enough:

> There is only one law binding all the members [...] sections and federations of the International [...]. It is the international solidarity of workers in all jobs and all countries in their economic struggle against the exploiters of labour. It is the real organisation of that solidarity through the spontaneous action of the working classes, and the absolutely free federation [...] which

[127] See note 52.

constitutes the real, living unity of the International. Who can doubt that it is out of this increasingly widespread organisation of the militant solidarity of the proletariat against bourgeois exploitation that the political struggle of the proletariat against the bourgeoisie must rise and grow? The Marxists and ourselves are unanimous on this point. But now comes the question that divides us so deeply from the Marxists. We think that the policy of the proletariat must necessarily be a revolutionary one, aimed directly and solely at the destruction of States. We do not see how it is possible to talk about international solidarity and yet to intend preserving States [...] because by its very nature the State is a breach of that solidarity and therefore a permanent cause of war. Nor can we conceive how it is possible to talk about the liberty of the proletariat or the real deliverance of the masses within and by means of the State. State means dominion, and all dominion involves the subjugation of the masses and consequently their exploitation for the sake of some ruling minority. We do not accept, even in the process of revolutionary transition, either constituent assemblies, provincial government or so called revolutionary dictatorships; because we are convinced that revolution is only sincere, honest and real in the hand of the masses, and that when it is concentrated into those of a few ruling individuals it inevitably and immediately becomes reaction.[128]

Thus, although Bakunin had in common with Proudhon an intransigent opposition to any form of political authority, especially in the direct form of the state, it would be quite wrong to tar him with the same brush as the mutualists. Whereas the latter had in effect abstained from all political activity, weighing heavily on the early years of the International, the autonomists – as Guillaume stressed in one of his last interventions at the Hague Congress – fought for 'a certain politics, of social revolution, of the destruction of bourgeois politics and of the state'.[129] It should be recognized that they were among the revolutionary components of the International, and that they offered an interesting critical contribution on the questions of political power, the state and bureaucracy.

How, then, did the 'negative politics' that the autonomists saw as the only possible form of action differ from the 'positive politics' advocated by the

---

[128] Mikhail Bakunin, 'A Letter to the Editorial Board of *La Liberté*', in Arthur Lehning (ed.), *Michael Bakunin: Selected Writings*, op. cit., pp. 236–7.
[129] From document 76, p. 290.

centralists? In the resolutions of the International Congress of Saint-Imier, held between 15 and 16 September 1872 on the proposal of the Italian Federation and attended by other delegates returning from The Hague, it is stated that 'all political organization can be nothing other than the organization of domination, to the benefit of one class and the detriment of the masses, and that if the proletariat aimed to seize power, it would itself become a dominant and exploiting class.' Consequently, 'the destruction of all political power is the first task of the proletariat', and 'any organization of so-called provisional and revolutionary political power to bring about such destruction can only be a further deception, and would be as dangerous to the proletariat as all governments existing today'.[130] As Bakunin stressed in another incomplete text, 'The International and Karl Marx', the task of the International was to lead the proletariat 'outside the politics of the State and of the bourgeois world'; the true basis of its programme should be 'quite simple and moderate: the organization of solidarity in the economic struggle of labour against capitalism'.[131] In fact, while taking various changes into account, this declaration of principles was close to the original aims of the organization and pointed in a direction very different from the one taken by Marx and the General Council after the London Conference of 1871.[132]

This profound opposition of principles and objectives shaped the climate in The Hague. Whereas the majority looked to the 'positive' conquest of political power,[133] the autonomists painted the political party as an instrument necessarily subordinate to bourgeois institutions and grotesquely likened Marx's conception of communism to the Lassallean *Volksstaat* that he had always tirelessly combated.[134] However, in the few moments when the antagonism left some space for reason, Bakunin and Guillaume recognized

---

[130] From document 78, p. 294.
[131] Mikhail Bakunin, 'The International and Karl Marx', in Sam Dolgoff (ed.), *Bakunin on Anarchy*. New York: Alfred A. Knopf, 1971, p. 303.
[132] On Bakunin's rejection of the conquest of the State by the working class organized in politican party see Arthur Lehning, 'Introduction', in Idem. (ed.), *Bakunin – Archiv*, vol. VI: *Michel Bakounine sur la Guerre Franco-Allemande et la Révolution Sociale en France (1870–1871)*, op. cit., p. cvii.
[133] See Guillaume, op. cit., p. 342.
[134] This accusation was reiterated by Bakunin in the only major work he ever completed: 'Marx's theory provided a meeting point: a vast, unified, strongly centralized state. This was what Lassalle wanted, and Bismarck was already doing it. Why should they not join forces?' Mikhail Bakunin, *Statism and Anarchy*. Cambridge: Cambridge University Press, 1990, p. 184.

that the two sides shared the same aspirations.[135] In *The Fictitious Splits in the International*, which he wrote together with Engels, Marx had explained that one of the preconditions of socialist society was the elimination of the power of the state:

> All socialists see anarchy as the following program: Once the aim of the proletarian movement – i.e., abolition of classes – is attained, the power of the state, which serves to keep the great majority of producers in bondage to a very small exploiter minority, disappears, and the functions of government become simple administrative functions.

The irreconcilable difference stemmed from the autonomist insistence that the aim must be realized immediately. Indeed, since they considered the International not as an instrument of political struggle but as an ideal model for the society of the future in which no kind of authority would exist, (in Marx's description) Bakunin and his supporters proclaim

> anarchy in proletarian ranks as the most infallible means of breaking the powerful concentration of social and political forces in the hands of the exploiters. Under this pretext, [they ask to] the International, at a time when the Old World is seeking a way of crushing it, to replace its organization with anarchy.[136]

Thus, despite their agreement about the need to abolish classes and the political power of the state in socialist society, the two sides differed radically over the fundamental issues of the path to follow and the social forces required to bring about the change. Whereas for Marx the revolutionary subject par excellence was a particular class, the factory proletariat, Bakunin turned to the 'great rabble of the people', the so-called 'lumpenproletariat', which, being 'almost unpolluted by bourgeois civilization, carries in its inner being and in its aspirations, in all the necessities and miseries of its collective life, all the seeds of the socialism of the future'.[137] Marx the communist had learned that social transformation required specific historical conditions, an effective organization and a long process of the formation of class consciousness

---

[135] See, for example, Guillaume, op. cit., pp. 298–9.
[136] From document 75, p. 289.
[137] Bakunin, 'The International and Karl Marx', op. cit., p. 294.

among the masses[138]; Bakunin the anarchist was convinced that the instincts of the common people, the so-called 'rabble', were both 'invincible as well as just', sufficient by themselves 'to inaugurate and bring to triumph the Social Revolution'.[139]

Another disagreement concerned the instruments for the achievement of socialism. Much of Bakunin's militant activity involved building (or fantasizing about building) small 'secret societies', mostly of intellectuals: a 'revolutionary general staff composed of dedicated, energetic, intelligent individuals, sincere friends of the people above all',[140] who will prepare the insurrection and carry out the revolution. Marx, however, believed in the self-emancipation of the working class and was convinced that secret societies conflicted with 'the development of the proletarian movement because, instead of instructing the workers, these societies subject them to authoritarian, mystical laws which cramp their independence and distort their powers of reason'.[141] The Russian exile opposed all political action by the working class that did not directly promote the revolution, whereas the stateless person with a fixed residence in London did not disdain mobilizations for social reforms and partial objectives, while remaining absolutely convinced that these should strengthen the working-class struggle to overcome the capitalist mode of production rather than integrate it into the system.

---

[138] Marx's critique of Bakunin's ideas is evident is his 'Conspectus of Bakunin's *Statism and Anarchy*', in MECW, vol. 24, p. 518: 'Schoolboyish rot! A radical social revolution is bound up with definite historical conditions of economic development; these are its premises. It is also only possible, therefore, where alongside capitalist production the industrial proletariat accounts for at least a significant portion of the mass of the people. [...] Mr Bakunin [...] understands absolutely nothing of social revolution, only its political rhetoric; its economic conditions simply do not exist for him. Now since all previous economic formations, whether developed or undeveloped, have entailed the enslavement of the worker (whether as wage-labourer, peasant, etc.), he imagines that radical revolution is equally possible in all these formations. What is more, he wants the European social revolution, whose economic basis is capitalist production, to be carried out on the level of the Russian or Slav[ic] agricultural and pastoral peoples, and that it should noy surpass this level [...] Willpower, not economic conditions, is the basia of his social revolution'.

[139] Bakunin, 'The International and Karl Marx', op. cit., pp. 294–5.

[140] Mikhail Bakunin, 'Programme and Purpose of the Revolutionary Organization of International Brothers', in Arthur Lehning (ed.), *Michael Bakunin: Selected Writings*, op. cit., p. 155. Evidence of Bakunin's deficient sense of reality is his claim: 'Therefore there should be no vast number of these individuals. A hundred powerfully and seriously allied revolutionaries are enough for the international organization of the whole Europe. Two or three hundred revolutionaries are enough for the largest country's organization', ibid.

[141] Karl Marx, 'Record of Marx's speech on Secret Societies', in MECW, vol. 22, p. 621.

The differences would not have diminished even after the revolution. For Bakunin, 'abolition of the state [was] the precondition or necessary accompaniment of the economic emancipation of the proletariat'[142]; for Marx, the state neither could nor should disappear from one day to the next. In his *Political Indifferentism*, which first appeared in *Almanacco Repubblicano* in December 1873, he challenged the hegemony of the anarchists in Italy's workers' movement by asserting that

> if the political struggle of the working class assumes violent forms and if the workers replace the dictatorship of the bourgeois class with their own revolutionary dictatorship, then [according to Bakunin] they are guilty of the terrible crime of *lèse-principe*; for, in order to satisfy their miserable profane daily needs and to crush the resistance of the bourgeois class, they, instead of laying down their arms and abolishing the state, give to the state a revolutionary and transitory form.[143]

It should be recognized, however, that despite Bakunin's sometimes exasperating refusal to distinguish between bourgeois and proletarian power, he foresaw some of the dangers of the so-called 'transitional period' between capitalism and socialism – particularly the danger of bureaucratic degeneration after the revolution. In his unfinished *The Knouto-Germanic Empire and the Social Revolution*, on which he worked between 1870 and 1871, he wrote:

> But in the People's State of Marx, there will be, we are told, no privileged class at all. All will be equal, not only from the juridical and political point of view, but from the economic point of view. [...] There will therefore be no longer any privileged class, but there will be a government, and, note this well, an extremely complex government, which will not content itself with governing and administering the masses politically, as all governments do today, but which will also administer them economically, concentrating in its own hands the production and the just division of wealth, the cultivation of land, the establishment and development of factories, the organization and direction of commerce, finally the application of capital to production by the only banker, the State. [...] It will be the reign of scientific intelligence,

---

[142] Mikhail Bakunin, 'Aux compagnons de la Fédération des sections internationales du Jura', in Arthur Lehning, A. J. C. Rüter, P. Scheibert (eds), *Bakunin – Archiv*, vol. II: *Michel Bakounine et les Conflits dans l'Internationale*. Leiden: Brill, 1965, p. 75.
[143] Karl Marx, 'Political Indifferentism', MECW, vol. 23, p. 393.

the most aristocratic, despotic, arrogant and contemptuous of all regimes. There will be a new class, a new hierarchy of real and pretended scientists and scholars, and the world will be divided into a minority ruling in the name of knowledge and an immense ignorant majority. [...] Every state, even the most republican and most democratic state [...] are in their essence only machines governing the masses from above, through an intelligent and therefore privileged minority, allegedly knowing the genuine interests of the people better than the people themselves.[144]

Partly because of his scant knowledge of economics, the federalist path indicated by Bakunin offered no really useful guidance on how the question of the future socialist society should be approached. But his critical insights already point ahead to some of the dramas of the twentieth century.

XII After Marx: The 'Centralist' and the 'Autonomist' International

The International would never be the same again. The great organization born in 1864, which had successfully supported strikes and struggles for 8 years, adopted an anticapitalist programme and established a presence in all European countries, finally imploded at the Hague Congress. Nevertheless, the story does not end with Marx's withdrawal, since two groupings, much reduced in size and without the old political ambition and capacity to organize projects, now occupied the same space. One was the 'centralist' majority issuing from the final congress, which favoured an organization under the political leadership of a General Council. The other was the 'autonomist' or 'federalist'[145] minority, who recognized an absolute autonomy of decision making for the sections.

In 1872, the strength of the International was not yet diminished. Displaying the uneven development that had characterized it in the past, its expansion in certain countries (above all, Spain and Italy) had compensated for its contraction in others (Britain, for example). The dramatic outcome at The Hague had split

---

[144] Mikhail Bakunin, *Marxism, Freedom and the State*. London: Freedom Press, 1950, p. 21.
[145] In the text, one has opted for the term 'autonomist' International, as utilized by Georges Haupt, *L'Internazionale socialista dalla Comune a Lenin*, op. cit., p. 70. Jacques Freymond, 'Introduction', in PI, III, p. VIII, on the contrary, preferred the use of the expression 'federalist' International.

the organization, making many activists, especially in the 'centralist' camp, realize that an important chapter in the history of the workers' movement had run its course. Along with the North American Federation, limited forces in Europe aligned themselves in support of the new General Council in New York: the Romande Federation and a number of German-speaking sections in Switzerland, both shored up by Becker's unflagging initiative; the German Social Democratic Workers' Party, which gave its unreserved but barely visible support; the new Austrian sections, which, unlike the ghostly Germans, actually scraped together a little money to forward from their members' dues; and the remote federations of Portugal and Denmark. In Spain, Italy and the Netherlands, however, few followed the new directives; the organization had not made a name for itself in Ireland; and by 1873 no section of the International remained in France. There was also Britain, of course, but in November 1872 – owing to personal clashes going back to long before the Hague Congress – the British Federal Council split into two feuding groups that each claimed to represent the International in the country. Hales, acting in the name of 16 sections and with the backing of such eminent Internationalists as Hermann Jung (1830–1901) and Thomas Motterhead (1825–84), disavowed the General Council in New York and called a new congress of the British Federation for January 1873. Both Hales and Eccarius performed some astounding political somersaults, for although they were reformists by conviction and argued for participation in elections – their idea was to convert the International into a political party with trade union support that would ally itself with the liberal wing of the bourgeoisie – they officially lined up with abstentionists led by Guillaume and Bakunin. Engels responded to these developments with two circulars recognizing the decisions taken at The Hague; they were signed by important leaders in Manchester and on the 'official' British Federal Council, plus the well-known former members of the General Council Dupont and Friedrich Lessner (1825–1910). The congress of the council then took place in June, but those taking part in it had to swallow the bitter truth that, with the departure of the General Council for New York (which everyone saw as the end of the organization) the British trade unions no longer felt involved.[146] Thus, all that the two groups had in common was a rapid decline.

---

[146] See Collins and Abramsky, op. cit., p. 275.

The general congress of the 'centralists' took place in the city that had once hosted the first congress of the International: Geneva. Thanks to Becker's efforts, it was attended by 30 delegates – including (for the first time) two women. But 15 of these were from Geneva itself, and the representation of sections from other countries was limited to a German, a Belgian, and a delegate from Austria-Hungary.[147] Having seen the climate of demobilization in Europe, the General Council decided not to send a representative from New York, and even Serrailler, the man appointed by the British Federation, failed to make the trip. In fact, this was the end of the centralist International.

Across the Atlantic, where Sorge was trying hard to keep the flame alight, the North American Federation was on the verge of collapse. Its financial situation, worsening with the decline in membership to less than 1,000 (few of whom paid dues), made even the buying of postage stamps a difficult proposition. Reduced to matters concerning only the United States, it found American workers alternating between attitudes of hostility and indifference, even in response to the *Manifesto to the Working People of North America*[148] that it issued in November 1873. Sorge eventually resigned as general secretary, and from then on the two-and-a-half remaining years of its history were little more than a chronicle of a death foretold. The final dissolution came on 15 July 1876, when ten delegates representing 635 members[149] met in Philadelphia, before hurrying to the founding congress of the Workingmen's Party of the United States, timed to coincide with the first US world fair, the Centennial Exhibition.

Although the 'centralist' organization only continued to operate for a short while in a couple of countries and they made no further contribution to the development of theory; the autonomists, on the other hand, had a real, active existence for some years to come. At the congress in Saint-Imier, attended by Swiss, Italians, Spanish and French, it was established that 'no one has the right to deprive the autonomous federations and sections of the incontestable right to determine for themselves and pursue the line of political conduct that they believe to be best' – an option for federalist autonomy within the International that underlay the offer of a 'pact of friendship, solidarity and mutual defence'.

---

[147] See PI, IV, note 355: 640–2.
[148] See Bernstein, op. cit., p. 221.
[149] Ibid., p. 283.

This position was the work of Guillaume. Unlike Bakunin, who would have preferred something more intransigent, the younger but more prudent Swiss activist had set his sights on expanding their support beyond the Jura, Spain and Italy, and winning over all the other federations opposed to the London line.[150] His tactics won the day. The birth of a new International would be carefully prepared, without forcing matters through high-sounding declarations.

New affiliations came one after another over the next few months. The autonomist stronghold remained Spain, where the persecutions launched by Práxedes Mateo Sagasta (1825–1903) failed to prevent the organization from flourishing. By the time of its federal congress in Cordoba, held between December 1872 and January 1873, it had some 50 federations comprising more than 300 sections, with a total membership of more than 25,000 (7,500 in Barcelona).[151] From late 1872 on, the autonomists also widened their support in new countries. In December, the Brussels congress of the Belgian Federation declared the resolutions of The Hague null and void, refused to recognize the General Council in New York, and added its signature to the Saint-Imier Pact.[152] In January 1873, the British rebels headed by Hales and Eccarius followed suit, and the Dutch Federation joined them the next month.[153]

Although the autonomists – who had also retained contacts in France, Austria and the United States – became the majority of a new International, the coalition was in reality a congeries of the most varied doctrines. It included: the Swiss anarcho-collectivists headed by Guillaume and Schwitzgébel (Bakunin withdrew from public life in 1873 and died in 1876); the Belgian federation under the leadership of De Paepe, for which the people's state (*Volksstaat*) should acquire greater powers and competences, beginning with the management of all public services; the ever more radical Italians, who eventually adopted insurrectionary positions ('propaganda of deeds') doomed to failure; and British advocates of participation in elections and an alliance

---

[150] See Lehning, 'Introduction', in Arthur Lehning, A. J. C. Rüter and P. Scheibert (eds), *Bakunin – Archiv*, vol. II: *Michel Bakounine et les Conflits dans l'Internationale*, op. cit., p. LII. Lehning also quoted a remark from Max Nettlau's manuscript, *Michael Bakunin: eine Biographie* (later printed by Milano: Feltrinelli, 1971): 'The autonomist International was the work of Guillaume', in Lehning, p. LXII.

[151] See Max Nettlau, *La Première Internationale en Espagne*. Dordrecht: D. Reidel, 1969, pp. 163–4.

[152] See PI, III, p. 163.

[153] Ibid., p. 191.

with progressive bourgeois forces. In 1874, contacts were even established with the Lassalleans of the General Association of German Workers.

The above scenario demonstrates that the prime antagonism that led to the split at the Hague Congress was neither between a group ready to stoop to deals with the state and an intransigent party more inclined to revolution, nor between proponents and opponents of political action. Rather, the chief cause of the radical and widespread opposition to the General Council was the turn rushed through at the London Conference in 1871. The Jura and Spanish federations, and later the newly formed Italian federation, would never have accepted Marx's call to build working-class political parties: above all, the socio-economic conditions in those countries made it unthinkable. A more cautious approach, however, might have kept the support of the Belgians – who for a number of years had been key to the balance within the Association – and other recently formed federations like the Dutch. A lower level of internal conflict would also have averted the split in Britain, which had more to do with personality clashes than with disagreements over policy. And, as some autonomists had foreseen, the moving of the General Council to New York left them with greater political scope and helped them to assert themselves after 1872. The fact remains, however, that in Marx's view the 'first' International had completed its historical task and the time had come to bring the curtain down.

The autonomists' 'first' congress – or, as they said, the 'sixth congress', counting the five of the International – was attended by 32 delegates, from Belgium, Spain, France, Italy, Britain, the Netherlands and Switzerland. It met in Geneva from 1 to 6 September 1873, the week before the congress of the centralists, and declared that it opened a 'new era in the International'.[154] It was unanimously decided to abolish the General Council, and for the first time at a congress of the International there was a debate about anarchist society.[155] The theoretical-political armoury of the Internationalists was also enriched by the idea of the general strike as a weapon to achieve the social revolution.

---

[154] See PI, IV, p. 5.
[155] Ibid., pp. 54–8. Remarkable was the position taken by Hales, mirroring the contradictions present in the autonomist International from the beginning: 'I oppose anarchy [...]. Anarchy is incompatible with collectivism'.

The groundwork was thus laid for what came to be known as anarcho-syndicalism.[156]

The next congress, held in Brussels from 7 to 13 September 1874, brought together 16 delegates: one from Britain (Eccarius), one from Spain and the rest from Belgium. Of the latter fourteen, two had the mandate of a French (Paris) or Italian (Palermo) section, while another two were German Lassalleans resident at the time in Belgium. Guillaume stated that one of these, Karl Frohme (1850–1933), actually represented the General Association of German Workers. Yet despite the fact that anarchists and Lassalleans were poles apart on the map of socialism, Guillaume motivated their presence by referring to the new rules approved by the Geneva Congress in 1873, under which the workers of each country were free to decide the best means of achieving their emancipation.[157] All the same, this International had mostly become a place where an ever smaller (and ever less representative) number of leaders met to discuss *in abstracto* the workers' material conditions and the action required to change them. The debate in 1874 was between anarchism and the people's state (*Volksstaat*), and De Paepe, returning after 3 years to a congress of the International, was the main protagonist. In one of his interventions, he claimed that 'in Spain, in parts of Italy and in the Jura, they are pro-anarchist, [whereas] in Germany, the Netherlands, Britain and America, they are for a workers' state (with Belgium still fluctuating between the two)'.[158] Once again no collective decision was taken, and the congress agreed unanimously that it was up to 'any federation and socialist democratic party in each country to decide which political line it thought it should follow'.[159]

The discussion at the Eighth Congress, held in Berne between 26 and 30 October 1876, followed the same lines. There were 28 delegates, including 19 Swiss (17 from the Jura Federation), 4 from Italy, 2 each from Spain and France, and De Paepe representing Belgium and the Netherlands. The proceedings showed the total incompatibility between the positions of De Paepe and Guillaume,[160] but they ended in agreement on a proposal from

---

[156] See the debate among the delegates which took place during the sessions of 4 September, 1873, in PI, IV, pp. 59–63 and 75–7. Cf. also Eugène Hins (1839–1933) document 18.
[157] See PI, IV, p. 646.
[158] César De Paepe, 7 September 1874, PI, IV, p. 347.
[159] PI, IV, p. 350.
[160] From document 40, pp. 192–3, and from document 41, pp. 194–8.

the Belgian Federation to call a world socialist congress for the following year, with invitations to be sent to 'all fractions of the socialist parties of Europe'.[161]

Before that could happen, however, the last congress of the International was held in Verviers, between 6 and 8 September 1877. It brought together 22 delegates: 13 from Belgium, 2 each from Spain, Italy, France and Germany, and Guillaume representing the Jura Federation. There were also three observers from socialist groups with a purely consultative function – one was Peter Kropotkin (1842–1921), later to become the founding father of anarcho-communism – but the only active participants were anarchists, including some like the Italian Andrea Costa (1851–1910) who would shortly go over to socialism. Thus, the autonomist International too, which had retained mass roots only in Spain, had run its course. Their perspective was overtaken by a growing realization throughout the European workers' movement that it was crucially important to participate in the political struggle by means of organized parties. With the end of the autonomist experience, there was also a definitive parting of the ways between anarchists and socialists.

XIII The new International

From 9 to 16 September 1877, the city of Ghent hosted the Universal Socialist Congress, with more countries represented than at any comparable event before. Some 3,000 workers welcomed delegates from nine countries (France, Germany, Switzerland, Britain, Spain, Italy, Hungary, Russia and Belgium), some of whom additionally held a mandate from an organization in another country (Denmark, the United States and, for the first time, labour groups in Greece and Egypt). Historic leaders of the International such as De Paepe and Liebknecht were present, as were Frankel, Guillaume, Hales and others, testifying to the importance of the organization for a whole generation of the European labour movement.

---

[161] PI, IV, p. 498.

In the concluding *Manifesto to Workers' Organizations and Societies in All Countries*, written by De Paepe and the future Belgian Socialist leader Louis Bertrand (1856–1943), the congress called for the establishment of a 'General Union of the Socialist Party'. A large majority also signed a 'pact':

> Inasmuch as social emancipation is inseparable from political emancipation; inasmuch as the proletariat, organized in a separate party opposed to all the parties of the possessing classes, must avail itself of all the political means tending to promote the liberation of its members; and inasmuch as the struggle against the dominion of the possessing classes must be worldwide in its scope and not merely local or national, and success in this struggle will depend upon harmonious and united activity on the part of the organizations in different lands – the undersigned delegates to the Universal Socialist Congress at Ghent decide that it is incumbent on the organizations they represent to furnish one another with material and moral support in all their industrial and political endeavours.

Six years after the London Conference of 1871, the Ghent theses confirmed that Marx had merely been in advance of the times. For the same document affirmed:

> We urge the necessity of political action as a powerful means of agitation, propaganda, popular education and association. The present organization of society must be combated on all sides at once and with all the means at our disposal. [...] Socialism should not be just theoretical speculation about the likely organization of future society; it should be real and living, involved with the actual aspirations, immediate needs and daily struggles of the proletarian class against those who control the social capital as well as social power.

> To wrest a political right from the bourgeoisie, to organize formerly isolated workers into an association, to obtain a reduction in working hours through strike action or resistance societies: these mean both working to build a new society and engaging in actual explorations with regard to the social arrangements of the future.

> Let the still unassociated workers organize and form associations! Let those who are organized only at the level of the economy descend into the political arena; they will find there the same adversaries and the same battle, and any victory scored at one of these levels will signal a triumph in the other!

Let the disinherited class in each nation form itself into a vast party distinct from all the bourgeois parties, and let this social party march hand in hand with those of other countries!

To claim all your rights, to abolish all privileges, workers of the world, unite![162]

In later decades, the workers' movement adopted a socialist programme, expanded throughout Europe and then the rest of the world, and built new structures of supranational coordination. Apart the continuity of names (the Second International from 1889 to 1916, the Third International from 1919 to 1943), each of these structures constantly referred to the values and doctrines of the First International. Thus, its revolutionary message proved extraordinarily fertile, producing results over time still greater than those achieved during its existence.

The International helped workers to grasp that the emancipation of labour could not be won in a single country but was a global objective. It also spread an awareness in their ranks that they had to achieve the goal themselves, through their own capacity for organization, rather than by delegating it to some other force; and that – here Marx's theoretical contribution was fundamental – it was essential to overcome the capitalist mode of production and wage labour, since improvements within the existing system, though necessary to pursue, would not eliminate dependence on employers' oligarchies.

An abyss separates the hopes of those times from the mistrust so characteristic of our own, the antisystemic spirit and solidarity of the age of the International from the ideological subordination and individualism of a world reshaped by neoliberal competition and privatization. The passion for politics among the workers who gathered in London in 1864 contrasts sharply with the apathy and resignation prevalent today.

And yet, while the world of labour has been reverting to conditions of exploitation similar to those of the nineteenth century, the project of the International has once again acquired an extraordinary topicality. Today's barbarism of the 'world order', ecological disasters produced by the present

---

[162] César De Paepe and Louis Bertrand, 'Manifeste aux Organisations ouvrières et Sociétés de tous les pays', in PI, IV, pp. 591–3.

mode of production, the growing gulf between the wealthy exploitative few and the huge impoverished majority, the oppression of women, and the blustery winds of war, racism and chauvinism, impose upon the contemporary workers' movement the urgent need to reorganize itself on the basis of two key characteristic of the International: the multiplicity of its structure and radicalism in objectives. The aims of the organization founded in London 150 years ago are today more vital than ever. To rise to the challenges of the present, however, the new International cannot evade that twin requirements: it must be plural and it must be anticapitalist.

Appendix: International Working Men's Association: Timeline and Membership

The first part of this appendix lists in chronological order all the congresses and conferences of the International: the unitary ones from the foundation in 1864 to the split at the Hague Congress in 1872; then the separate 'autonomist' and 'centralist' events beginning in 1873.

The second part is a table containing membership data for the International in various countries. Precise figures are impossible to establish for several reasons: (1) only a small number of workers' movement organizations at the time – above all, the British trade unions and the German socialist parties – kept an exact count; (2) workers mostly joined the International not on an individual basis but through the affiliation of trade unions and other collective bodies and (3) the International was illegal for some of the period in a number of countries, making it especially difficult to evaluate its size.

This is perhaps why – with the exception of the invaluable collective work *La Première Internationale: l'institute, l'implantation, le rayonnement* (Paris: Éditions du Centre national de la recherche scientifique, 1968) – none of the many books on the International have ventured to calculate its total membership. If it has seemed useful to attempt this here, at the risk of some approximation and imprecision, this is largely because most publications in the past bandied around excessive figures that created a misleading picture of the reality.

The first column of the table lists – in chronological order of foundation – the countries where the International established a presence; it does not include Australia, New Zealand or India, for example, where it had only sporadic contacts with small groups of workers. Nor does it cover Russia, since the International never managed to penetrate that country (although some exiles founded a circle in Switzerland). The second column gives the years in which the organization reached its peak in the respective countries, while the third offers an approximate figure for the size of its membership. These totals have been calculated from the studies in *La Première Internationale: l'institute, l'implantation, le rayonnement* and other monographs listed in the bibliography at the end of this book.

Timeline

Conferences and Congresses (1864–1872)

London Conference: 25–29 September 1865
I Congress: Geneva, 3–8 September 1866
II Congress: Lausanne, 2–8 September 1867
III Congress: Brussels, 6–13 September 1868
IV Congress: Basel, 6–12 September 1869
London Delegate Conference: 17–23 September 1871
V Congress: The Hague, 2–7 September 1872

The "Autonomist" International

VI Congress: Geneva, 1–6 September 1873
VII Congress: Brussels, 7–13 September 1874
VIII Congress: Berne, 26–30 October 1876
IX Congress: Verviers, 6–8 September 1877

The "Centralist" International

VI Congress: Geneva, 7–13 September 1873
Philadelphia Delegate Conference: 15 July 1876

Membership Table

Country	Peak Year	Membership
Britain	1867	50,000
Switzerland	1870	6,000
France	1871	More than 30,000
Belgium	1871	More than 30,000
USA	1872	4,000
Germany	1870	11,000 (including the members of the Social Democratic Workers' Party)
Spain	1873	About 30,000
Italy	1873	About 25,000
Netherlands	1872	Less than 1,000
Denmark	1872	A couple of thousands
Portugal	1872	Less than 1,000
Ireland	1872	Less than 1,000
Austria-Hungary	1872	A couple of thousands

The International Working Men's Association: Addresses, Resolutions, Interventions, Documents

Part One

The Inaugural Address

1

Karl Marx, *Inaugural Address of the International Working Men's Association*[1]

Workingmen:

It is a great fact that the misery of the working masses has not diminished from 1848 to 1864, and yet this period is unrivalled for the development of its industry and the growth of its commerce. In 1850 a moderate organ of the British middle class, of more than average information, predicted that if the exports and imports of England were to rise 50 per cent, English pauperism would sink to zero. Alas! On 7 April 1864, the Chancellor of the Exchequer delighted his parliamentary audience by the statement that the total import and export of England had grown in 1863 'to 443,955,000 pounds! That astonishing sum about three times the trade of the comparatively recent epoch of 1843!' With all that, he was eloquent upon 'poverty'.

'Think,' he exclaimed, 'of those who are on the border of that region,' upon 'wages... not increased'; upon 'human life... in nine cases out of ten but a struggle of existence!' [...]

When, consequent upon the Civil War in America, the operatives of Lancashire and Cheshire were thrown upon the streets, the [...] House of Lords sent to the manufacturing districts a physician commissioned to investigate into the smallest possible amount of carbon and nitrogen, to be administered in the cheapest and plainest form, which on an average might just suffice to 'avert

---

[1] Written between 21 and 27 October 1864, the text was approved by the GC in its session of 1 November. It was published 3 days later in the London weekly *The Bee-Hive*, and was then re-issued in the same month, along with the statutes of the organization, in a booklet entitled *Address and Provisional Rules of the Working Men's International Association*. Karl Marx [1818–83] was the brain of the IWMA. He wrote all its major resolutions, was a member of the GC from its founding until 1872, and participated in the two London Conferences (1865 and 1871) and in the Hague Congress (1872). The complete text appears in GC, I: 277–87.

starvation diseases'. Dr Smith, the medical deputy, ascertained that 28,000 grains of carbon and 1,330 grains of nitrogen were the weekly allowance that would keep an average adult... just over the level of starvation diseases, and he found furthermore that quantity pretty nearly to agree with the scanty nourishment to which the pressure of extreme distress had actually reduced the cotton operatives.[2] But now mark! The same learned doctor was later on again deputed by the medical officer of the Privy Council to enquire into the nourishment of the poorer labouring classes. The results of his research are embodied in the 'Sixth Report on Public Health', published by order of Parliament in the course of the present year. What did the doctor discover? That the silk weavers, the needlewomen, the kid glovers, the stock weavers, and so forth, received on an average, not even the distress pittance of the cotton operatives, not even the amount of carbon and nitrogen 'just sufficient to avert starvation diseases'. [...]

'It must be remembered', adds the official report, 'that privation of food is very reluctantly borne, and that, as a rule, great poorness of diet will only come when other privations have preceded it.... Even cleanliness will have been found costly or difficult, and if there still be self-respectful endeavors to maintain it, every such endeavor will represent additional pangs of hunger. These are painful reflections, especially when it is remembered that the poverty to which they advert is not the deserved poverty of idleness; in all cases it is the poverty of working populations. Indeed the work which obtains the scanty pittance of food is for the most part excessively prolonged.' [...]

Such are the official statements published by order of Parliament in 1864, during the millennium of free trade, at a time when the Chancellor of the Exchequer told the House of Commons that:

'the average condition of the British labourer has improved in a degree we know to be extraordinary and unexampled in the history of any country or any age.'

---

[2] We need hardly remind the reader that, apart from the elements of water and certain inorganic substances, carbon and nitrogen form the raw materials of human food. However, to nourish the human system, these simple chemical constituents must be supplied in the form of vegetable or animal substances. Potatoes, for instance, contain mainly carbon, while wheaten bread contains carbonaceous and nitrogenous substances in a due proportion [Note written by Karl Marx].

Upon these official congratulations jars the dry remark of the official Public Health Report:

'The public health of a country means the health of its masses, and the masses will scarcely be healthy unless, to their very base, they be at least moderately prosperous.'

Dazzled by the 'Progress of the Nation' statistics dancing before his eyes, the Chancellor of the Exchequer exclaims in wild ecstasy:

'From 1842 to 1852, the taxable income of the country increased by 6 per cent; in the eight years from 1853 to 1861, it has increased from the basis taken in 1853, 20 per cent! The fact is so astonishing to be almost incredible! ... This intoxicating augmentation of wealth and power,' adds Mr Gladstone, 'is entirely confined to classes of property.'

If you want to know under what conditions of broken health, tainted morals, and mental ruin that 'intoxicating augmentation of wealth and power... entirely confined to classes of property' was, and is, being produced by the classes of labour, look to the picture hung up in the last Public Health Report of the workshops of tailors, printers, and dressmakers! [...]

Open the census of 1861 and you will find that the number of male landed proprietors of England and Wales has decreased from 16,934 in 1851 to 15,066 in 1861, so that the concentration of land had grown in 10 years 11 per cent. If the concentration of the soil of the country in a few hands proceeds at the same rate, the land question will become singularly simplified, as it had become in the Roman Empire when Nero grinned at the discovery that half of the province of Africa was owned by six gentlemen.

We have dwelt so long upon these facts 'so astonishing to be almost incredible' because England heads the Europe of commerce and industry. It will be remembered that some months ago one of the refugee sons of Louis Philippe publicly congratulated the English agricultural labourer on the superiority of his lot over that of his less florid comrade on the other side of the Channel. Indeed, with local colours changed, and on a scale somewhat contracted, the English facts reproduce themselves in all the industrious and progressive countries of the Continent. In all of them there has taken place, since 1848, an unheard-of development of industry, and an unheard-of expansion of imports and exports. In all of them, as in England, a minority of the working classes got their real wages somewhat advanced; while in most cases the monetary rise of wages denoted no more a real access of comforts than the inmate of the metropolitan poorhouse or orphan asylum, for instance, was in the least benefited by his first necessaries costing £9 15s. 8d. in 1861 against £7 7s. 4d. in 1852. Everywhere the great mass of the working classes were sinking down to a lower depth, at the same rate at least that those above them were rising in the social scale. In all countries of Europe it has now become a truth demonstrable to every unprejudiced mind, and only decried by those whose interest it is to hedge other people in a fool's paradise, that no improvement of machinery, no appliance of science to production, no contrivances of communication, no new colonies, no emigration, no opening of markets, no free trade, not all these things put together, will do away with the miseries of the industrious masses; but that, on the present false base, every fresh development of the productive powers of labour must tend to deepen social contrasts and point social antagonisms. Death of starvation rose almost to the rank of an institution, during this intoxicating epoch of economical progress, in the metropolis of the British empire. That epoch is marked in the annals of the world by the quickened return, the widening compass, and the deadlier effects of the social pest called a commercial and industrial crisis.

After the failure of the Revolution of 1848, all party organizations and party journals of the working classes were, on the Continent, crushed by the iron hand of force, the most advanced sons of labour fled in despair to the transatlantic republic, and the short-lived dreams of emancipation vanished before an epoch of industrial fever, moral marasm, and political reaction. [...] The discoveries of new gold lands led to an immense exodus, leaving an irreparable void in the ranks of the British proletariat. Others of its formerly active members were caught by the temporary bribe of greater work and wages, and turned into 'political blacks'. All the efforts made at keeping up, of remodelling, the Chartist movement failed signally; the press organs of the working class died one by one of the apathy of the masses, and in point of fact never before seemed the English working class so thoroughly reconciled to a state of political nullity. If, then, there had been no solidarity of action between the British and the continental working classes, there was, at all events, a solidarity of defeat.

And yet the period passed since the Revolutions of 1848 has not been without its compensating features. We shall here only point to two great factors.

After a 30 years' struggle, fought with most admirable perseverance, the English working classes, improving a momentaneous split between the landlords and money lords, succeeded in carrying the Ten Hours' Bill. The immense physical, moral, and intellectual benefits hence accruing to the factory operatives, half-yearly chronicled in the reports of the inspectors of factories, are now acknowledged on all sides. Most of the continental governments had to accept the English Factory Act in more or less modified forms, and the English Parliament itself is every year compelled to enlarge its sphere of action. But besides its practical import, there was something else to exalt the marvellous success of this workingmen's measure. Through their most notorious organs of science, such as Dr Ure, Professor Senior, and other sages of that stamp, the middle class had predicted, and to their heart's content proved, that any legal restriction of the hours of labour must sound the death knell of British industry, which, vampirelike, could but live by sucking blood, and children's blood, too. In olden times, child murder was a mysterious rite of the religion of Moloch, but it was practiced on some very solemn occasions only, once a year perhaps, and then Moloch had no exclusive bias for the children of the poor. This struggle about the legal restriction of the hours of labour raged the more fiercely since, apart from frightened avarice, it told indeed upon the great contest between the blind rule of the supply and demand laws which form the political economy of the middle class, and social production controlled by social foresight, which forms the political economy of the working class. Hence the Ten Hours' Bill was not only a great practical success; it was the victory of a principle; it was the first time that in broad daylight the political economy of the middle class succumbed to the political economy of the working class.

But there was in store a still greater victory of the political economy of labour over the political economy of property. We speak of the cooperative movement, especially the cooperative factories raised by the unassisted efforts of a few bold 'hands'. The value of these great social experiments cannot be overrated. By deed instead of by argument, they have shown that production on a large scale, and in accord with the behests of modern science, may be carried on without the existence of a class of masters employing a class of hands; that to bear fruit, the means of labour need not be monopolized as a means of dominion over, and of extortion against, the labouring man himself; and that, like slave labour, like serf labour, hired labour is but a transitory and inferior form, destined to disappear before associated labour plying its toil with a willing hand, a ready mind, and a joyous heart. In England, the seeds of the cooperative system were sown by Robert Owen; the workingmen's experiments tried on the Continent were, in fact, the practical upshot of the theories, not invented, but loudly proclaimed, in 1848.

At the same time the experience of the period from 1848 to 1864 has proved beyond doubt that, however, excellent in principle and however useful in practice, cooperative labour, if kept within the narrow circle of the casual efforts of private workmen, will never be able to arrest the growth in geometrical progression of monopoly, to free the masses, nor even to perceptibly lighten the burden of their miseries. It is perhaps for this very reason that plausible noblemen, philanthropic middle-class spouters, and even keen political economists have all at once turned nauseously complimentary to the very cooperative labour system they had vainly tried to nip in the bud by deriding it as the utopia of the dreamer, or stigmatizing it as the sacrilege of the socialist. To save the industrious masses, cooperative labour ought to be developed to national dimensions, and, consequently, to be fostered by national means. Yet the lords of the land and the lords of capital will always use their political privileges for the defence and perpetuation of their economic monopolies. So far from promoting, they will continue to lay every possible impediment in the way of the emancipation of labour. Remember the sneer with which, last session, Lord Palmerston put down the advocates of the Irish Tenants' Right Bill. The House of Commons, cried he, is a house of landed proprietors.

To conquer political power has, therefore, become the great duty of the working classes. They seem to have comprehended this, for in England, Germany, Italy and France, there have taken place simultaneous revivals, and simultaneous efforts are being made at the political organization of the working men's party.

One element of success they possess – numbers; but numbers weigh in the balance only if united by combination and led by knowledge. Past experience has shown how disregard of that bond of brotherhood which ought to exist between the workmen of different countries, and incite them to stand firmly by each other in all their struggles for emancipation, will be chastised by the common discomfiture of their incoherent efforts. This thought prompted the workingmen of different countries assembled on 28 September 1864, in public meeting at St Martin's Hall, to found the International Association.

Another conviction swayed that meeting.

If the emancipation of the working classes requires their fraternal concurrence, how are they to fulfil that great mission with a foreign policy in pursuit of criminal designs, playing upon national prejudices, and squandering in piratical wars the people's blood and treasure? It was not the wisdom of the ruling classes, but the heroic resistance to their criminal folly by the working classes of England, that saved the west of Europe from plunging headlong into an infamous crusade for the perpetuation and propagation of slavery on the other side of the Atlantic. The shameless approval, mock sympathy, or idiotic indifference with which the upper classes of Europe have witnessed the mountain fortress of the Caucasus falling a prey to, and heroic Poland being assassinated by, Russia: the immense and unresisted encroachments of that barbarous power, whose head is in St Petersburg, and whose hands are in every cabinet of Europe, have taught the working classes the duty to master themselves the mysteries of international politics; to watch the diplomatic acts of their respective governments; to counteract them, if necessary, by all means in their power; when unable to prevent, to combine in simultaneous denunciations, and to vindicate the simple laws or morals and justice, which ought to govern the relations of private individuals, as the rules paramount of the intercourse of nations.

The fight for such a foreign policy forms part of the general struggle for the emancipation of the working classes.

Proletarians of all countries, unite!

Part Two

The Political Program

2

Karl Marx, *[Resolutions of the Geneva Congress (1866)]*[3]

[...]

Limitation of the working day

A preliminary condition, without which all further attempts at improvement and emancipation must prove abortive, is the *limitation of the working day.*

It is needed to restore the health and physical energies of the working class, that is, the great body of every nation, as well as to secure them the possibility of intellectual development, sociable intercourse, social and political action.

We propose 8 *hours work* as the *legal limit* of the working day. This limitation being generally claimed by the workmen of the United States of America, the vote of the Congress will raise it to the common platform of the working classes all over the world.

For the information of continental members, whose experience of factory law is comparatively short-dated, we add that all legal restrictions will fail and be broken through by capital if the *period of the day* during which the 8 working hours must be taken, be not fixed. The length of that period ought to be determined by the 8 working hours and the additional pauses for meals. For instance, if the different interruptions for meals amount to *one hour*, the legal period of the day ought to embrace 9 hours, say from 7 a.m. to 4 p.m.,

---

[3] This selection is excerpted from the *Instructions for the Delegates of the Provisional General Council. The Different Question*. Written by Karl Marx (see note 1) in August 1866, the text was read at the Geneva Congress, during which all the parts here included were approved, except for 'Direct and indirect taxation'. A revised version was published between February and March 1867, in *The Courrier International*, and appears also in GC, I: 340–51.

or from 8 a.m. to 5 p.m., etc. Nightwork to be but exceptionally permitted, in trades or branches of trades specified by law. The tendency must be to suppress all nightwork [...].

Juvenile and children's labour (both sexes)

We consider the tendency of modern industry to make children and juvenile persons of both sexes co-operate in the great work of social production, as a progressive, sound and legitimate tendency, although under capital it was distorted into an abomination. [...]

It may be desirable to begin elementary school instruction before the age of 9 years; but we deal here only with the most indispensable antidotes against the tendencies of a social system which degrades the working man into a mere instrument for the accumulation of capital, and transforms parents by their necessities into slave-holders, sellers of their own children. The *right* of children and juvenile persons must be vindicated. They are unable to act for themselves. It is, therefore, the duty of society to act on their behalf.

If the middle and higher classes neglect their duties towards their offspring, it is their own fault. Sharing the privileges of these classes, the child is condemned to suffer from their prejudices.

The case of the working class stands quite different. The working man is no free agent. In too many cases, he is even too ignorant to understand the true interest of his child, or the normal conditions of human development. However, the more enlightened part of the working class fully understands that the future of its class, and, therefore, of mankind, altogether depends upon the formation of the rising working generation. They know that, before everything else, the children and juvenile workers must be saved from the crushing effects of the present system. This can only be effected by converting *social reason* into *social force*, and, under given circumstances, there exists no other method of doing so, than through *general laws*, enforced by the power of the state. In enforcing such laws, the working class do not fortify governmental power. On the contrary, they transform that power, now used against them, into their own agency. They effect by a general act what they would vainly attempt by a multitude of isolated individual efforts.

Proceeding from this standpoint, we say that no parent and no employer ought to be allowed to use juvenile labour, except when combined with education. [...]

Cooperative labour

It is the business of the International Working Men's Association to combine and generalize the *spontaneous movements* of the working classes, but not to dictate or impose any doctrinary system whatever. The Congress should, therefore, proclaim no *special system* of cooperation, but limit itself to the enunciation of a few general principles.

a. We acknowledge the cooperative movement as one of the transforming forces of the present society based upon class antagonism. Its great merit is to practically show, that the present pauperizing and despotic system of the *subordination of labour* to capital can be superseded by the republican and beneficent system of *the association of free and equal producers.*
b. Restricted, however, to the dwarfish forms into which individual wages slaves can elaborate it by their private efforts, the cooperative system will never transform capitalist society. To convert social production into one large and harmonious system of free and cooperative labour, *general social changes* are wanted, *changes of the general conditions of society,* never to be realized save by the transfer of the organized forces of society, viz., the state power, from capitalists and landlords to the producers themselves.
c. We recommend to the working men to embark in *cooperative production* rather than in *cooperative stores*. The latter touch but the surface of the present economical system, the former attacks its groundwork.
d. We recommend to all cooperative societies to convert one part of their joint income into a fund for propagating their principles by example as well as by precept, in other words, by promoting the establishment of new cooperative fabrics, as well as by teaching and preaching.
e. In order to prevent cooperative societies from degenerating into ordinary middle-class joint stock companies (*sociétés par actions*), all workmen employed, whether shareholders or not, ought to share alike. As a mere temporary expedient, we are willing to allow shareholders a low rate of interest.

Trades' Unions: Their past, present and future

(a) Their past

Capital is concentrated social force, while the workman has only to dispose of his working force. The *contract* between capital and labour can therefore never be struck on equitable terms, equitable even in the sense of a society which places the ownership of the material means of life and labour on one side and the vital productive energies on the opposite side. The only social power of the workmen is their number. The force of numbers, however is broken by disunion. The disunion of the workmen is created and perpetuated by their *unavoidable competition among themselves.*

Trades' Unions originally sprang up from the *spontaneous* attempts of workmen at removing or at least checking that competition, in order to conquer such terms of contract as might raise them at least above the condition of mere slaves. The immediate object of Trades' Unions was therefore confined to everyday necessities, to expediences for the obstruction of the incessant encroachments of capital, in one word, to questions of wages and time of labour. This activity of the Trades' Unions is not only legitimate, it is necessary. It cannot be dispensed with so long as the present system of production lasts. On the contrary, it must be generalized by the formation and the combination of Trades' Unions throughout all countries. On the other hand, unconsciously to themselves, the Trades' Unions were forming *centres of organization* of the working class, as the mediaeval municipalities and communes did for the middle class. If the Trades' Unions are required for the guerrilla fights between capital and labour, they are still more important as *organized agencies for superseding the very system of wages labour and capital rule.*

(b) Their present

Too exclusively bent upon the local and immediate struggles with capital, the Trades' Unions have not yet fully understood their power of acting against the system of wage slavery itself. They therefore kept too much aloof from general social and political movements. Of late, however, they seem to awaken to some sense of their great historical mission, as appears, for instance, from their participation, in England, in the recent political movement, from the enlarged views taken of their function in the United States, and from the following resolution passed at the recent great conference of Trades' delegates at Sheffield:

'That this Conference, fully appreciating the efforts made by the International Association to unite in one common bond of brotherhood the working men of all countries, most earnestly recommend to the various societies here represented, the advisability of becoming affiliated to that body, believing that it is essential to the progress and prosperity of the entire working community.'

(c) Their future

Apart from their original purposes, they must now learn to act deliberately as organizing centres of the working class in the broad interest of its *complete emancipation*. They must aid every social and political movement tending in that direction. Considering themselves and acting as the champions and representatives of the whole working class, they cannot fail to enlist the non-society men into their ranks. They must look carefully after the interests of the worst paid trades, such as the agricultural labourers, rendered powerless by exceptional circumstances. They must convince the world at large[4] that their efforts, far from being narrow and selfish, aim at the emancipation of the downtrodden millions.

Direct and indirect taxation

a. No modification of the form of taxation can produce any important change in the relations of labour and capital.
b. Nevertheless, having to choose between two systems of taxation, we recommend the *total abolition of indirect taxes*, and the *general substitution of direct taxes* because direct taxes are cheaper to collect and do not interfere with production.[5]

---

[4] The French and German versions refer instead to 'the broad masses of workers'.
[5] The explanation contained in the last part of this sentence is taken from the French and German versions.

Because indirect taxes enhance the prices of commodities – the tradesmen adding to those prices not only the amount of the indirect taxes, but the interest and profit upon the capital advanced in their payment;

Because indirect taxes conceal from an individual what he is paying to the state, whereas a direct tax is undisguised, unsophisticated, and not to be misunderstood by the meanest capacity. Direct taxation prompts therefore every individual to control the governing powers while indirect taxation destroys all tendency to self-government. [...]

Standing armies; their relation to production[6]

a. The deleterious influence of large standing armies upon *production*, has been sufficiently exposed at middle-class congresses of all denominations, at peace congresses, economical congresses, statistical congresses, philanthropical congresses, sociological congresses. We think it, therefore, quite superfluous to expatiate upon this point.
b. We propose the general armament of the people and their general instruction in the use of arms. [...]

---

[6] In the English text this heading is simply 'Armies'.

3
Various Authors, *[Resolutions of the Brussels Congress (1868)]*[7]

Trades unions and strikes

1. That strikes are not a means to the complete emancipation of the working classes, but are frequently a necessity in the actual situation of the struggle between labour and capital.
2. That it is requisite to subject them to certain rules of organization, opportunity, and legitimacy.
3. In trades where no unions and benefit societies exist as yet, it is necessary to create them. The unions of all trades and countries must combine. In each local federation of trade societies a fund destined to support strikes ought to be established. In one word, the work undertaken by International Working Men's Association is to be continued so as to enable working men to enter the association en masse.
4. It is necessary to appoint in each locality a committee consisting of delegates of the various societies, who shall act as umpires, deciding eventually upon the advisability and legitimacy of a strike. For the rest, the different sections will, of course, in the mode of appointing these committees, follow the particular manners, habit, and laws of their respective places.

---

[7] On 6 October 1868, the GC decided to publish the principal resolutions of the Congresses of Geneva (1866) and Brussels (1868). The *Resolutions of the Third Congress of the International Working Men's Association* were of fundamental importance for the IWMA. They signalled the defeat of the mutualists and, with it, the collectivist turn of the entire organization. This text first appeared in *The Bee-Hive*, between November and December 1868, and, subsequently, still in London, with the Westminster Printing Company, in February of the following year, as a booklet entitled *The International Working Men's Association. Resolutions of the Congress of Geneva, 1866, and the Congress of Brussels, 1868*. For the complete text, see GC, III: 292–8.

The effects of machinery in the hands of the capitalist class

Considering that on the one side machinery has proved a most powerful instrument of despotism and extortion in the hands of the capitalist class, and that on the other side the development of machinery creates the material conditions necessary for the superseding of the wages system by a truly social system of production;

Considering that machinery will render no real service to the working men until by a more equitable, social organization, it be put into their own possession, the Congress declares:

1. That it is only by means of cooperative associations and an organization of mutual credit that the producer can obtain possession of machinery.
2. That even in the existing state of things it is possible for working men organized in trade societies to enforce some guarantees or compensation in cases of sudden displacement by machinery. [...]

The question of education

Cognizant that it is impossible at present to organize a rational system of education, the Congress invites the different sections to establish courses of public lectures on scientific and economical subjects, and thus to remedy as much as possible the shortcomings of the education actually received by the working man. It is understood that reduction of the hours of labour is an indispensable preliminary condition of any true system of education.

Property in land, mines, railroads, & etc.

1. *In relation to mines, collieries, railways, etc.* – Considering that these great productive forces are fixed in, and occupy a large portion of the soil, the common gift of nature,

That they can only be worked by means of machinery and collective labour power,

That the machinery and the collective labour power, which today exist only for the advantage of the capitalists ought in future to benefit the whole people;

The Congress resolves:

a. That the quarries, collieries, and other mines, as well as the railways, ought in a normal state of society to belong to the community represented by the state, a state itself subject to the laws of justice.
b. That the quarries, collierries, and other mines, and Railways, be let by the state, not to companies of capitalists as at present, but to companies of working men bound by contract to guarantee to society the rational and scientific working of the railways, etc., at a price as nearly as possible approximate to the working expense. The same contract ought to reserve to the state the right to verify the accounts of the companies, so as to present the possibility of any reconstitution of monopolies. A second contract ought to guarantee the mutual right of each member of the companies in respect to his fellow workmen.

2. *In Relation to Agricultural Property*: – Considering that the necessities of production and the application of the known laws of agronomy require culture on a large scale, and necessitate the introduction of machinery and the organization of agricultural labour power, and that generally modern economical development tends to agriculture on a large scale;

Considering that consequently agricultural labour and property in arable soil ought to be put on the same footing as mines;

Considering that the productive properties of the soil are the prime materials of all products, the prime source of all means of production, and of all desirable things that cost no labour;

The Congress thinks that the economical development of modern society will create the social necessity of converting arable land into the common property of society, and of letting the soil on behalf of the state to agricultural companies under conditions analogous to those stated in regard to mines and railways.

3. *In Relation to Canals, Highways and Telegraphs.* – Considering that the roads and other means of communication require a common social direction, the Congress thinks they ought to remain the common property of society.

4. *In Relation to Forests.* – Considering that the abandonment of forests to private individuals causes the destruction of woods necessary for the conservation of springs, and, as a matter of course, of the good qualities of the soil, as well as the health and lives of the population, the Congress thinks that the forests ought to remain the property of society.

Reduction of the hours of labour

A resolution having been unanimously passed by the Congress of Geneva, 1866, to the effect that the legal limitation of the working day is a preliminary condition to all ulterior social improvement of the working classes, the Congress is of opinion that the time has arrived when practical effect should be given to that resolution, and that it has become the duty of all the branches to agitate that question practically in the different countries where the International Working Men's Association is established.

War and standing armies

Considering that our social institutions as well as the centralization of political power are a permanent cause of war, which can only be removed by a thorough social reform;

that the people even now can diminish the number of wars by opposing those who declare and make war;

that this concerns above all the working classes, who have almost exclusively to shed their blood;

that to do this there is a practical and legal means which can be immediately acted upon; that as the body politic could not go on for any length of time without labour, it would suffice for the working men to strike work to render war impossible;

the International Working Men's Congress recommends to all the sections, and to the members of working men's societies in particular and to the working classes in general, to cease work in case a war be declared in their country. The Congress counts upon the spirit of solidarity which animates the working men of all countries, and entertains a hope that means would not be wanting in such an emergency to support the people against their government. [...]

Part Three

Labour

4

Karl Marx, *[Inquiry on the Situation of the Working Classes]*[8]

[...]

International combination of efforts, by the agency of the association, in the struggle between labour and capital

a. From a general point of view, this question embraces the whole activity of the International Association which aims at combining and generalizing the till now disconnected efforts for emancipation by the working classes in different countries.
b. To counteract the intrigues of capitalists always ready, in cases of strikes and lockouts, to misuse the foreign workman as a tool against the native workman, is one of the particular functions which our Society has hitherto performed with success. It is one of the great purposes of the Association to make the workmen of different countries not only *feel* but *act* as brethren and comrades in the army of emancipation.
c. One great 'International combination of efforts' which we suggest is a *statistical inquiry into the situation of the working classes of all countries to be instituted by the working classes themselves*. To act with any success, the materials to be acted upon must be known. By initiating so great a work, the workmen will prove their ability to take their own fate into their own hands. We propose therefore:

---

[8] This is an excerpt from the text set out in note 3. These statements were also approved by the participants at the conference.

That in each locality, where branches of our Association exist, the work be immediately commenced, and evidence collected on the different points specified in the subjoined scheme of inquiry.

That the Congress invite all workmen of Europe and the United States of America to collaborate in gathering the elements of the statistics of the working class; that reports and evidence be forwarded to the Central Council. That the Central Council elaborate them into a general report, adding the evidence as an appendix.

That this report together with its appendix be laid before the next annual Congress, and after having received its sanction, be printed at the expense of the Association.

General Scheme of Inquiry, which may of course be modified by each Locality

1. Industry, name of.
2. Age and sex of the employed.
3. Number of the employed.
4. Salaries and wages: *(a)* apprentices; *(b)* wages by the day or piece work; scale paid by middlemen. Weekly, yearly average.
5. *(a)* Hours of work in factories. *(b)* The hours of work with small employers and in home work, if the business be carried on in those different modes. *(c)* Nightwork and daywork.
6. Meal times and treatment.
7. Sort of workshop and work: overcrowding, defective ventilation, want of sunlight, use of gaslight. Cleanliness, etc.
8. Nature of occupation.
9. Effect of employment upon the physical condition.
10. Moral condition. Education.
11. State of trade: whether season trade, or more or less uniformly distributed over year, whether greatly fluctuating, whether exposed to foreign competition, whether destined principally for home or foreign consumption, etc.
12. Condition of nutrition and housing of the worker.[9]

---

[9] The original English text comprised points 1 to 10; the French and German versions included point 11; the German also included point 12.

5
François Dupleix – Ferdinand Quinet – Jean Marly – Adrien Schettel – Jean Henri de Beaumont, *[On Machinery and its Effects]*[10]

[…] The Committee acknowledges that, of all the means used to date, machinery is the most powerful to achieve the outcome we seek, namely the betterment of the material conditions of the working class; yet, to arrive at this end, it is of the utmost urgency that labour take hold of the means of production, by association and through the aid of mutual credit banks, to make them serve the benefit of all, rather than allowing them to remain in the hands of capitalists who, until this day, have used them only in their own interests, to the detriment of the working class, in moral as much as in material terms, through the employment of a large number of women and children in factories.

Machines, eliminating a great many hands, must be put into balance with the number of workers through a shortening of the working day, so that each may be employed and thereby have access to the means of consumption; this is precisely what has not occurred up until now and what is responsible for the large-scale disturbances caused by the utilization of machinery, which has been supplying products in quantities that surpass consumption.

With the invention of machinery, the division of labour becomes necessary to be able to supply products equal to those produced by machinery in both

---

[10] This text is an excerpt from one of the *Reports of the Committeee of the Congress on the on Programmatic Questions* (PI, I: 189–236), presented at the Congress of Lausanne (1867). The report here partially reproduced was elaborated by the committee on labour and capital. Its members were: François Dupleix [unk.], a bookbinder, a leader of the Geneva section and a delegate at the Congresses of Geneva (1866) and Basel (1867); Ferdinand Quinet [unk.] (rapporteur of the committee), a Swiss craftsman and activist of the Geneva section; Jean Marly [unk.], a weaver and delegate of the Paris section; Adrien Schettel [unk.], a mechanic and one of the organizers of the Lyon section; Jean Henri de Beaumont [1821–unk.], a Parisian bronze worker. The report was published in L1867 and is also found in PI, I: 209–10.

manufacture and selling price. Unfortunately, in this way, all noble ambition in man has been annihilated and his liberty completely nullified as he passes into the condition of a machine, henceforth the property of the one who employs him and holds him in a state of complete dependence.

The capitalist takes great care of his machinery; but he does the opposite with the worker, to whom he affords hardly enough to suffice; for him, the machine is everything, the man a mere appendage. What concern is it of his the many forms of deprivation suffered by the worker owing to the paltriness of his wage? For him, the objective is to give little and gain much; the result is immense misery for the masses and immense riches for the few.

Only through association can this state of affairs be remedied by means of the equal distribution of work and profit, which will eliminate wage labour by giving everyone a share.

We conclude, for the reasons given above, that labour, by every possible means, must take the place of capital. One of the means used to date is the strike. […]

6

P. Eslens – Eugène Hins – Paul Robin, [On Woman's Emancipation and Independence][11]

Ancient religions considered work a punishment; today man sees in work his true destiny. Work then becomes a sacred right that cannot be denied to anyone. Woman can therefore claim this right by the same token as man, since only in work will she find independence and dignity.

Many arguments have been made against extending this right to women. We shall examine the most specious of them:

1. Hiring women in industry is said to lower the wages of men. This is simply a result of the current organization of work. One could just as well say that hiring too large a number of men would lower the wages of all of them, and then conclude that it is necessary to limit the number of workers and reestablish the ancient guilds. An easy way to prevent this problem would be to include women in the future system by which work is organized.
2. Workplaces are said to be sites of immoral behaviour. This arises from various causes that have nothing to do with the work itself – for example, pressure exercised by licentious bosses and foremen; inadequate wages, which drive women to debauchery; and ignorance, which leaves woman no other pleasures than those of the senses.

---

[11] This text is a document presented in the reports described in note 10. In the debate on the role of man and woman in society (the fifth issue discussed), the Belgian branch submitted two reports expressing opposed positions. The first, that of the majority, written by César de Paepe (see note 14) and two other internationalists, expressed conservative views and called for woman to return to the family, arguing that her emancipation could be achieved only through that of the working man. By contrast, the minority report prefigured certain goals that would later be advanced by the feminist movement, such as the socialization of domestic labour. Its three exponents were P. Eslens [unk.], of whom nothing is known; Eugène Hins [1839-1933], first a Proudhonian and later a Bakuninist, director of the newspaper *La Liberté*, member of the Belgian federal committee and a delegate to the Congresses of Brussels (1868) and Basel (1869); and Paul Robin [1837-unk.], a French schoolteacher who moved between Belgium, Switzerland and London, a follower of Bakunin since 1869, and member of the GC in 1870-71. The text may be found in PI, I: 220-1.

3. Woman is said to be weak. But if man is endowed with strength, woman may make up for this with dexterity. The field open to woman is therefore vast, and the machines that more and more diminish the importance of physical strength will increase the number of occupations that she can practice.
4. Motherhood. It is said that woman is destined for marriage and therefore will not have time to work. But one can answer that she may perhaps not marry, or she may be a widow without children, or she may have finished raising her children. Moreover, we should take away from the married women all that could be better carried out, with the division of labour, through specific institutions, such as preparing food, washing and ironing, making clothes, and teaching children in pre-school. Woman will then only be unable to work during the last months of pregnancy and the first three years of a child's life. During that time, the woman will be supported either by her husband (assuming the continuation of marriage) or by a special fund earmarked for this purpose.

If we reckon an average of four children for each woman, and if we allow roughly 4 years for each child, this would add up to no more than 16 years removed from work, and even then, not completely. There will therefore remain in the life of woman a sufficient part to be devoted to work.

A man can be free to support a woman entirely if he wants a full-time housewife, but the woman should not be bound to him as a matter of necessity. If she wants to leave him, she should be able to retrieve, in the exercise of her profession, an independent existence.

Conclusion. The International Working Men's Association should promote the development among women of associations that currently exist only for men. The women's associations should federate with the men's associations so as to fight together for the emancipation of labour, which alone will be able to assure independence for everyone.

7

Karl Marx, *[The Influence of Machinery in the Hands of Capitalists]*[12]

Marx [...] said what strikes us most is that all the consequences which were expected as the inevitable result of machinery have been reversed. Instead of diminishing the hours of labour, the working day was prolonged to 16 and 18 hours. Formerly, the normal working day was 10 hours, during the last century the hours of labour were increased by law here as well as on the Continent. The whole of the trade legislation of the last century turns upon compelling the working people by law to work longer hours.

It was not until 1833 that the hours of labour for children were limited to 12. In consequence of overwork there was no time left whatever for mental culture. They also became physically deteriorated; contagious fevers broke out amongst them, and this induced a portion of the upper class to take the matter up. The first Sir Robert Peel was one of the foremost in calling attention to the crying evil, and Robert Owen was the first mill-owner who limited the hours of labour in his factory. The 10 hours' bill was the first law which limited the hours of labour to ten and a half per day for women and children, but it applied only to certain factories.

This was a step of progress, in so far as it afforded more leisure time to the work-people. With regard to production, the limitation has long since been overtaken. By improved machinery and increased intensity of the labour of individuals there is now more work done in the short day than formerly in the long day. People are again overworked, and it will soon become necessary to limit the working day to 8 hours.

---

[12] This text is a synopsis of a speech made by Marx (see note 1) on 28 July 1868 in a session of the GC. It is located in the GC, II: 231–3. A comprehensive discussion of this issue can be found in the thirteenth chapter of *Capital*, published less than a year earlier.

[...] Another consequence of the use of machinery was that it entirely changed the relations of the capital of the country. Formerly there were wealthy employers of labour, and poor labourers who worked with their own tools. They were to a certain extent free agents, who had it in their power effectually to resist their employers. For the modern factory operative, for the women and children, such freedom does not exist, they are slaves of capital.

There was a constant cry for some invention that might render the capitalist independent of the working man; the spinning machine and power-loom has rendered him independent, it has transferred the motive power of production into his hands. By this the power of the capitalist has been immensely increased. The factory lord has become a penal legislator within his own establishment, inflicting fines at will, frequently for his own aggrandisement. The feudal baron in his dealings with his serfs was bound by traditions and subject to certain definite rules; the factory lord is subject to no controlling agency of any kind.

One of the great results of machinery is organized labour which must bear fruit sooner or later. The influence of machinery upon those with whose labour it enters into competition is directly hostile. Many, hand-loom weavers were positively killed by the introduction of the power-loom both here and in India.

We are frequently told that the hardships resulting from machinery are only temporary, but the development of machinery is constant, and if it attracts and gives employment to large numbers at one time it constantly throws large numbers out of employment. There is a continual surplus of displaced population, not as the Malthusian asserts a surplus population in relation to the produce of the country, but a surplus whose labour has been superseded by more productive agencies.

Employed on land machinery produces a constantly increasing surplus population whose employment is not fluctuating. This surplus flocks to the towns and exercises a constant pressure, a wage lowering pressure upon the labour market. [...]

8

Eugène Steens, [*The Effect of Machinery on the Situation of Workers*][13]

[…] Thanks to human knowledge, which, in our time, eludes all authoritarian and political constriction, the old organization is breaking down.

From one day to the next, science sheds a vivid light upon the most obscure points of the social question, and drives the irresistible movement of the old world towards its dissolution.

Also, we see social injury expand in direct proportion to inventions and discoveries. Indeed, do we not remark that the improvements introduced by the driving force of steam, weaving and spinning machines, the development of tools and mechanisms, though lessening the hardships of labour, lead to a depression in wages and give rise to successive crises and periodic disturbances?

To formulate an overall judgement upon the good and the harm that machinery exerts on the situation of the worker, we believe that it must be considered from the view point of each of the following three phases: Its introduction into industry. The period of transition. Its role in the future.

The introduction of machinery in the manufacturing, commercial, agricultural and extractive industries threw into disarray the old system of labour; the character of demonstrations for and against machinery left no doubt as to the fair assessment of those involved. The antagonism between

---

[13] This text is an excerpt from a report of the Brussels section presented at the Brussels Congress (1868) to a session of 9 September dedicated to the question of machinery. Likely written collectively, it was read by Eugène Steens [unk.], director of *La Tribune du Peuple* of Brussels and also a delegate to the London Conference of 1871. The full version is in PI, I: 291–4.

the monopolizers and the exploited, the basis of the existing order, became sharper and fiercer. The exploiters, filled with delight in anticipation of immense profits and the considerable reduction of their operating costs, sang the praises of the inventor of a marvel so favourable to their speculations; while labourers, appalled to see steam supplanting human force and machinery doing away with millions of workers, were filled with great loathing for the infernal genius behind the aggravation of their destitution in present society, and devoted themselves to the destruction of its instruments of grief and exploitation.

The future justified in part these cries of joy and sounds of alarm. Employers and workers were aware of the transformative role of these new and immense engines of production and consumption: the equilibrium was upset and crisis was generalized. [...]

Steam engines existing in England today replace by themselves the work of thirty-five million labourers.

This simple factual statement, clear, precise and irrefutable, brings to the fore all of the grievances that workers have against machinery. It demonstrates beyond dispute that, when monopolized in the hands of employers, machinery is the prime agent of the rapid and prodigious rise of their wealth, and the cause of the frightful reduction of pay.

What adds to these disastrous effects is that, as machinery is improved, competition is redoubled and becomes ever more frantic. The masters of industry that have not adopted the new machinery, or cannot acquire it, make recourse to the lowering of wages to keep up an impossible battle, and, in this way, oblige the possessor of machinery to lower them equally.

This is evidently one of the most alarming causes of modern pauperism and the utopia of riots so fatal to the worker.

And this competition between the owners of older sophisticated machinery, does it not extend as far as nations? For a long time Belgium and France, faced with the superiority of English machinery and its products, and terrified by the immense centralization of English capital, imposed an import tariff on manufactured products from England in order to shut off access to their markets. Today, this exclusive protectionism still partially exists, to the great advantage of speculators, and to the detriment of labour's prosperity.

But the loss of a few million jobs does not, however, bring about the immediate danger of social demise. The momentary crisis, intense as it was at the appearance of steam in industry, was, in the long run, averted by a series of compensations which the labourer, in his first moments of terror, did not fully grasp.

The indispensable needs of steam machinery gave rise to a lucrative chain reaction. Previously unknown industries sprang into being, while others experienced a new and rapid growth. The railways, the manufacture of mechanisms and machinery, the iron industry, coal mining, etc., have in part reclaimed the hands sacrificed by steam engines; but such compensations are only illusory. The same phenomena erupt in these new industries; there, as everywhere, owing to machinery, employees suffer a reduction disproportionate to their needs.

In vain economists try to convince us that, with the aid of machinery, immeasurable improvements have, in the span of a few years' time, been introduced in the plight and the living conditions of the poor classes; that life is sweeter and toil less tedious owing to the fallacious claim that industrial products of all kinds are at the disposition of the less fortunate. We see the facts of daily life refute these pretentious assertions. Periodic and rapidly-succeeding riots, as never before seen, unmask such affirmations with bitter irony.

Admittedly, since the invention of steam engines, cheapness is the order of the day. The products of labour have decreased notably in price, one of the improvements invoked by economists; we would be happy if we could applaud such a result, if economic laws did not demonstrate to us that it is by compressing wages, turned into a raw material, that cheapness is established and competition maintained.

It is therefore a total error to affirm that the abundance of products and their favourable price, when compared to the past, represent a new comfort for the worker.

The opposite is true, as simple reason suffices to show. Indeed, what satisfaction can the worker derive from the cheapness of the products of his labour if the lowering of product prices flows directly from the reduction of his wages? Evidently none; his position will be only more precarious than ever if the rise of foodstuffs coincides with successive decreases in his earnings. Consequently, how can he be expected to enjoy the benefits of inexpensive goods if his earnings hardly permit him to restore the energies he expends in labour; in a word, how would you have him clothe himself decently when he has nothing to eat? After that, to claim, as bourgeois economists are inclined to do, that the worker gains in consumption what he loses in production, is a bitter joke.

However, as the worker advances in his career, he modifies his first impression of his formidable rivals, and his fears are assuaged with the progress of enlightenment.

A revolution has been accomplished in his ideas and in fact; initiated today into the mysteries of social renewal, he considers machinery from the point of view of its results in the future; he recognizes the great alleviation that it has brought, through the immense aid of its resources and its force, to the most arduous forms of labour; finally, the labourer plunges into the new transformation.

This is the flight of the past into the future; such that these fatal and dangerous crises, generated by machinery in the phase of transition, are phenomena utilizing the experience of the past for the benefit of the future.

On the day in which steam engines cease to be the monopoly of capital and pass, along with all other instruments of labour, into the hands of labourers organized in agricultural and industrial associations, the worker will be liberated, peace will be achieved and justice will reign.

Originally intended for the exclusive benefit of employers, this gigantic machinery of production has taken its place, as of now, among the salutary means of precipitating social decomposition; it will exercise an extraordinary influence on the prosperity of the future; multiplying by an incalculable proportion the sum of public wealth, it will render life sweeter and more agreeable by the large and constant diminishing of the hours of labour made more appealing; once machinery is placed at the disposal of all, as a fateful compensation for lost well-being, evil will cease to exist; already now, it presses towards the full emancipation of the worker.

9

Pierre Fluse, [*The Effect of Machinery on the Wages and Situation of Workers*][14]

Society, considered in its totality, stands to gain from the introduction of machinery, as it permits the production of a greater output with the same number of hands and in the same frame of time.

But this phenomenon is taking place in a society composed of two groups in a state of perpetual antagonism: one, *the exploited*, quite significant in size, the other, *the exploiters*, relatively small but all-powerful, and both engaged in competition.

The introduction of machinery in an industrial centre always results in the dismissal of a certain number of workers, who, in finding themselves without resources, are forced to change their social status, which is rather distressing at a certain age, to live on public charity or to die of hunger and the illnesses it begets.

Moreover, even if they all managed to find new employment immediately, this would only create a labour surplus, which is always the cause of a lowering of wages for the other workers owing to competition.

It could be objected that, as competition leads to products being sold at a better rate, workers are the first to benefit from the introduction of machinery.

It is easy to refute this argument; labourers without bread can hardly benefit from a drop in prices, which is always by the smallest possible amount and never equivalent to the reduction of their wages. In addition, the goods produced are usually those that the labourer never consumes.

---

[14] This text is a report from the Liege section presented at the same session referred to in note 13. Probably a collective work, it was read by Pierre Fluse [unk.]. He was a Belgian weaver, first a Proudounian and later close to Bakunin. He also participated in the London Conference of 1871 and The Hague Congress (1872). It may be found in PI, I: 294–6.

The working class gains nothing from this price drop, since they alone shoulder its costs while the greater part of its profits are returned to their exploiters.

If, as economists affirm, workers always profited from this decline in the price of products, it would necessarily happen that, by everywhere replacing a certain ratio of workers by machinery, they would stand to gain considerably from it. Yet, we see, to the contrary, that in this case, all the replaced labourers would run the great risk of dying of hunger or would, at the very least, witness their destitution mount.

It is true that a certain time after the price drop, demand tends generally to increase, but this phenomenon is produced bit by bit and its real effects are felt only long afterwards.

The laid-off workers would, thus, often have to wait years before finding a new employment and, without means of existence, would naturally be delivered over to the deepest destitution.

If the introduction of machinery causes a significant laying-off of workers, it is understandable that the expectation of profiting from the additional output becomes entirely preposterous, for the destitution of a great number of consumers would prevent production from realizing its full potential.

To sum up, the introduction of machinery brings about, for the *exploiters*, the retention of a portion of wages acquired by laying-off workers and increasing competition among them, the lowering of the prices of products that they can buy, an increase in profits resulting from an increase in demand; for the *exploited*, the loss of a part of their wages through lay-offs and the competition of their companions, a partial enjoyment in the lowering of the prices of products, a partial compensation by the growth in demand over time, delayed by the destitution of the masses.

We can therefore conclude that, in current society, the introduction of machinery is harmful to the great many and favourable to the exploitation of workers.

In a society composed of federated and solidary associations, where capital representing accumulated labour would not be a source of exploitation, but simply an auxiliary of exchange, machinery, far from breeding destitution, would increase the well-being of all.

No longer used in the interests of exploitation, machinery would represent, like any other labour, a value that the inventor would receive in selling it to the federated associations of workers.

These would draw from it an immense profit that would be translated into less hours to earn their day's labour and the capacity to produce much more.

The introduction of new machinery and inventions would become the interest of all engineers, who, far from being detested by their comrades, would be encouraged everywhere and by everyone.

The man deprived of his bread, rewarded for his toil by an expulsion from the workshop, was wrong to curse machinery, for his hatred and his anger must be directed higher up.

Social anarchy is the cause of evil; justice in social relations is its remedy.

Let us, therefore, overturn the old world, let us put an end to the exploitation of man by man.

The future belongs to the principles of solidarity and fraternity, to the workers' International.

10

Eugène Tartaret, [*For the Reduction of Working Hours*][15]

[…] The purpose of reducing the number of hours of work is to assure the material and intellectual development of the workers, to allow them the free exercise of their civil and political rights.

In modern society, work should no longer be punishment, servitude, or a mark of indignity; it should be a duty imposed on all citizens.

If work is to be really the exercise of a common duty, it should be carried out under conditions that guarantee workers their health, the satisfaction of their needs and those of their families, and protection against the pain and misery of old age and disability.

Under present conditions, does work meet the goal set by the *International*? – No.

Work as practiced under the pressure of competition is a struggle to the death among workers, people against people, individual against individual. Everywhere exploitation produces antagonism and servitude of the workers.

Production bears the weight of enormous charges, imposed by excessive taxes, to pay exorbitant salaries to officials whose main occupation is to keep workers subjugated to capital.

Exploitation, fostering and maintaining competition by lowering wages, forces workers to work long hours. In some very painful occupations – construction, digging, etc. etc. – the workers tire quickly and receive no training.

---

[15] This report was prepared by the committee on reduction of the workday of the Brussels Congress (1868). It was read in the session of 12 September 1868, by the Parisian cabinet-maker Eugène Tartaret [unk.], who was also a delegate to the Lausanne Congress (1869). Part of it was published in B1868. The complete text is in PI, I: 385–7.

Finally, wherever the workday is not limited, the worker becomes physically and intellectually exhausted. From a citizen destined to learn, carry out responsibilities, and exercise civil and political rights, the worker is turned into a pariah, a slave indifferent to progress and incapable of learning anything. Tired of his pain and his misery, the worker puts up with exploitation and servitude without daring to protest such injustice. And how would he learn, how would he resist? He doesn't have the time.

This initial goal of reducing work hours is therefore indispensable, because without it, the task of organizing international solidarity, proposed by our Association, would be hopeless. (...)

The necessary increase of production and lowering of prices must be achieved [not by forcing workers to work longer hours, but rather] through the use of appropriate raw materials, the professional training of workers, and the wise use of machines.

But the intervention of machines further complicates the unfortunate situation of the workers, because the machines belong exclusively to the owners of capital.

It is sometimes objected that the worker at the machine will play a passive role, as nothing more than the *operator of the machine*. It is also said that in certain occupations the worker will no longer do anything but regular and uniform operations, which will limit his knowledge of the industrial process as a whole. But we are not afraid that this will happen.

Machinery is inert and is a human creation; it cannot function usefully without cooperation and without intelligent direction.

If man's industrial role is diminished through a reduction of working hours, justice is served, because man has not only work to do, but also a family to support, children to educate, civil and political rights to exercise. If machinery when first introduced harms workers through excess production and a forced unemployment that impoverishes them, this is because, as the International has recognized, it is not owned by the workers, who can acquire it only through solidarity.

Machinery, a fruit of human intelligence, must serve man as a means of emancipation and must not be a cause of ruin. If it produces too much, it should run for less time, and its human operator will benefit from the reduction of work hours.

This reduction of work hours should bring man wellbeing, intelligence, and freedom. [...]

V. Tinayre, [On Working Women's Equality and the Inclusion of Different Political Opinions][16]

Considering first: that the working woman's needs are equal to those of the working man and that the pay for her work is much less, the central Section of Working Women requests the Congress to include in its resolutions that henceforth agreements reached between employers and strikes of a trade in which women are employed will stipulate the same advantage for them as for men as this has been adopted by the Congress of the Romance Federation held this year at Vevey.

Considering, secondly: that the more different groups of opinion there are on the ways of achieving the same aim, *the emancipation of labour,* the easier it is to generalize the working class movement without losing any of the forces (even the most widely diverging) to concur in the final result; that it is advisable to leave to individuals, within the principles of the International, the right to group according to their tastes and their opinions.

Consequently: the Working Women of the Central Section demand: that the general Council shall not have the power to reject any section, whatever particular purpose it proposes, whatever its principles, provided that purpose and principles are not capable of harming those of the International Working Men's Association and are compatible with the General Rules.

---

[16] This text is an excerpt from the mandate given by the Central Section of Working Women of Geneva to Harriet Law [1832–97], a feminist and only woman of the GC from 1867 until 1872, as their representative at the The Hague Congress (1872). This mandate was likely drafted by the General Secretary, V. Tinayre [unk.], and contains the signatures of sixteen working women. Besides the demand for equal rights between men and women workers, of particular interest is the exhortation to allow the different currents of thought to coexist within the struggle for the emancipation of labour. The full version is in HAGUE: 313–14.

Part Four

Trade Union and Strike

12

Karl Marx, [*The Necessity and Limits of Trade Union Struggle*][17]

[…] The cry for an *equality of wages* rests, therefore, upon a mistake, is an inane wish never to be fulfilled. It is an offspring of that false and superficial radicalism that accepts premises and tries to evade conclusions. Upon the basis of the wages system the value of labouring power is settled like that of every other commodity; and as different kinds of labouring power have different values, or require different quantities of labour for their production, they *must* fetch different prices in the labour market. To clamour for *equal or even equitable retribution*[18] on the basis of the wages system is the same as to clamour for *freedom* on the basis of the slavery system. What you think just or equitable is out of the question. […]

Having shown that the periodical resistance on the part of the working men against a reduction of wages, and their periodical attempts at getting a rise of wages, are inseparable from the wages system, and dictated by the very fact of labour being assimilated to commodities, and therefore subject to the laws, regulating the general movement of prices; having furthermore, shown that a general rise of wages would result in a fall in the general rate of profit, but not affect the average prices of commodities, or their values, the question now ultimately arises, how far, in this incessant struggle between capital and labour, the latter is likely to prove successful.

I might answer by a generalization, and say that, as with all other commodities, so with labour, its *market price* will, in the long run, adapt itself

---

[17] This text consists of excerpts from *Value, Price and Profit*, London: Swan Sonnenschein, 1898, which was originally a report read by Karl Marx (see note 1) to the GC on 20 and 27 June 1865. The report was in response to the position previously put forward by the Owenite John Weston that meaningful increases in wages were not possible and that trade union action to raise wages therefore had undesirable consequences.

[18] 'Retribution' in the sense of 'payment'.

to its *value*; that, therefore, despite all the ups and downs, and do what he may, the working man will, on an average, only receive the value of his labour, which resolves into the value of his labouring power, which is determined by the value of the necessaries required for its maintenance and reproduction, which value of necessaries finally is regulated by the quantity of labour wanted to produce them. […]

Besides this mere physical element, the value of labour is in every country determined by a *traditional standard of life*. […]

This historical or social element, entering into the value of labour, may be expanded, or contracted, or altogether extinguished, so that nothing remains but the *physical limit*. […] And why cannot we fix that limit? Because, although we can fix the *minimum* of wages, we cannot fix their *maximum*. […]

The fixation of its actual degree is only settled by the continuous struggle between capital and labour, the capitalist constantly tending to reduce wages to their physical minimum, and to extend the working day to its physical maximum, while the working man constantly presses in the opposite direction.

The matter resolves itself into a question of the respective powers of the combatants.

As to the *limitation of the working day* in England, as in all other countries, it has never been settled except by *legislative interference*. Without the working men's continuous pressure from without that interference would never have taken place. But at all events, the result was not to be attained by private settlement between the working men and the capitalists. This very necessity of *general political action* affords the proof that in its merely economical action capital is the stronger side. […]

[T]he very development of modern industry must progressively turn the scale in favour of the capitalist against the working man, and that consequently the general tendency of capitalistic production is not to raise, but to sink the average standard of wages, or to push the *value of labour* more or less to its *minimum limit*. Such being the tendency of *things* in this system, is this saying that the working class ought to renounce their resistance against the encroachments of capital, and abandon their attempts at making the best of the occasional chances for their temporary improvement? If they did, they would be degraded to one level mass of broken wretches past salvation. I think I have shown that their struggles for the standard of wages are incidents inseparable from the whole wages system, that in 99 cases out of 100 their efforts at raising wages are only efforts at maintaining the given value of labour, and that the necessity of debating their price with the capitalist is inherent to their condition of having to sell themselves as commodities. By cowardly giving way in their everyday conflict with capital, they would certainly disqualify themselves for the initiating of any larger movement.

At the same time, and quite apart from the general servitude involved in the wages system, the working class ought not to exaggerate to themselves the ultimate working of these everyday struggles. They ought not to forget that they are fighting with effects, but not with the causes of those effects; that they are retarding the downward movement, but not changing its direction; that they are applying palliatives, not curing the malady. They ought, therefore, not to be exclusively absorbed in these unavoidable guerilla fights incessantly springing up from the never ceasing encroachments of capital or changes of the market. They ought to understand that, with all the miseries it imposes upon them, the present system simultaneously engenders the *material conditions* and the *social forms* necessary for an economical reconstruction of society. Instead of the *conservative* motto: '*A fair day's wage for a fair day's work!*' they ought to inscribe on their banner the *revolutionary* watchword: '*Abolition of the wages system!*' [...]

13

Karl Marx, *[Against Strike Breaking]*[19]

Some time ago the London journeymen tailors formed a general association to uphold their demands against the London master tailors, who are mostly big capitalists. It was a question not only of bringing wages into line with the increased prices of means of subsistence, but also of putting an end to the exceedingly harsh treatment of the workers in this branch of industry. The masters sought to frustrate this plan by recruiting journeymen tailors, chiefly in Belgium, France and Switzerland. Thereupon the secretaries of the Central Council of the International Working Men's Association published in Belgian, French and Swiss newspapers a warning which was a complete success. The London masters' manoeuver was foiled; they had to surrender and meet their workers' just demands.

Defeated in England, the masters are now trying to take counter-measures, starting in *Scotland*. The fact is that, as a result of the London events, they had to agree, initially, to a 15 per cent wage rise in Edinburgh as well. But secretly they sent agents to Germany to recruit journeymen tailors, particularly in the Hanover and Mecklenburg areas, for importation to Edinburgh. The first group has already been shipped off. The purpose of this importation is the same as that of the importation of Indian coolies[20] to Jamaica, namely, *perpetuation of slavery*. If the Edinburgh masters succeeded, through the import of German labour, in nullifying the concessions they had already made, it would inevitably lead to repercussions in England. *No one would suffer more than the German*

---

[19] This article was prepared on behalf of the GC in April of 1866, after some Scottish capitalists had recruited German and Danish tailors to replace striking local ones. The GC sent two representatives (Haufe and Lessner) to Edinburgh who were able to persuade them to break their contracts and return to their countries of origin. Karl Marx (see note 1) compiled this short text for the German press. It appeared on 13 May 1866 in *Der Bote vom Niederrheim* under the title *A Warning*, and may be found in the GC, I: 367–8.

[20] A term used at the time to refer to Asian labourers.

workers themselves, who constitute in Great Britain a larger number than the workers of all the other Continental nations. And the newly-imported workers, being completely helpless in a strange land, would soon sink to the level of pariahs.

Furthermore, it is a point of honour with the German workers to prove to other countries that they, like their brothers in France, Belgium and Switzerland, know how to defend the common interests of their class and will not become *obedient mercenaries of capital* in its struggle against labour.

14

Various Authors, [Interference in Trades' Disputes][21]

One of the best means of demonstrating the beneficent influence of international combination is the assistance rendered by the International Working Men's Association in the daily occurring trades' disputes. It used to be a standard threat with British capitalists, not only in London, but also in the provinces, when their workmen would not tamely submit to their arbitrary dictation, that they would supplant them by an importation of *foreigners.* The possibility of such importations taking place was in most cases sufficient to deter the British workmen from insisting on their demands. The action taken by the Council has had the effect of putting a stop to these threats being made publicly. Where anything of the kind is contemplated it has to be done in secret, and the slightest information obtained by the workmen suffices to frustrate the plans of the capitalists. As a rule, when a strike or a lock-out occurs concerning any of the affiliated trades, the Continental correspondents are at once instructed to warn the workmen in their respective localities not to enter into any engagements with the agents of the capitalists of the place where the dispute is. However, this action is not confined to affiliated trades. The same action is taken on behalf of other trades upon application being received. This generally leads to the affiliation of the trades that invoke our aid.

Now and then it happens that the capitalists succeed in getting a few stragglers, but they generally repudiate their engagements upon being informed of the reason why they were engaged.

---

[21] Extract from the *Third Annual Report of the International Working Men's Association* to the Lausanne Congress (1867), approved from the GC on 20 August – a collectively authored document that built on various inputs of information from local sections of the IWMA. First published in the weekly *The Bee-Hive* on 14 September 1867. The full version is reproduced in GC, II: 292–303.

During the London basket-makers' dispute last winter information was received that six Belgians were at work under the railway arches in Blue Anchor Lane, Bermondsey. They were as strictly guarded against coming in contact with the outside public as a kidnapped girl in a nunnery. By some stratagem a Flemish member of the Council succeeded in obtaining an interview, and upon being informed of the nature of their engagement the men struck work and returned home. Just as they were about to embark a steamer arrived with a fresh supply. The new arrivals were at once communicated with; they too repudiated their engagements, and returned home, promising that they would exert themselves to prevent any further supplies, which they accomplished.

In consequence of the appeals made by deputations from the Council to various British societies, the Paris bronze-workers received very considerable pecuniary support during their lockout, and the London tailors on strike have in turn received support from Continental associations through the intercession of the Council. The good offices of the Council were also employed on behalf of the excavators, the wire-workers, the block-cutters, the hairdressers, and others.

15

César De Paepe, *[Strikes, Unions, and the Affiliation of Unions with the International]*[22]

[…] First we should state that in our view the strike is not even a partial solution to the great problem of the abolition of poverty, but we do think it is an instrument of struggle that can lead in the end to the solution of the problem. This is why we think we should speak out against the single-minded cooperativists, who see no serious movement among the workers apart from consumption, credit and production societies, and who in particular regard the strike as useless or even injurious to the workers' interests. […]

The strike is just and legitimate and necessary when the employer breaks a collective agreement, and it may be tried then even if the chances are that it will be unsuccessful. Is it not always a great and fine thing to see slaves protest against barbaric and inhuman measures? And what measure can be more barbaric and inhuman than ceaseless whittling down of the rations of those whose life consists only of deprivations?

Given the minimal wages in certain industries (large manufactories and collieries, for instance), given the great centralization of capital which means that capitalists are in permanent league with one another to reduce workers to their last gasp, given the huge capital that these workers would need to run vast factories and collieries, and given the lack of any organization of credit that might make it easier to create production associations in these industries, we ask what other weapon than the strike, even unorganized, is left to these

---

[22] The following text is excerpted from a report presented by the Brussels section at the 8 September 1868 session of the IWMA congress which took place in the same city. César De Paepe [1841–90] was second only to Marx as a theoretician of the IWMA. Leader of the association in Belgium, he participated in all the congresses (except those of Geneva 1866 and The Hague 1872) and conferences of the IWMA. He joined the 'autonomist' IWMA and was a delegate at its congresses of Brussels (1874) and Bern (1876). In 1885 he was among the founders of the Belgian Socialist Party. This text was published in B1868 and may be found in PI, I: 271–85.

proletarians against the indefinite lowering of their wages. Is it better that they starve to death on the job, without uttering a cry of indignation and without making any effort to get back on their feet? Well, even if it was proved like 2 + 2 = 4 that the strike cannot bring the workers any improvement in such cases, it would have to be accepted as the ultimate protest of the downtrodden against the vices of our organization of society.

We said at the beginning of this report that the strike may be useful and necessary; that consequently we favour resistance societies[23] with a view to giving resources and wise, energetic leadership to strike actions. Yes, despite our wish and certainty that we shall one day see the social order completely transformed – that is, that the exploitation of man by man will be ended and replaced with the equal exchange of products and reciprocity among producers – we hold that it is necessary to establish resistance societies so long as there exist categories of workers whose complete liberation is today impossible.

[…]

The resistance society is still necessary because it instils a certain fear in the exploiter. He will refrain from infringing agreements unless he is almost sure of success, since he knows that he will lose his authority if his arbitrary moves end in failure. This remark is so true that it is applicable to the exploited. For workers who are forced to go back to work, having initially refused to do so because of a cut in the price offered for it, are much more aware of the authority exercised over them by a disdainful employer when need forces them to return with bowed heads to their workplace, which, instead of a site of slavery, ought to be one of happiness and satisfaction, because it is there that life, wealth and well-being have their origin.

The resistance society is indisputably necessary so long as the exploitation of man by man persists, so long as the idle extract anything whatsoever from the labour of others. It is necessary not only because of what we have already said but also because it is the only way that the bosses and the workers will know who they are dealing with when someone comes looking for work. The Association

---

[23] The resistance society (*société de résistance*) was one of several types of workers' organizations in the nineteenth century, following abolition of guilds during the Revolution. Unlike other types of organization, the resistance societies provided little by way of benefits and existed fundamentally to improve wages and the and conditions of employment by coordinating strikes and exerting other forms of pressure on employers, as a result of which they were illegal.

gives each of its members a certificate of morality and honesty. Bosses and workers will know that the Association has within it only workers who are free from any taint.

We further note that one of the reasons for the constant lowering of the price of manpower is that unemployed workers go round the houses offering their labour – which gives the exploiter the idea that there is a greater abundance of men without work than there is in reality. Through the Association, demands for workers should be made directly to the committees, which can then send workers only where the need for them has made itself felt.

Apart from its usefulness for strikes, the placement of workers, etc., the price maintenance society is also useful by virtue of one of the complementary institutions it should comprise: we mean the unemployment insurance fund, an indispensable complement to the resistance fund proper. For while it is necessary that the Association should collect funds to provide for members in the event of strike action, that is, in the event of unemployment resulting from a dispute with the bosses, it is at least useful that it should do as much in the event of unforeseen unemployment due to more or less temporary industrial crises.

If, to be successful, strikes need to be waged and led by resistance societies, it is also the case that resistance societies will be serious only when they are all federated with one another – not only at the level of a trade or country, but across different countries and trades. Hence the necessity of an international federation.

A word of explanation will not be out of place here. Thus, it is readily understandable that, even if a resistance society succeeds in rallying all the workers in one trade in a particular locality, it will have not have achieved anything stable and worthwhile unless the boss is unable to find anywhere – in neighbouring areas, in other parts of the country or abroad – the workers he needs to replace those who have withdrawn their labour for a legitimate reason.

[…]

The strike, we maintain, is useful only for a limited period of time; a perpetual strike would mean making the wages system perpetual, and we want the abolition of the wages system; a perpetual strike would mean struggle with no end or truce between capital and labour, and our aim is precisely not what is nowadays called the *association of labour and capital* (a hybrid whereby the capitalist funder comes to an agreement with the workers to do away with the boss, while continuing to extract interest and dividends from their labour) but the absorption of capital by labour. For since capital is accumulated labour that should have a simple exchange-value equal to the value of the labour it cost, it cannot be taken into account in the distribution of products. As the product of labour, capital can only be the worker's property; it cannot be his associate.

Thus, since this transformation of resistance societies does not take place in just one country but in all, or at least in those at the forefront of civilization, since, in short, all these associations of all federated countries will intervene at first for the purposes of struggle, building on this federation to apply it to the reciprocal exchange of products at cost price, international mutual exchange will replace both protectionism and the free trade advocated by bourgeois economists. And since this universal organization of labour and exchange, of production and circulation, coincides with an inevitable and necessary transformation in the organization of landed property as well as an intellectual transformation starting with a complete education for all, the regeneration of society shall be brought about in both the material and mental domains. Based henceforth upon science and labour, not, as today, upon ignorance and the domination of capital, mankind will peacefully accomplish its destiny as it marches from progress to progress in every branch of the arts, sciences and industry.

16

Karl Marx, *The Belgian Massacre*[24]

To the workmen of Europe and the United States

There passes hardly a week in England without strikes — and strikes upon a grand scale. If, on such occasions, the government was to let its soldiers loose upon the Working Class, this land of strikes would become a land of massacres. [...] There exists but one country in the civilized world where every strike is eagerly and joyously turned into a pretext for the official massacre of the Working Class. That country of single blessedness is *Belgium!* the model state of continental constitutionalism, the snug, well-hedged, little paradise of the landlord, the capitalist, and the priest. [...]

The Belgian capitalist has won fair fame in the world by his eccentric passion for, what he calls, *the liberty of labour (la liberté du travail)*. So fond is he of the liberty of his hands to labour for him all the hours of their life, without exemption of age or sex, that he has always indignantly repulsed any factory law encroaching upon that liberty. He shudders at the very idea that a common workman should be wicked enough to claim any higher destiny than that of enriching his master and natural superior. He wants his workman not only to remain a miserable drudge, overworked and underpaid, but, like every other slave-holder, he wants him to be a cringing, servile, broken-hearted, morally prostrate, religiously humble drudge. Hence his frantic fury at strikes. With him, a strike is a blasphemy, a slave's revolt, the signal of a social cataclysm. Put, now, into the hands of such men – cruel from sheer cowardice – the

---

[24] This text, reproduced here in part, was written by Karl Marx (see note 1) after the decision taken by the GC on 20 April 1869 to disseminate as much as possible news about the extreme violence of unprovoked attacks by both cavalry and infantry on unarmed metalworkers striking in Belgium. It was partially published in *The Bee-Hive* on 8 May and printed as a booklet 4 days later. The full version is in the GC, III: 312–18.

undivided, uncontrolled, absolute sway of the state power, as is actually the case in Belgium, and you will no longer wonder to find the sabre, the bayonet, and the musket working in that country as legitimate and normal instruments for keeping wages down and screwing profits up. […]

It will easily be understood that the *International Working Men's Association* was no welcome guest in Belgium. Excommunicated by the priest, calumniated by the respectable press, it came soon to loggerheads with the government. The latter tried hard to get rid of it by making it responsible for the Charleroi colliery strikes of 1867–68, strikes wound up, after the invariable Belgian rule, by official massacres, followed by the judicial prosecution of the victims. Not only was this cabal baffled, but the Association took active steps, resulting in a verdict of *not guilty* for the Charleroi miners, and, consequently, in a verdict of *guilty* against the Government itself? Fretting at this defeat, the Belgian ministers gave vent to their spleen by fierce denunciations, from the tribune of the Chamber of Deputies, against the *International Working Men's Association,* and pompously declared they should never allow its General Congress to meet at Brussels. […] [The] culpable complicity [of Belgian government] during the recent events has been proved beyond the possibility of doubt. The emissaries of the Brussels Central Committee for Belgium and some of the Local Committees stand convicted of several flagrant crimes. In the first instance, they have tried hard to calm the excitement of the workmen on strike, and warn them off the government traps. In some localities they have actually prevented the effusion of blood. And last, not least, these ill-boding emissaries observed on the spot, verified by witnesses, noted carefully down and publicly denounced the sanguinary vagaries of the defenders of order. […]

The General Council of the *International Working Men's Association* hereby calls upon the workmen of Europe and the United States to open monetary subscriptions for alleviating the sufferings of the widows, wives, and children of the Belgian victims, and also for the expenses incident upon the legal defence of the arrested workmen, and the inquiry proposed by the Brussels Committee.

17

Jean Louis Pindy, *[Resolution on Resistance Funds]*[25]

There seem to be two distinct aspects to the question: how resistance societies should be organized to prepare for the future and, as far as possible, to make the present more secure; and how our ideas about the organization of work in the future can help us to establish resistance societies in the present. These two sides of the question complement and reinforce each other.

We envisage two ways for workers to group together: a local group that allows workers in the same place to maintain day-to-day relations with one another; and a group stretching across different localities, basins, regions, etc.

First mode. This form of grouping corresponds to political relations in present-day society and replaces them in an advantageous manner; it has up to now been the form employed by the International Working Men's Association.

This state of affairs entails that the local resistance societies in a federation help one another by means of cash loans, organize meetings to discuss social issues, and jointly take measures in the collective interest.

But as industry expands, a second kind of grouping becomes necessary alongside the first.

Workers in all countries feel that they have a solidarity of interests, but that they collide with one another. At the same time, the future demands an

---

[25] This resolution was presented at the morning session of 11 September 1869, at the Basel Congress by the rapporteur of the committee on resistance societies, and subsequently approved. At first a supporter of the theories of Pierre-Joseph Proudhon [1809–65], Jean Louis Pindy [1840–1917] was an activist in Paris and Brest. Also a delegate to the Brussels Congress (1868), he was a prominent leader of the Paris Commune. Later, he moved to Switzerland, became an anarchist, joined the 'autonomist' IWMA and participated to the conferences in Geneva (1873) and Bern (1876). The resolution was included in B1869 and was published in PI, II: 108–9.

organization that goes beyond the limits of a town and, no longer recognizing frontiers, establishes a vast allocation of labour from one end of the world to the other. From these two points of view, resistance societies should organize internationally: every trade must engage in correspondence and the exchange of information within its own country and with other nations, must work to set up new branches where none exist, must agree with fellow workers on common action, and must even pool its funds with others when this is possible, as the English do already. This kind of grouping becomes an agency of decentralization, for it is no longer a question of establishing in every country a common centre for all industries; each will have as its centre the locality where it is most developed.

Once these two groupings have taken effect, labour will organize for the present and future by doing away with the wages system as follows: working hours will be reduced across the board within the same occupation, the work will be divided up equitably, and competition among the workforce will be eliminated. This way of proceeding, together with a limit on the number of apprentices through free and rational statistical calculation applying to all occupations, will allocate workers within all industries, prevent accumulation in one and shortages in another, and make the right to work a reality.

The grouping of corporations by town and by country has another advantage. Since each trade will strike by turns, and be supported by the others, it will pursue its struggle until it reaches the level common to all.

Furthermore, this kind of grouping forms the commune of the future, as the other kind forms the workers' representation of the future. The grouping will be replaced with the associated councils of the various trades and a committee of their respective delegates, thereby regulating the work relations that will replace politics.

To conclude – and since grouping by town and by country already exists in part – we propose the following resolution:

Congress takes the view that all workers should actively engage in creating resistance funds in the various trades.

To the extent that such societies take shape, Congress asks sections, federal groups and central councils to give notification of this to societies of the same corporation, in order to bring about national associations of the various trades.

These federations will be charged with the collection of information regarding their respective industry, the operation of common measures, the regulation of strikes and activity to ensure their success, until such time as the wages system is replaced with the federation of free producers.

18

Eugène Hins, *[Resistance Societies as the Organization of the Future]*[26]

Yes, resistance societies will persist after the abolition of the wages system, not by that name but in terms of what they do: they will organize work. They will solve the problem of free exchange, by operating a vast allocation of labour from one end of the world to the other. They will replace the old political systems: there will be representation of labour instead of confused, heterogeneous representation.

At the same time, this will be an agency of decentralization. For the centres will vary according to industry, each in its way forming a state apart and preventing for ever a return to the old form of centralist state – which will not preclude another form of government for local relations.

As you see, if we are open to the reproach of indifference to any form of government, it is not because we are content with the first government that comes along; it is because we detest them all equally, and because we think that a society true to the principles of justice can be established only on their ruins.

---

[26] This text is a synopsis of a speech given by Eugène Hins (see note 11) during the morning session of 11 September 1869, at the Basel Congress. This is the first statement outlining the basic features of anarcho-syndicalism. It is located in PI, II: 111. For other interesting observations on this subject, refer to the debate on the question of the general strike which took place in one of the sessions of 4 September 1873, at the 'autonomists' IWMA Geneva Congress, published in PI, IV: 75–7.

Robert Applegarth, [On the Resistance Societies][27]

1. In the present age of competition, industrialists who embark upon risky undertakings and senseless financial speculation in order to bid a lower sum than their rivals, in many cases stirring the workers of one country against those of another, have made resistance societies an absolute necessity in each country for the effective protection of workers, and a federation among all nationalities one of the conditions for their existence.

2. Since the interests of labour are the same all over the world, and since Congress represents the interests of almost all nations, it recommends to societies that have not yet established themselves as resistance societies to do so without delay, in every country and every branch of industry, whether the workers in them are men or women.

3. Congress seriously urges societies in all nations to form themselves into federations that send one another monthly reports with information on wages, working hours, and the general conditions of workers in their country. [...]

6. Although the present system of competition should give way to cooperation for production, it is evident – to judge from past experience – that the resistance society is the first and best form of organization to which workers have resorted for their protection and should continue to resort as long as the present reign of competition continues, and that this organization is incontestably the best way of introducing knowledge and the spirit of order and discipline, which are inseparable conditions to ensure the success of cooperation in production.

---

[27] This text reproduces part of a resolution approved during the afternoon session of 11 September 1869, at the Basel Congress. The presenter was Robert Applegarth [1834–1924], a carpenter and union leader, as well as a member of the GC in 1865, and from 1868 until 1872. The full version is in PI, II: 114–15.

7. Congress recommends that, in their future programme, resistance societies should include a demand on the state for a system of compulsory secular education; this should precede any great social or political reform, being the only guarantee that such reforms will be permanent and beneficial.

[…] There is no point in discussing the need for resistance societies, since these exist only because of their indispensable necessity. He has years of experience and, in his view, trades union will remain a necessity so long as the relations between labour and capital remain what they are today. The coming generation should be educated in such a way that it can live in a higher social organization. If we were to design the workers' education with a view to productive cooperation, they would no longer feel the necessity of resistance societies.

20

Adhémar Schwitzguébel, *[On Resistance Funds]*[28]

We do not think so [that the commodification of labour is an eternal condition], since labour, the source of all wealth, should also be the condition for all happiness, all freedom. To restore the law of justice in relations between labour and capital, we need a profound revolution that only the classes representing the interests of labour can bring about; a general and universal organization of workers therefore becomes an absolute necessity, not only for the complete and radical demand for labour rights, but also to resist with success the exclusive domination of capital under present conditions, so that the proletariat does not fall into a state of poverty and degradation that makes it incapable of bringing about the social revolution.

The need to organize labour with a view to resisting the unjust demands of capital has long been felt by workers in the most industrious countries, and the founding of trade unions answered this need to group and combine the workers' forces for the purposes of resistance. To oppose the pretensions of the capitalist boss, the power of the associated workers – that is, collective resistance to the domination of one individual – should be the means of counterbalancing the power of capital for the benefit of labour. Resistance societies are not only the sole means for workers to have rights in fixing the price of their labour; they also have the great advantage of preparing the general organization of the proletariat, of accustoming workers to identify their interests, to practise

---

[28] This text reproduces a portion of a report adopted at the general assembly of 29 August 1869 of the District Courtelary section (Switzerland) of the IWMA. Possibly written collectively, one certain author was Adhemar Schwitzguébel [1844–95], an engraver who published numerous writings. He was a delegate to the Congresses of Geneva (1866), Basel (1869) and The Hague (1872), and later a prominent figure of the 'autonomist' IWMA, as well as a participant at its Geneva (1873) and Brussels (1874) Congresses. The full version may be found in PI, II: 123–6.

solidarity and to act in common for the interests of all. In short, they are the basis for the coming organization of society, since workers' associations will have to do no more than take over the running of industrial and agricultural enterprises, while the tools, land, mines, etc. will be accorded to them by the collective once it has become their owner by virtue of company liquidations.

But let us keep to the present.

While the power of labour resistance is being organized, capital – which, with all the wheels of the economy operating to its advantage, is further taking over financial companies by means of large enterprises – becomes master of a large part of industry and all the means of circulation that are ever easier to acquire. The struggle between capital and labour then takes on a new aspect: isolated associations can no longer fight effectively against big capital, and the bosses can bring in foreign workers overnight to replace striking national workers. The federation of all the workers' societies thus becomes an absolute necessity for the present struggle, but also the only possible way of achieving general emancipation.

The foundation of the International Working Men's Association is simply the result of this new necessity, and it is time that, with the help of practical institutions, it enabled itself to achieve some of the hopes of the proletariat and to increase its power of action. To organize resistance internationally: such is one of the duties of our Association. An international federation of resistance funds is the logical counterpart to the international federation of workers' societies.

Thanks to the international solidarity that workers increasingly practise among themselves, it has been possible up to a point to correct the disadvantages resulting from the lack of a general resistance fund, but we are convinced that regular organization would allow us to support strikes more effectively and even make them unnecessary. When a strike breaks out, the societies involved (if they have nearly exhausted their capital) make an appeal to the workers' societies, which then begin fund-raising in support of it; funds come in slowly and often arrive only after the struggle is over; if several subscriptions are opened within a short space of time, the members grow discouraged, the incoming funds slow to a trickle, and the strikes fail for lack of support. If instead we set up one or more central funds, with a capital drawn from contributions by all resistance societies belonging to the fund plus an extra half-yearly or quarterly contribution from all members of the International (which would advantageously replace special ad hoc subscriptions), we would have a considerable capital that we could use at any moment, strikes could always be supported at the time of the struggle, and workers' associations would acquire a power of resistance that they do not have at present. The bosses would know there was a central standing organization to support strikes, and, having learned from experience that this gives workers an invincible power to resist, they would be more readily disposed to accept the workers' demands, so that many strikes would be averted without any sacrifice of the right of resistance.

We conclude:

In the struggle now taking place between labour and capital, an essentially international struggle, it is indispensable to organize resistance internationally.

This can be organized only by means of a general resistance fund.

The capital for this fund may come: from a contribution by all workers' societies belonging to the general fund; from an additional half-yearly or quarterly contribution by all members of the International.

These funds will serve to support all strikes requiring assistance from the Association.

21

Alfred Herman, [Promoting Solidarity for Strikers][29]

Comrades,

The General Council has just received a delegation of engineers from Newcastle. These workers, as you know, have been on strike for several weeks in order to get a cut in working hours of one hour a day, that is, to bring their working day down to 9 hours. This movement, as you see, is just the same as the one started by the Verviers engineers. But the Newcastle workers, who thought themselves about to win and gain full satisfaction for all their claims, have just learned that their employers have gone to the Continent to recruit workers whom they are tricking by false promises, as they generally do. It would appear that the employers have gone to recruit 3000 workers, mostly Belgian, who will come over here shortly to supplant their English brothers. The General Council cannot let this action take place. It must naturally do all it can to prevent workers from themselves aggravating their own condition by a disastrous competition among themselves. It has therefore decided that two delegates shall be sent to Belgium to appeal to the best feeling of the Belgian workers and try to make them understand that it is their duty to help the English workers and not to attempt to supplant them. The Belgian Federal Council will not want to lag behind. We therefore hope, comrades, that you will do everything possible to stop such action on the part of the Belgians.

---

[29] In support of a strike by the metalworkers of Newcastle on 8 August 1871, the GC sent to workers in Belgium a document entitled *To The Belgian Federal Council*. Its author, the craftsman Alfred Herman [1843–1900], was founder of the IWMA in the city of Liege, and a delegate to the Brussels Congress (1868). He immigrated to London in 1871 and became a member of the GC and Corresponding Secretary for Belgium from 1871 to 1872. He participated in the London Conference of 1871 and The Hague Congress (1872), and later joined the 'autonomist' IWMA. In 1885 he was among the founders of the Workers' Party of Belgium. This text was published in Brussels in *L'Internationale* on 20 August 1871. Its full version may be found in GC, IV: 486–7.

We hope above all that they will understand what ingratitude it will be on their part if they cause the defeat of the just claims of the English workers while the latter have quite recently given such a good example of solidarity in backing the strike of the cigar-makers of Antwerp. […]

We vigorously call on the Belgian Federal Council to inform all Belgian sections of the arrival of the English delegates, to summon the engineers without further delay, to explain to them the situation of their brothers and to request them not to come to supplant them but rather to given them help and assistance. […]

22

Johann Philipp Becker, [*International Trade Union Organization*][30]

Considering,

That the struggle of labour against capital is neither local nor national but a social problem embracing all countries in which modern society exists;

That there is an international understanding among capitalists for the exploitation and oppression of the working class, and that for this reason the workers' efforts at resistance have failed because of the lack of solidarity among workers of different occupations within the same country, and of fraternal union among the working classes of various countries;

That the principle of solidarity enjoins workers to help one another everywhere;

That the emigration or exporting of labour power from one country to another necessarily increases competition among workers in the latter country;

For these reasons, the General Council of the International Working Men's Association submits to the various resistance societies (trade unions) of all countries the following plan for ways of organizing to expand the activity and prosperity of trade unions in all countries.

All (resistance) societies of a particular trade in a country shall meet to elect a central executive for their country.

---

[30] This passage is an excerpt from the summary of resolutions adopted at the 'centralist' IWMA Geneva Congress (1873). They were published on 24 September, in the biweekly of Leipzig *Der Volksstaat*, with the title *Vom Der Kongress der Internationalen Arbeiterassoziation*. Its author, Johann Philipp Becker [1809–86], was editor of *Der Vorbote* and a key leader of the IWMA of which he was a tireless organizer in Switzerland and Germany. Delegate to the London Conference of 1865 and to all IWMA Congresses, he was also the promoter of the 'centralist' IWMA Geneva Congress (1873). The full version is in PI, IV: 222–4.

In so far as the laws permit it, all these executive committees shall maintain permanent communications with one another through the intermediary of a general executive council, so that they are always in touch with the real state of the trade and of labour in all countries.

Funds shall be raised and controlled by the executives of the various countries, to help members of the union in case of need wherever that may be, and to cover the expenses of the general executive council.

All the central executives of the various trades in each country shall meet for mutual assistance in the event that a particular trade does not have the means to continue the struggle against its exploiters.

In the event of relocation or migration, each member of the international union shall enjoy the same rights in his new country as those enjoyed by members of longer standing in that country.

Each member of any international society who has to leave his country for political reasons shall receive the same support in the new country as that which was due to him in the country he has left.

As far as possible, these international unions shall prevent, through a central executive, the import or export of labour power under contracts relating to strikes, emigration and immigration.

Part Five

Cooperative Movement and Credit

23

César De Paepe, *[Credit and the Emancipation of the Working Class]*[31]

The question submitted for your Commission to examine was *how the working classes can use for their emancipation the credit they give to the bourgeoisie and the government.* […]

'Congress urgently requests members of the International Association in the various countries to use their influence so that trade unions apply their funds for cooperation in production, this being the best way to employ, for the emancipation of the working classes, the credit they presently give to the middle class and to governments.'

'Those trade unions that do not think it appropriate to commit their funds to the formation of cooperative establishments on their own account should employ them to assist the establishment of productive cooperation in general, and endeavour to establish a national credit system corresponding to the means of those who ask for its help, independently of metallic values, and to establish a system of cooperative banks.'

---

[31] This is a resolution introduced by César De Paepe (see note 22) in the same report set out in note 15. This is located in PI, I: 201.

24

Ludwig Buechner – César De Paepe – André Murat – Louis Müller – R. L. Garbe, [On the Cooperative Movement][32]

The efforts that the associations are making today for the emancipation of the working class can be summed up in what has been called the *cooperative movement*. In its various manifestations, however – so-called mutual credit society,[33] consumer cooperative, production cooperative – the cooperative movement still recognizes the old principle of the productivity of capital, that is, the right of capital to dip into the fruits of labour, and practises it on a wide scale.

Thus, in credit societies, [...] the funds first produce an interest, then dividends proportional to what each associate member has put in. But since that contribution is unequal, the inevitable result is that those who put in the most will not take long to enrich themselves [...], and that they will all eventually improve their situation a little at the expense of the mass of proletarians, from whom the payment of the interest and dividends will be levied in the last instance.

---

[32] This text is an excerpt from one of the reports set out in note 10. Probably the fruit of a collective effort, the report here reproduced was produced by a committee, whose topic was the emancipation of the fourth estate, mutualism, and workers' solidarity. Its member were: Ludwig Büchner [1824–99], well known philosopher and physiologist originary from Darmstadt; César De Paepe (see note 22); André Murat [1833–93], among the founder of the Mechanics' syndical chamber of Paris and a delegate to all the Congresses of the IWMA (except that of The Hague in 1872); Louis Müller, shoemaker and member of the Stuttgart's section, he was a delegate also at the Congress of Geneva (1866); and R. L. Garbe [unk.], plumber of Paris. Published in L1867, the complete may be found in PI, I: 201–5.

[33] Mutual savings and credit societies represented one of the key solutions advanced by mutualists in order to establish socialism. They were created in accordance with Pierre-Joseph Proudhon's idea of the People's Bank. This political demand was preponderant among French and Belgian internationalists until 1869.

In consumer cooperatives, either associates buy goods in order to make a profit by reselling them to members of the public, or they allocate the goods they buy among themselves alone. In the first case, a collective intermediary simply replaces the individual trader. In the second case, two situations are possible: either the cooperatives are restricted to a few men, having no influence on the situation of the masses, and therefore only improve the lot of a few; or the cooperatives spread to the masses, and then their ultimate effect is zero because they soon lead to a lowering of wages proportional to the fall in prices of consumption articles, since the competition among workers, the excess of supply over demand for manpower in present-day society, means that for most workers the wage always tends to decline to the minimum required to obtain strict necessities.

In production cooperatives, profits are usually allocated between capital and labour. [...] The share of capital is made up as follows: first an interest fixed in advance, then a dividend proportional to the volume of business and each contribution to the capital. Since this contribution generally varies – one associate's share due to labour may be ten against a share of one (or even 0) due to capital, while another associate's *labour share* may be one against the *capital share* of 20 (e.g., 5 as interest and 15 as dividend) – those associates whose capital share gets larger and larger soon find it possible to live on the revenue, and that is indeed what has happened in many associations.

In other cases there is no labour share at all in the allocation, and once wages and interest have been paid out the profits are distributed in proportion to the number of shares or, more generally, in proportion to each associate's capital stake in the enterprise, with the same result as in the foregoing. Moreover, most production associations consist of a few privileged workers who systematically detach themselves from their colleagues; they are not willing to spread and take in entire trades, so that there is already a division of the proletariat.

To conclude this critique, we should add that, apart from the inequalities we have just noted in the internal organization of these three kinds of association, the fundamental vice of these cooperatives lies in the way they behave towards the rest of society: that is, instead of exchanging services and products at *cost price*, they all intend to make profits, to increase their share capital, to swell their coffers; and the more an association increases its capital and profits in this way, the more bourgeois economists encourage it, and the more people with limited views go into raptures. But those profits do not fall from the skies like manna from the Lord; they must be extracted from someone, and that someone is the public. And the section of the public who live off profits, interest, farm rents and housing rent are careful to make good by leaning on labour, so that in the end these associations levy their profits from the mass of proletarians outside them. Such profits therefore represent a new exploitation of labour, in addition to the old bourgeois exploitation. If such associations keep spreading, the result must be: on the one hand, the creation of a new class consisting of members who share the profits among themselves; and on the other hand, the creation of another class consisting of those from whom the profits are levied, one more wretched than ever because more exploited. Hence there is a real tendency for a new privileged *fourth estate* to be constituted alongside the *third estate* or bourgeoisie. […]

The question Congress posed to us was twofold.

1. The question speaks of a fourth estate between the third estate or bourgeoisie and the proletariat (which therefore becomes the fifth estate);
2. It asks whether this fifth estate is not even more wretched than before.

To avoid the outcome spoken of in the second part of the question, it is enough that the credit, consumption and production associations, instead of making profits out of the mass of proletarians, should not make profits and therefore not impoverish the proletariat. For this to be the case, however, these associations must be based upon the principle of mutuality; their members must practise among themselves a reciprocity of lending, discounting, insurance, guarantees, services and products, by exchanging all products and services for what they are worth, that is, for what they cost in labour and expenses, or, more clearly still, in producer's consumption costs and the costs of tools and raw materials.

As to the first part of the question, we should make it clear that even if the existing associations were all based on the reciprocity principle their members would experience an improvement in their lot through application of that principle and would therefore still constitute, not a new exploiting class (since they would not extract a tribute from anyone's labour), but a new intermediate class between the capitalist bourgeoisie and the vast plebs outside those associations – in short, a fourth estate that has a fifth estate beneath it. Consequently, to guard against the formation of such a fourth and fifth estate, we think that it is not enough to practise even the purest principles of justice in isolation, at a restricted level among particular groups or in a few corners of society, but that it is absolutely necessary to employ general measures that apply straightaway to the whole of society and whose action is immediately felt throughout the social collective. [...]

It is always good to see workers group together and seek to improve their lot by their own practical efforts, even if they should make mistakes along the way. In this respect, the cooperative movement is in our view the great school at which the worker is initiated into economic matters; it is the most powerful lever of social progress.

25

Johann Georg Eccarius – Henri Louis Tolain, [Fourth Estate and Modern Production][34]

1. Congress thinks that, if the workers' associations become widespread in their existing form, their present efforts will tend to constitute a fourth estate that has an even more wretched fifth estate beneath it.

The supposed danger that the present efforts of the workers' associations will lead to the creation of a fifth estate will disappear in so far as the development of modern industry makes small-scale production impossible. Modern production on a large scale fuses individual efforts and makes cooperative labour a necessity for all.

2. To guard against this danger, Congress thinks the proletariat needs to convince itself of this idea: that the radical and definitive transformation of society can take place only through measures that operate on the whole of society and conform to the principles of reciprocity and justice.

3. Nevertheless, Congress thinks that all the efforts of the workers' associations should be encouraged, save only that the levy of capital on labour is eliminated as far as possible and the idea of mutuality and federation is introduced into these associations.

---

[34] This is an excerpt from the same report described in note 15. The main authors of this part were Johann Georg Eccarius [1818–89] and Henri Louis Tolain [1828–97]. Eccarius, a tailor from Thuringia who emigrated to London, was a member of the GC from its inception until 1872, its general secretary from 1867 to 1871, and its corresponding secretary for the United States from 1867 to 1871. He was a delegate to all the congresses and conferences of the IWA. After 1872 he adhered to the 'autonomist' IWMA and took part in its Geneva Congress in 1873. Tolain, a French engraver, was a mutualist and one of the founders of the IWMA in France. A delegate to all Conferences and Congresses of the organization except that of The Hague (1872), he was expelled in April 1871 after expressing support for the Versailles government against the Paris Commune, following his election to the French Senate. This is located in PI, I: 208–9.

26

Various Authors, [The Question of Mutual Credit Among Workers][35]

Considering:

1. That interest and profits of every kind accruing to capital, whatever form it may assume, is a blackmail levied upon the labour of today for the benefit of him whom the labour of yesterday has already enriched, and that if he has the right to accumulate, he has no right to do so at the expense of others;
2. That, therefore, the interest on capital is a permanent source of injustice and inequality, and that the cooperative associations by continuing this practice, do simply transfer the principle of egoism – the gnawing worm of the actual state of society – from the individuality to the collectivity;
3. That the application of the principle of solidarity on a large scale is the only practical means at the disposal of the working class to struggle against the moneyed interest.

The Congress believes that the foundation of banks of exchange, based upon cost price, to be the means of rendering credit democratic and equal, of simplifying the relations between producer and consumer, of withdrawing labour from the domination of capital, and reducing the latter to its natural and legitimate function, that of being the agent of labour.

---

[35] This text corresponds to the conclusion of the debate on the issue of credit. This report, written collectively by the member of the committee on the questions of education and credit, was approved on 12 September 1868 at the Brussels Congress. Published in B1868, the full version is also found in GC, III: 293–4.

27

Aimé Grinand, [Cooperative and Workers' Emancipation][36]

[…] In the last few years, workers got the idea that something could be done to mitigate the terrible plague of pauperism that has been eating away at them. No longer counting on the rulers and saviours of humanity, they tried to find their own solution to these economic questions and did not take long to raise their cry of 'war on capital'.

But they lacked experience at first and gave in to appetites for gain and pleasure, which are always in the human heart when not offset by a sense of law and justice. Production and consumption cooperatives were created in which workers, while protesting against the constrictions of capital, attempted to create capital of their own and to collect the profits. Constitution of capital in their hands, collection of a dividend from consumers, conservative sentiments and an appetite for pleasures, purchase of annuities: these were the thoughts and desires that such a conception of cooperatives developed, thereby justifying all the accusations that workers direct daily against the holders of capital. Such practices soon end up creating an entrenched fourth class, a bourgeois class which, on the day of reckoning, will join the ranks of reaction and again beat back the unfortunate ones who have not been able to put any money aside.

The associations contained in the principles of the International have no other aim than to wrest the instruments of production from the capitalists and to put them in the hands of their rightful owners, the worker-producers.

The International seeks to wage war on the stranglehold of capitalist interests; the old society is founded on an antagonism of interests; it is war, so

---

[36] This text corresponds to a report prepared by the committee on cooperation, submitted on 13 September 1868 to the Brussels Congress. Its rapporteur was Aimé Grinand [1842-unk.] of the Lyon section. Published in B1868, the full version is also found in PI, I: 407–8.

okay, we shall wage war! We shall unite our forces, and from these collective efforts will perhaps emerge a humanity less pitiful than the one whose long procession of woes has been unfolding in our times. We shall wrest away the machines, those instruments of death, and turn them into instruments of life; we shall smash those institutions from which an annuity, a fortune, a whole life of idleness emerges out of an inert metal. To live free and work free, that is our right; to let others live free and work free, that is our duty. The International shall not fail in its task; the workers shall organize.

How will these associations take shape without kindling in men the desire to own things without work? The answer is that they will be created in such a way that money interest can never be paid out. Since any price demanded above the cost price of the labour is a form of theft, any interest charged must return to labour, to the consumer. What is a cooperative association? It is an association in which all the members sell and trade only among themselves. It is necessary to widen the circle, to sell to everyone, but without ever charging compensation other than a payment for the labour supplied. Otherwise, if all the profits that such transactions give to capitalists are drawn from the market, there will be nothing to distinguish the association of small worker-capitals from the associations of entrepreneurs, directors and tricksters in today's enterprises.

Let the workers collect the scraps remaining to them, let them group together and create at once these consumer associations that do not require a lot of capital; later it will be possible to create productive associations, and then we will have in our hands all the resources of human wealth.

The commission on cooperative association proposes the following resolutions:

Any society based upon democratic principles rejects all levies on behalf of capital, whatever the form in which they present themselves – rents, interest, profit – and therefore leaves to labour its full entitlement, its just remuneration.

Through the reduction in working hours, through just remuneration of the fruits of his efforts, through the education that a secure life will permit him to acquire, through the disappearance of those heartless vampires who were choking the life out of him, the free worker will alone have changed the face of the old world.

28

Eugène Hins, [Cooperative Associations as a Model of the Future Society][37]

The question is the following: to give these cooperative societies a means of emancipation for the working class. But that depends on the organization of these associations, which, according to how they are constituted, often become a scourge instead of a remedy.

Moreover, only a few trades allow such associations to be established at once; in many others, that is totally impossible. [...]

Such workers then constitute a new caste that is all the more dangerous for having one foot in the bourgeois camp and the other in the workers' camp, while in the end all it does is perpetuate the exploitation of the workers.

In all cooperative associations founded among workers, the distribution must take place according to the labour performed, not according to the capital paid in.

A sum should first be fixed, but with a facility to pay it in whole or in parts, and once the sum is complete everyone should have a right to all the profits produced by their labour.

In the end, these associations will not be able to spread very widely and will inevitably be restricted to certain trades where it will not cost much to establish them. As for mines, coalfields, etc., it will be necessary to start by changing the whole organization of society, either by establishing collective ownership or by making credit free of charge.

Cooperation is therefore not a means of achieving the total emancipation of the working class. It can be considered only as a kind of workshop of the future, when the bosses have been abolished for good along with the other causes of exploitation.

---

[37] This text is an excerpt from the synopsis of a speech by Eugène Hins (see note 11), following the submission of the report referred to in note 36. The full version is in PI, I: 410.

Part Six

On Inheritance

29

Karl Marx, *[On Inheritance]*[38]

The working class, who had nothing to inherit, had no interest in the question.

The Democratic Alliance was going to commence the social revolution with the abolition of the right of inheritance. He [Marx] asked would it be policy to do so?

The proposition was not new. St Simon had proposed it in 1830.

As an economical measure, it would avail nothing. It would cause so much irritation that it would be sure to raise an almost insurmountable opposition which would inevitably lead to reaction. If at the time of a revolution it was proclaimed, he did not believe that the general state of intelligence would warrant its being sustained. Besides, if the working class had sufficient power to abolish the right of inheritance, it would be powerful enough to proceed to expropriation, which would be a much simpler and more efficient process.

To abolish the right to the inheritance of land in England would involve the hereditary functions connected with the land, the House of Lords, etc., and 15,000 lords and 15,000 ladies would have to die before it became available. If, on the contrary, a workingmen's parliament decreed that the rent should be paid into the treasury instead of to the landlord, the government would obtain a fund at once without any social disturbance, while by abolishing the right of inheritance everything would be disturbed and nothing got.

Our efforts must be directed to the end that no instruments of production should be private property. The private property in these things was a fiction, since the proprietors could not use them themselves; they only gave them

---

[38] This text is the synopsis of a speech by Karl Marx (see note 1) to the GC, on 20 July 1869, during debate on the agenda for the Basel Congress. Partly reproduced here, its full version is in GC, III: 128–32.

dominion over them, by which they compelled other people to work for them. In a semi-barbarous state, this might have been necessary, but it was no longer so. All the means of labour must be socialized, so that every man had a right and the means to exercise his labour power. If we had such a state of things, the right of inheritance would be of no use. As long as we had not, the family right of inheritance could not be abolished. The chief aim of people in saving for their children was to insure them the means of subsistence. If a man's children were provided for after his death, he could not care about leaving them wherewith to get a living, but as long as this was not the case, it would only result in hardships, it would irritate and frighten people and do no good. Instead of the beginning it could only be the end of a social revolution. The beginning must be to get the means to socialize the means of labour.

The testamentary right of inheritance was obnoxious to the middle class; with this the state could safely interfere any time. We had legacy duties already, all we had to do was to increase them and make them progressive, as well as the income tax, leaving the smaller amounts, £50, for instance, free. Insofar only it was a working-class question.

All that was connected with the present state of things would have to be transformed, but if testaments were suppressed they would be avoided by gifts during life, therefore it would be better to tolerate then on certain conditions than do worse. First, the means for a transformed state of things must be got, then the right would disappear of itself. [...]

If the state had the power to appropriate the land, inheritance was gone. To declare the abolition of inheritance would be foolish. If a revolution occurred, expropriation could be carried; if there was no power to do that, the right of inheritance would not be abolished.

30

Mikhail Bakunin, [On Abolition of Inheritance][39]

There is a difference between collectivists who think it *pointless* to vote for the abolition of inheritance rights and collectivists who think it *necessary* to vote for the same: the former take the future as their starting point – that is, a situation where collective ownership of the land and the instruments of labour has already been achieved – whereas we, the latter, take the present as our starting point, that is, individual inherited property running at full power.

Eccarius said that right is only a result of facts, and that once the fact of individual property has been abolished the right of inheritance will die out by itself. It is certain that in history facts have always preceded legal rights: the latter have always enshrined the former. But it is also indisputable that, having been an effect, right becomes in its turn a cause of other effects; and that it first has to be reversed if we are to arrive at different effects. Thus, the right of inheritance has become the basis and chief condition for state-guaranteed individual property.

Some have said that it would not be practical to abolish this right, because when the workers are powerful enough to abolish the right of inheritance they should profit from that power to proclaim and carry out the social liquidation. But it is in the name of practice that I urge on you the abolition of the right of inheritance. There has been talk of the difficulty of dispossessing small peasant landowners; and certainly an attempt to dispossess them would throw them

---

[39] This text is the synopsis of a speech given on 10 September 1869 at the Basel Congress. This intervention closed the debate on the issue of inheritance and, although not approved because it did not win the vote of the majority of the delegates, it received 32 votes in favour, 23 in opposition and 13 abstentions. Mikhail Bakunin [1814–76], one of the leading exponents of anarchism, joined the IWMA in 1869 and was a delegate to the Basel Congress the same year. Expelled in 1872, he was one of the progenitors of the 'autonomist' IWMA. Originally published in B1869, the text is also found in PI, II: 94–5.

into the arms of the counter-revolution. That must be avoided. Therefore, they will probably remain for some time in de facto possession of the plots of land they own today. And if the right of inheritance is maintained, they will be not only in possession of those plots but their actual owners, and they will pass on their entitlement to their children.

But if the right of inheritance is abolished, and in general all juridical and political rights bound up with the state, all that will be left them is the fact of possession – a fact which, no longer protected by the state, will be easily transformed and overthrown by the force of revolutionary events.

31

Karl Marx, *[On the Right of Inheritance]*[40]

The right of inheritance is only of social import insofar as it leaves to the heir the power which the deceased wielded *during his lifetime* – viz., the power of transferring to himself, by means of his property, the produce of other people's labour. For instance, land gives the living proprietor the power to transfer to himself, under the name of rent, without any equivalent, the produce of other people's labour. Capital gives him the power to do the same under the name of profit and interest. The property in public funds gives him the power to live without labour upon other people's labour, etc.

Inheritance does not *create* that power of transferring the produce of one man's labour into another man's pocket – it only relates to the change in individuals who yield that power. Like all other civil legislation, the laws of inheritance are not the cause, but the effect, the juridical consequence of the existing economical organization of society, based upon private property in the means of production; that is to say, in land, raw material, machinery, etc. In the same way, the right of inheritance in the slave is not the cause of slavery, but on the contrary, slavery is the cause of inheritance in slaves.

What we have to grapple with is the cause and not the effect – the economical basis, not the juridical superstructure. Suppose the means of production transformed from private into social prosperity, then the right of inheritance (so far as it is of any social importance) would die of itself, because a man only leaves after his death what he possessed during his lifetime. Our great aim must, therefore, be to supersede those institutions which give to some people,

---

[40] This text is an excerpt from the *Report of the General Council on the Right of Inheritance*. It was written by Karl Marx (see note 1) on 2 and 3 August 1869, and was presented by Johann Georg Eccarius (see note 34) on 10 September 1869, at a session of the Basel Congress. It received 19 votes in favour and 37 against, making it the first report of the GC not approved at an IWMA Congress. It was originally published in B1869 and is located in the GC, III: 322–4.

during their lifetime, the economical power of transferring to themselves the fruits of labour of the many. Where the state of society is far enough advanced, and the working class possesses sufficient power to abrogate such institutions, they must do so in a *direct way*. For instance, by doing away with the public debt, they get of course, at the same time, rid of inheritance in public funds. On the other hand, if they do not possess the power to abolish the public debt, it would be a foolish attempt to abolish the right of inheritance in public funds.

The disappearance of the right of inheritance will be the natural result of a social change superseding private property in the means of production; but the abolition of the right of inheritance can never be the starting point of such a social transformation.

It was one of the great errors committed about 40 years since by the disciples of St Simon, to treat the right of inheritance not as the legal effect but as the economic cause of the present social organization. This did not at all prevent them from perpetuating in their system of society private property in land and the other means of production. Of course, elective and lifelong proprietors, they thought, might exist as elective kings have existed.

To proclaim the abolition of the right of inheritance as the starting point of the social revolution would only tend to lead the working class away from the true point of attack against present society. It would be as absurd a thing as to abolish the laws of contract between buyer and seller, while continuing to present state of exchange of commodities.

It would be a thing false in theory, and reactionary in practice.

In treating of the laws of inheritance, we necessarily suppose that private property in the means of production continues to exist. If it did no longer exist among the living, it could not be transferred from them, and by them, after their death. All measures, in regard to the right of inheritance, can therefore only relate to a state of social transition, where, on the one hand, the present economical base of society is not yet transformed, but where, on the other hand, the working masses have gathered strength enough to enforce transitory measures calculated to bring about an ultimate radical change of society.

Considered from this standpoint, changes of the laws of inheritance form only part of a great many other transitory measures tending to the same end.

These transitory measures, as to inheritance, can only be:

a. Extension of the inheritance duties already existing in many states, and the application of the funds hence derived to purposes of social emancipation.
b. Limitation of the testamentary right of inheritance, which – as distinguished from the intestate or family right of inheritance – appears as arbitrary and superstitious exaggeration even of the principles of private property themselves.

Part Seven

Collective Ownership and the State

32

Jean Vasseur, [Definition and Role of the State][41]

1. The state is or should be only the strict executor of the laws enacted and recognized by citizens.
2. The efforts of nations should aim at state ownership of the means of transport and circulation, in order to abolish the powerful monopoly of large companies which, by subjecting the working class to their arbitrary laws, attack both human dignity and individual liberty. By this means, both the collective interest and the individual interest will be given satisfaction.
3. We express the hope that citizens appointed by universal suffrage will judge the guilty; that the citizen-judges will have a thorough knowledge of the culprit; and that they will investigate the main factors that led the man into crime and error.

We also demand that no culprit should be tried outside his own country, so that it is possible to examine the main reasons that diverted him from his duties. For all too often society as a whole is the only guilty party. Lack of education leads to extreme poverty, extreme poverty leads to brutalization, brutalization leads to crime, crime to prison, and prison to an abasement that is worse than death.

---

[41] This text is a resolution presented, during the discussion on the reports set out in note 10, by the committee on the State. Its rapporteur was Jean Vasseur [1838–68], factory worker and correspondent for the GC on the International Committeee of Marseille. It may be found in PI, I: 233.

33

César De Paepe,
[On the Collectivization of the Land][42]

What for Proudhon is this social mission of individual landed property? Is it to guarantee the independence and freedom of the individual vis-à-vis society, vis-à-vis the state? [...] But in seeking to establish such a strong guarantee of individual independence, what guarantee is one giving to society vis-à-vis the absolutism of property ownership?

Next, in a society founded on justice, this guarantee of individual independence would have to exist for all, and everyone would therefore have to own a share of landed property. But that is inadmissible in a society such as ours, where along with agricultural industry there also exist extraction, haulage, manufacturing and other industries. [...]

We may be told that the point is not to give every individual a guarantee of independence from the state by assigning him eminent domain over a piece of land, but rather to create a large social body of peasant-landowners who, by virtue of their ownership rights, are able to counterbalance the influence of the state; that the point, in short, is to make landed property a kind of political function served by the body of farmer-landowners. But it may be said in response that the independence of this large social body does not necessarily require individual appropriation of the land; it fits just as well with collective appropriation of the land by agricultural associations, or even by all groups of rural workers together. [...]

Therefore, we shall not seek a guarantee of individual independence and freedom in the existence of individual landownership. In our view, such independence of each in relation to all can result only from the relative, mutual

---

[42] This text is an excerpt from the *Report of the Brussels Section on the Issue of Land Ownership*. It was read by César De Paepe (see note 22) during the session of 11 September 1868, at the Brussels Congress debating the same topic. The full version may be found in PI, I: 365–79.

dependence of each on all (that is, the solidarity of each individual in a given group with fellow-members of the same group, and of each group with other groups), not from the complete independence of any one social body from the rest of society. [...]

So, however we look at the question – from the economic viewpoint of a better production of wealth or the socialist viewpoint of a better distribution of wealth, from an agronomic or an egalitarian viewpoint, in terms of large or small landholdings, concentration in a few hands or division among many, alienation of the land to a few privileged families or its financial mobilization, with the peasant-owner's consent or against his will, slowly or suddenly, peacefully or violently – we invariably end up with collective ownership. Economic tendencies are pushing us in that direction; logic and facts are leading us there. *Collective ownership*: that will be the form in which the land is appropriated in future society. That is what a close, impartial observation of social phenomena allows us to predict.

But how should we conceive of collective ownership? How far will the collective in question actually stretch? Will it relate only to agricultural groups or to the whole of society? In other words, the land may belong collectively to an independent agricultural association; it may belong without division to all agricultural groups together, first of one nation, then of a federation of nations; or it may belong to the entire society and be made over *conditionally* to the agricultural associations, or even, while awaiting the creation of such associations, to the existing farmers. It is difficult, if not impossible, under present circumstances to state in advance that collective ownership will take this form rather than that; nothing in our observation of economic phenomena shows that society as a whole will tend more towards one mode than another; the most we might say is that a particular mode is more suited to the spirit and traditions of a particular race. [...]

First of all, the most elementary system – landed property belonging to free and independent agricultural associations – has two main advantages in its favour:

1. It places the agricultural worker who jointly owns a large farm in the same position as the worker who, in the new society, has a share in industry as the joint owner of his factory or workshop;

2. It removes the association from all influence of the state or local authority, which could be a source of privilege and despotism.

In this system, ground rent would no longer exist, or it would merge with the repayment of advances made by the farmer on the land: that is, the net product and the gross product would merge into one. [...]

The second system presents a situation of collective landownership on a larger scale; it would involve assigning all the ownership of farmland, prairie, etc. to all the agricultural associations together in a particular nation or confederation of nations, and centralizing the high-level management of territorial holdings in the hands of a council appointed by the various farmers' associations. It would have the advantage over the first system of making it easier to carry out major projects of drying out, clearance, channelling and irrigation. [...]

In this system, either ground rent would be abolished as in the previous system, or it might be preserved and paid to the totality of agricultural groups represented by their central council, rather than to the state, the local authority or industrial groups; the rent would then serve to pay the running costs of the council, or perhaps even the costs of major projects of public utility that the council undertakes.

Furthermore, it is easy to predict that the first system – the one involving landed property in the hands of independent associations – would gradually tend to establish links among various associations: that is, a whole series of institutions, mutual insurance systems, exchanges of services, agreements to place products and producers, cooperation on major joint projects. This would eventually lead to a situation like that which the second system claims to introduce all at once.

But this is where supporters of a third kind of collective ownership, at a higher level than the previous two, have their say. In the two systems we have just examined, there is always alienation of land to one or more groups; in the third system, the land is inalienable.

Starting from the fact that the land is (directly or indirectly) the raw material of all products, the passive source of all wealth, supporters of the latter system fear that landed property – whether in the hands of all agricultural groups or of different associations, among which a coalition would be easy to establish – constitutes a dangerous monopoly for the rest of society. Let us suppose, they say, that the land is inhabited by no more than two families, one of which owns all the land, while the other is dispossessed. Is it then not clear that the property-owning family, which controls the permanent source of all fixed assets and real estate, is able if necessary to do without the services of the propertyless family, whereas the latter, controlling only capital that disappears through use, can do without the land and its produce for only a very short time? And can it therefore not be said that that the property-owning family has in its hands the fate of the landless family? If you then replace our two families with two classes – landowning farmers and workers outside the system of landownership – the situation will be the same as it was in relation to the two families.

It might be said that, while the industrial worker needs the farmer's produce, the farmer in turn needs the products supplied by the industrial worker: clothes, furniture, tools, etc. But the reply to this is that, once the landowning farmer has his clothes, furniture, tools, etc., he can if necessary go all his life without replacing them, whereas the industrial worker cannot go one day without the produce of the land; and that, in producing tools, clothes and other objects of use to the farmer, the industrial worker already depends on those who have the raw material indispensable for those objects: that is, the land.

This line of thinking leads one to conclude that the eminent domain over the land should be assigned to the whole of society (nation, then confederation of nations), under the management either of the central state or of the local commune; and that the land should be granted to the various agricultural associations, by giving them the right to the product of their labour and to the value they have added to the land, with certain guarantees to society covering such aspects as cultivation methods, the selling price of farm produce, etc.

In this way, the agricultural associations would do no more than occupy the land, either through a free land grant (the system of America's Anti-Renters or Herzen's and Bakunin's 'Slav ownership') or through a system of tenant-farming (as accepted by Colins de Ham and Louis de Potter).

In the latter case, the ground rent would be paid to society; it would be considered an instrument of compensatory equality among agricultural groups occupying land with differential fertility or topographical advantages, and might fully or partly replace taxes.

The main reproach made against this system of collective ownership by the whole of society (and it is a serious reproach) is that, in seeking to safeguard society against a coalition of landowning farmers, it places rural workers, and with them the whole society, under the yoke of the state and opens the gates to the most terrible government autocracy. It should be noted, however, that none of the supporters of this system call for it to be enshrined in present-day society with the state as it is presently constituted. They wait for the state, which today is purely political, to become economic: that is, for it to be no more than a federation of the various groups of workers represented by their delegates. Apart from that, this great transformation of landed property is in their view inseparable from a whole series of other economic reforms relating to capital or moveable property, and from a radical reform in people's attitudes.

Such, in rough outline, are the different forms of collective appropriation of the land. […] A system of fragmented smallholdings is condemned in the name of science, while one of large individual holdings is condemned in the name of justice. For us, then, there is no middle way: either the land should be the property of associated rural workers, or it should be the property of the whole of society. The future will decide.

34

Karl Marx, *[On Landed Property]*[43]

[…] The small peasantry is not at the Congresses, – but their idealistic representatives are there. The Proudhonists are very strong upon the point and they were at Brussels. […] The small man is only a nominal proprietor, but he is the more dangerous because he still fancies that he is a proprietor. In England the land could be transformed into common property by act of Parliament in the course of a fortnight. In France it must be accomplished by means of the proprietors' indebtedness and liability to taxation.

---

[43] This text is a short excerpt from a synopsis of an intervention made by Karl Marx (see note 1) on 6 July 1869 during a session of the GC in preparation for the Basel Congress. It provides a response by Marx to concerns raised by Elisée Reclus regarding the absence of farmers at IWMA Congresses. The full version is in GC, III: 120–3.

35

Mikhail Bakunin, *[On the Question of Landed Property]*[44]

Bakunin said that the absence of agricultural delegates is no reason to dispute the right of Congress to take a decision on the issue of ownership. Congress is only a minority, but in every historical epoch it is minorities that have represented the interests of humanity as a whole. In 1789 the minority of the middle class represented the interests of France and the world; it brought about the reign of the middle class. In the name of the proletariat, Babeuf and his friends protested against the domination of capital. We are only their continuators; our minority, which will soon be a majority, represents the entire working population of Europe.

Contrary to what has been said, the collective is the basis of the individual. It is society that shapes individuals; isolated men would not have learned to speak or think. Men of genius – the Galileos, Newtons, and so on – would have invented nothing, discovered nothing, without the acquisitions of previous generations. There is someone smarter than Voltaire, and that is everyone. Even the greatest genius would have produced nothing at all if he had lived in a desert from the age of 5. Private property has never been, nor is it now, anything but individual appropriation of the labour of the collective.

He is for collective ownership of the land in particular, and more generally for collective wealth by means of social liquidation. By social liquidation, he means abolition of the political and juridical state, which is the sanction and guarantee whereby a small number of men appropriate for themselves the products of everyone else's labour. All productive labour is first and foremost

---

[44] This text partially reproduces an intervention by Mikhail Bakunin (see note 39) during a session of 10 September 1869, at the Basel Congress. It was included in B1869 and its full version is also found in PI, II: 67.

social labour: since production is possible only by combining the labour of past generations with that of the present generation, there has never been labour that can be called individual labour. [...]

The speaker calls for the destruction of all national and territorial states, and the construction on their ruins of the international state of millions of workers. It will be the role of the International to build that state.

36

César De Paepe, [*On the Reorganization of Landed Property*][45]

[...]

Class antagonism, the struggle of labour against capital, has given rise to resistance societies or 'trades unions', which, through their federation or grouping together, organize the proletariat and eventually constitute a state within the state, an economic, workers' state in the midst of the political, bourgeois state. This state is naturally represented by the delegates of workers' corporations, who, while providing for current necessities, are also the embryo of the administration of the future; for in so far as new categories of workers go beyond their present isolation and associate with one another, that delegation will open its ranks to newcomers. This being so, it is quite possible that one fine day this new state will declare the old state dissolved, and that – with regard to the institutions of the old society, political centralization, legal system, army, religions, public education, banking, trade, industrial organization, landed property, etc. – it will take all the necessary measures to put an end to privileges and poverty and ensure equality and well-being for all. As far as landed property is concerned, this state that the workers have charged with carrying out the tasks of social liquidation and reorganization might well make a few little declarations such as the following:

1. Individual landed property is abolished; the land belongs to the social collective; it is inalienable;
2. Henceforth farmers shall pay to the state the rent they used to pay to the landowner; this rent will take the place of taxes and serve as payment for public services such as education, insurance, etc.

---

[45] This text is an excerpt from the *Report of the Brussels Section* presented by César De Paepe (see note 22) during a session on 10 September 1869, at the Basel Congress, devoted to the discussion on land ownership. Published in B1869, the full version is also found in PI, II: 79–88.

3. As a transitional measure, it is accepted that smallholders who work their land by their own labour may remain in possession of that land for their lifetime without paying rent; after they die, the land tax on their holding will be increased proportionally to the level of the rent on other land of the same value and will therefore be converted into ground rent; hence the land tax will be abolished for such land, as it is already for those who pay rent;
4. Leases shall be for the lifetime of individual farmers; they shall be for a fixed term ... in the case of agricultural associations (a longer term than the average lifetime);
5. Leases may nevertheless be terminated by individuals or agricultural associations, on clearly specified grounds of utility;
6. Leases are personal; subletting is forbidden;
7. The land is valued at the beginning and the end of each lease. If, at the end of the lease, there has been a gain in value, society shall pay it; if there has been a loss in value, the legacy shall pay it; if the legacy is worth nothing, society picks up the loss;
8. In order to simplify matters, the management of the real estate shall be entrusted in each commune to the communal (or municipal) council directly chosen by all adult inhabitants of the commune; this council shall in particular see to the combining of individual plots and the delimitation of ownership, in such a way as to stop fragmentation;
9. In concert with agricultural commissions appointed by farmers, the state shall concern itself with major projects of land clearance, reforestation, drying and irrigation. It shall reach agreement with groups of rural workers that may be formed to carry out these major works.

If the victorious organized proletariat takes these measures, adding any modifications and later introducing all the improvements that practice recommends, the agrarian revolution will be carried out and landed property will take shape in conformity with justice.

Emile Aubry, [*On Workers Capacity to Administer Society*][46]

The ruling classes, as they call themselves, far from striving to make the advancement of the people easy and peaceful as the most elementary moral laws require, declare on the contrary that they will make sure of everything to perpetuate modern slavery; never, they declare, will wage labour be abolished: it is indispensable for civilization! Thus argued the slave-owners of antiquity!

The idea that the proletariat will soon emancipate itself bewilders that section of the people which, it claims, achieved success by the sole power of its intelligence, and makes it advance the movement.

Profoundly ignorant of the causes which are hastening society's ruin, that section of the people persists in accelerating the movement instead of slowing it down by a few sacrifices.

Supported by the ignorance of a large portion of our class, the bourgeoisie, more prepared to increase its enjoyment than to decrease it, rushes ahead down to destruction.

Cupidity makes it increase the debt and the power of monopoly to a point where the already considerable disorder in the organization of its degenerate economy increases incessantly. [...]

The moral disorder reigning everywhere confirms the imminence of our triumph, because it is the harbinger of transformation and because the crassest ignorance dominates all the economic measures our adversaries will take; they seem to have made a pact with contradiction to hasten the disintegration of the social atoms. [...]

---

[46] This text is an excerpt from the *Report of the Rouen Federation* sent to The Hague Congress (1872). It was written by Hector Emile Aubry [1829–1900], a lithographer and delegate at the Geneva (1866) and Brussels (1868) Congresses, and Secretary of the IWMA in Rouen. The full version is in HAGUE: 248–56.

Does the worker possess the qualities necessary to administer society? We believe, after the short period of his activity in the [Paris] Commune, that the workers can today, without fear of creating chaos, take the place of those who really constitute the disorder in all branches of society; to become convinced of this it is sufficient to consider the votes of the Versailles Assembly. We know that it will be further objected that the fact that we have been defeated is proof that we have not the requisite qualities to direct a society such as we understand it.

To this we shall reply that labour is the antipode of war, it defends itself only in producing, and if it was defeated the reason was that it was naïve enough to entrust its battalions to those who said that, being specialists in defence, they entrusted its future victory, and because labour, with its habitual trust believed that these men said to ingratiate themselves with its rising power. [...]

We ask you in the name of liberty and justice, the fruit of our immortal year 89, to proclaim loudly to everybody that the proletariat will consider itself emancipated only on condition:

a. That the individual ownership of the product is available to all those who work, and is not a privilege granted to those who produce nothing.
b. That property which cannot be divided without violating social harmony is placed under the control of the corporation, commune, canton, the department or zone and of the national administration.

By collective property we mean the railways, roads and waterways linking the commune with the canton and the zone, and all the territorial divisions.

The post, telegraph and all public services as well as the equipment, on condition, of course, that each of these properties is under the control of the respective authorities.

For example, the equipment which plays the biggest role in social organization must belong to the corporations or working class companies which use it to work up materials.

c. That all private and collective interests are protected by the application of federative principles.

Karl Marx – Friedrich Engels – Paul Lafargue, [Critique of Bakunin's Politics][47]

[...]

Let us deal with [Bakunin's] programme.

[...] 'With the cry of peace for the workers, liberty for all the oppressed and death to the rulers, exploiters and guardians of all kinds, we seek to destroy all states and all churches along with all their institutions and laws, religious, political, juridical, financial, police, university, economic and social, so that all these millions of poor human beings, deceived, enslaved, tormented and exploited, delivered from all their directors and benefactors, official and officious, collective and individual, may breathe at last with complete freedom.'[48]

Here indeed we have revolutionary revolutionism! The first condition for the achievement of this astounding goal is to refuse to fight the existing states and governments with the means employed by ordinary revolutionaries, but on the contrary to hurl resounding, grandiloquent phrases at

---

[47] Extract from a text written by Karl Marx (see note 1), Friedrich Engels and Paul Lafargue [1842-1911]. Engels [1820-95] became a member of the GC in 1870, after his move from Manchester to London. He became corresponding secretary for a number of countries, and participated in the 1871 London Conference, in addition to being a delegate to The Hague Congress (1872). Lafargue, a writer, was a member of the General Council from 1866 to 1872, Corresponding Secretary for Spain from 1866 to 1869, and Spain and Portugal from 1871 to 1872, and a delegate to the Hague Congress (1872). The text, entitled *The Alliance of Socialist Democracy and the International Working Men's Association*, was written between April and July 1873 and published in French as a pamphlet in late August (London: A. Darson, 1873). The full original text may be found in PI, II: 383-478, and in English translation in HAGUE: 505-639.

[48] This quotation and the others that follow are taken from Bakunin's *Programme and Objectives of the Revolutionary Organisation of the International Brethren*, which also contains the articles cited, and was included as an appendix to the published pamphlet.

'the institution of the State and that which is both its consequence and basis — i.e., private property'.

Thus it is not the Bonapartist State, the Prussian or Russian State that has to be overthrown, but an abstract state, the state as such, a state that nowhere exists. […]

That is why the police shows so little concern over 'the Alliance or, to put it frankly, the conspiracy' of Citizen B.[49] against the abstract idea of the state.

The first act of the revolution, then, must be to decree the abolition of the state, as Bakunin did on 28 September in Lyons,[50] despite the fact that this abolition of the state is of necessity an authoritarian act. By the state he means all political power, revolutionary or reactionary,

'for it matters little to us that this authority calls itself church, monarchy, constitutional state, bourgeois republic, or even revolutionary dictatorship. We detest them and we reject them all alike as infallible sources of exploitation and despotism'.

And he goes on to declare that all the revolutionaries who, on the day after the revolution, want 'construction of a revolutionary state' are far more dangerous than all the existing governments put together, and that 'we, the international brethren, are the natural enemies of these revolutionaries' because to disorganize the revolution is the first duty of the international brethren. […]

Let us see, however, just what the consequences of the anarchist gospel are; let us suppose the state has been abolished by decree. According to Article 6, the consequences of this act will be: the bankruptcy of the state, an end to the payment of private debts by the intervention of the state, an end to the payment of all taxes and all contributions, the dissolution of the army, the magistrature, the bureaucracy, the police and the clergy (!); the abolition of official justice, accompanied by an auto-da-fé of all title-deeds and all judicial and civil junk, the confiscation of all productive capital and instruments of labour for the benefit of the workers' associations and an alliance of these

---

[49] Marx's sarcastic reference to Bakunin in this work.
[50] The people of Lyons established their own commune in early September 1870, declaring France a Republic even before the people of Paris. Bakunin tried to conform the Commune of Lyons to his anarchists principles, but failed and left France after the defeat.

associations, which 'will form the Commune'. This Commune will give individuals thus dispossessed the strict necessaries of life, while granting them freedom to earn more by their own labour.

What happened at Lyons has proved that merely decreeing the abolition of the state is far from sufficient to accomplish all these fine promises. Two companies of the bourgeois National Guards proved quite sufficient, on the other hand, to shatter this splendid dream and send Bakunin hurrying back to Geneva with the miraculous decree in his pocket. Naturally he could not imagine his supporters to be so stupid that they need not be given some sort of plan of organization that would put his decree into practical effect. Here is the plan:

'For the organisation of the Commune – a federation of permanently acting barricades and the functioning of a Council of the Revolutionary Commune by the delegation of one or two deputies from each barricade, and one per street, or per block, these deputies being invested with imperative mandates and always responsible and revocable at any time' (odd barricades, these barricades of the Alliance, where instead of fighting they spend their time writing mandates). 'The Commune Council, thus organized, will be able to elect from its membership special Executive Committees for each branch of the revolutionary administration of the Commune.'

The insurgent capital, thus constituted as a Commune, then proclaims to the other communes of the country that it renounces all claim to govern them; it invites them to reorganize themselves in a revolutionary way and then to send their responsible and recallable deputies, vested with their imperative mandates, to an agreed place where they will set up a federation of insurgent associations, communes and provinces and organize a revolutionary force capable of triumphing over reaction. This organization will not be confined to the communes of the insurgent country; other provinces or countries will be able to take part in it, while 'the provinces, communes, associations and individuals that side with the reaction shall be debarred from it'.

So the abolition of frontiers goes hand in hand with the most benevolent tolerance towards the reactionary provinces, which would not hesitate to resume the civil war.

Thus in this anarchistic organization of the tribune-barricades we have first the Commune Council, then the executive committees which, to be able to be anything at all, must be vested with some power and supported by a public force; this is to be followed by nothing short of a federal parliament, whose principal object will be to organize this public force. Like the Commune Council, this parliament will have to assign executive power to one or more committees which by this act alone will be given an authoritarian character that the demands of the struggle will increasingly accentuate. We are thus confronted with a perfect reconstruction of all the elements of the 'authoritarian State'; and the fact that we call this machine a 'revolutionary Commune organised from bottom to top', makes little difference. The name changes nothing of the substance; organization from bottom to top exists in any bourgeois republic and imperative mandates date from the Middle Ages. Indeed Bakunin himself admits as much when (in Article 8) he describes his organization as a 'new revolutionary State'. [...]

Now we shall reveal the secret of all the Alliance's double and triple-bottomed boxes. To make sure that the orthodox programme is adhered to and that anarchy behaves itself properly,

> 'it is necessary that in the midst of popular anarchy, which will constitute the very life and energy of the revolution, unity of revolutionary idea and action should find an organ. This organ must be the secret and world association of the international brethren. This association proceeds from the conviction that revolutions are never made either by individuals or by secret societies. They come about, as it were, of their own accord, produced by the force of things, by the course of events and facts. They are prepared over a long time deep in the instinctive consciousness of the popular masses, and then they flare up.... All that a well-organised secret society can do is, first, to assist in the birth of the revolution by spreading among the masses ideas corresponding to their instincts, and to organise, not the army of the revolution – the army must always be the people' (cannon fodder), 'but a revolutionary General Staff composed of devoted, energetic, intelligent and above all sincere friends of the people, who are not ambitious or vain, and who are capable of serving as intermediaries between the revolutionary idea' (monopolised by them) 'and the popular instincts. The number of these individuals should not, therefore, be too large. For the international

organisation in the whole of Europe a hundred firmly and seriously united revolutionaries would be sufficient. Two or three hundred revolutionaries would be enough for the organisation of the biggest country.'

So everything changes. Anarchy, the 'unleashing of popular life', of 'evil passions' and all the rest is no longer enough. To assure the success of the revolution one must have unity of thought and action. The members of the International are trying to create this unity by propaganda, by discussion and the public organization of the proletariat. But all Bakunin needs is a secret organization of 100 people, the privileged representatives of the revolutionary idea, the general staff in the background, self-appointed and commanded by the permanent 'Citizen B'. Unity of thought and action means nothing but orthodoxy and blind obedience. *Perinde ac cadaver*.[51] We are indeed confronted with a veritable Society of Jesus.

To say that the hundred international brethren must 'serve as intermediaries between the revolutionary idea and the popular instincts', is to create an unbridgeable gulf between the Alliance's revolutionary idea and the proletarian masses; it means proclaiming that these hundred guardsmen cannot be recruited anywhere but from among the privileged classes.

[...] The revolutionary movement in Lyons was just flaring up. [...] On 28 September, the day of his arrival, the people had occupied the Town Hall. Bakunin installed himself there. And then came the critical moment, moment anticipated for many years, when Bakunin could at last accomplish the most revolutionary act that the world had ever seen: he decreed the *Abolition of the State*. But the state, in the shape and form of two companies of bourgeois National Guards, made an entry through a door which had inadvertently been left unguarded, cleared the hall, and forced Bakunin to beat a hasty retreat to Geneva.

---

[51] 'Be like unto a corpse,' used by the Jesuits to describe the unquestioning obedience required of junior members.

39

César de Paepe, *[On the Organization of Public Services in the Society of Future]*[52]

A great number of socialists have cried out: War on the state! They do not want to hear talk about the state in any form, no matter how interpreted. They declare very plainly that they seek the absolute destruction of the state, of all states: and the more logical among them, perceiving rightly that the commune is, in the final analysis, merely a mini-state, a state with a tinier territory, whose functions are performed on a smaller scale than ordinary states, declare that they want no more to do with the communal state than with the state proper. Upon their standard they have daubed the device: An-archy! Not 'anarchy' in the sense of disorder, since, on the contrary, they believe in the possibility of arriving at true order through spontaneous organization of economic forces, but An-archy, in the sense in which Proudhon intended it, that is, absence of power, absence of authority, and in their minds, in the sense of abolition of the state, the terms authority and power being in their view absolute synonyms for the word state.

But alongside this traditional historical notion of the state, which, in fact, has thus far never been anything other than authority, power, and, further, despotism, (and the worst of despotisms at that, since it has always been exercised by an idle minority over the toiling majority), these socialists have taken account of a true fact and one that will become increasingly true, a fact that is one of the greatest economic phenomena of modern times: they have

---

[52] This text by César de Paepe (see note 22) is an excerpt from a pamphlet (Brussels: Brismée, 1874) that appeared just before the 'autonomist' IWMA Brussels Congress (1874), and also presented during a session of the latter on 12 September. A partial reprint of this paper was included in the collection edited by Daniel Guérin, *Ni dieu, Ni Maître*. Paris: Maspero, 1980, later translated into English by Paul Sharkey, and published under the title *No Gods, No Masters*. Oakland, CA: AK, 2005, pp. 221–9. To this version, partially reproduced here, have been added new parts, translated for the first time by Christine Henderson. The full version is in the PI, IV: 292–338.

seen, in the chief branches of modern production, large industry increasingly replacing small-scale industry, centralization of capital, more and more massive application of collective effort and division of labour, the incessant introduction of mighty steam-driven machinery powering a host of tools and machines, tools hitherto isolated, now requiring that huge masses of workers be gathered into enormous factories, and that all of this cannot but add day by day to the domain of big industry. They have seen that in this great modern production, the isolated worker or artisan gives way to collective labour force, to workers' collectives; they have seen that these workers' collectives, faced with the allied capitalists whose interests are diametrically and openly opposed to their own, had a necessity to form themselves into resistance groups, into trades unions, and indeed implicate the workers of small industries in this movement: that association by trade must spread, and their conclusion is that such spontaneous grouping is not unlike the spontaneous banding together into bourgeois communes in the Middle Ages: community of interests inevitably impelling trades bodies to spread in order to support one another, out of this grows a whole range of federations–at first local, then regional, then international. What is more, not content with these theoretical observations, they have embarked upon practice: like the English workers, they have founded trade unions, they have federated with one another, and they have quite rightly, sought to found the International Association upon this federative economic basis. Thus they have embraced this grouping of workers' bodies which is rooted in the depths of modern life as a counter to the more or less artificial and obsolete grouping into communes and purely political states, and predicted the future decline of these latter.

So far so good. But we wonder whether the workers' bodies, the associated trades bodies of the same locality, whether this commune of proletarians, in short, on the day that it replaces today's official commune or bourgeois commune, will not act just like the latter vis-a-vis certain public services whose survival is essential to the life of society? We wonder whether, in the new commune, there will be no need for security, a civil state, maintenance of roads and public squares, street lighting, drinking water in the houses, sewer maintenance, and a whole host of public services that we listed at the start of this work? Would there not be a need for workers' groups, the commune's trade bodies, to select from among their number delegates to each of the public services, delegates charged with operating these various services, unless these groups prefer instead to act as a bloc in appointing a delegation to share management of these various services? In either instance, do you still not have a local public service administration, a communal administration?

But all public services cannot be handled by a purely local administration, since many of them, and the most important of them at that, are by their very natures fated to operate over a territory larger than that of the commune: is one commune about to run the railways, maintain the highways, dam the rivers, channel the stream, see to delivery of mail and the despatching of telegrams to other localities, etc.? Obviously not! So communes have to come to some arrangement, organize themselves into a Federation of communes and choose a delegation to look after public services. Whether that delegation be appointed with a general remit to run all great regional public services, or with a special remit applicable to a particular service, matters not: in any event these delegates have to be in direct and ongoing contact with one another, so they still represent a regional or national public administration, the name having no bearing upon the thing. [...]

And what is that regional or national Federation of communes going to be, in essence, other than a state? Yes, a state, for we should call things by their name. Except that this will be a federative state, a state formed from the bottom up. A state having at bottom, at its origins, an economic association, the grouping of trades bodies making up the commune, and, in addition, having, no doubt, alongside its great public service administration directly emanating from the federal communes, a Labour Chamber emanating directly from the general unions (in England they call them amalgamated unions) made up of local unions from the same trade federated at regional level.

It will, perhaps, be objected that what we are here calling a state has nothing in common with what has hitherto been designated as such; until now, the state has represented nothing other than the organization of despotism, rather than a free association based upon economic forces. Well, if this free association has precisely as its principal objective and effect the delivery of public services by way of an ad hoc administration, which is the main function of all states (regardless of the many vicious forms taken by existing states and the many superfluities with which the dominant classes have burdened states past and present), why should we not call this a state? Because this institution has always been defective in its organization, because, thus far, it has only ever served as an instrument for the exploitation of the masses, must we seek to abolish it, even while recognizing the necessity of reconstructing it on a basis which corresponds to new ideas? Because public education has had, to date, the aim of instilling prejudice in the masses while, at the same time, providing the privileged classes with a means of oppression and exploitation, must we want its elimination? Because industry has, to this day, been the means of further enriching the wealthy and of further impoverishing the poor, must we preach its annihilation?

Not long ago, labourers, seeing that they were being supplanted by machinery in their workshops, threw themselves violently upon these machines and destroyed them. The voices of Luddites called out: War on machinery! Today, they say that machinery is useful, necessary even to a society that could not survive without large-scale production, and they cry out: Machinery belongs to us! The state is a machine, it is the instrument of the great public services.

Like any other machine, this one too is essential for large-scale modern production and for substantial circulation in the products resulting from the same: like any other machine, the latter too has been murderous for the workers and has thus far always worked for the exclusive benefit of privileged classes. If there is to be an end of that, the workers must take over that machine. But in taking it over, let us check whether the state machine does not stand in need of important modifications so that it cannot injure anyone: let us check whether certain gears which bourgeois exploitation had imposed do not need removing and others, which bourgeois carelessness had neglected, added: let us see indeed if it does not need to be established upon wholly new foundations. With those reservations, we can say, workers, the machine belongs to us, the state belongs to us! [...]

Is there anything very authoritarian about expressions like state postal service, state railways, state-sponsored clearance of scrubland, etc.? We have no difficulty conceiving of a non-authoritarian state. [...]

And so, to the commune fall the merely local and communal public services under the purview of the local administration appointed by the trades' bodies of the area and operating under the supervision of all local inhabitants. To the state fall the more widespread regional or national public services, under the management of a regional administration appointed by the Federation of communes and operating under the gaze of the regional Chamber of Labour. Is that all? No; there are and increasingly there will be public services which, by their very nature, are international or inter-regional (the actual name matters very little here). [...]

To the Jacobin conception of the omnipotent state and the subordinate commune, we oppose the idea of the liberated commune, itself appointing all its administrators, with no exceptions: shifting for itself in respect of laws, justice, and police. The liberal conception of the gendarme-state we counter with the nation of the state disarmed, but charged with educating the young and centralizing the great joint undertakings. The commune becomes essentially the organ of political functions or what are described as such: law, justice, security, the guaranteeing of contracts, the protection of the incapable, civil society, but at the same time it is the organ of all public and local services. The state becomes essentially the organ of scientific unity and of the great joint undertakings necessary to society.

Political decentralization and economic centralization, such is, it seems to us, the situation to which this new understanding of the double role of the commune and the state leads, an understanding based on the examination of the public services which logically fall within the powers of each of these organs of collective life.

James Guillaume, [*On the Abolition of the State*][53]

All kinds of fantasies have been dreamed up on this score. It has been claimed that *anarchists* or *Bakuninists* – that is usually what we are called – want to eliminate any social bond between people, any collective action; that they want not only to destroy political institutions like the army, judiciary, police, clergy, etc., but even what are called 'public services'. How could anyone seriously impute such absurdities to us?

When we speak of 'abolishing the state', we mean abolition of that authoritarian organization which, instead of being the natural form of society, is an artificial institution created for the sole purpose of ensuring the supremacy of one class over the rest of the people; abolition of the state is for us abolition of government by a class.

Do not the German Socialists pursue exactly the same goal? Do they not want to abolish what they call the *Klassenstaat*, the state based on classes? Yes. Well, as you see, with regard to what is negated, we do not differ as some claim but are in agreement: the Germans want to abolish the *Klassenstaat*, we want to abolish the state. We say the state *tout court* because, as we define it, every state is the organization through which one class rules over the others, every state is a *Klassenstaat*. So, in speaking of the abolition of *the state*, we are necessarily speaking of the abolition of a *Klassenstaat*.

It remains to examine the positive side of the question, and here begin the differences – serious differences this time, no longer just a quarrel over words.

---

[53] This text is an excerpt from the synopsis of a speech given on 27 October 1876 at the 'autonomist' IWMA Berne Congress. James Guillaume [1844–1916], a typographer, teacher and author of an IWMA history, was one of the main leaders of the Jura Federation. Delegate to all IWMA Congresses, he was expelled in 1872. Afterwards, he was the main organizer of the 'autonomist' IWMA and participated in all its Congresses. This intervention was published in B1876 and its complete version is also found in PI, IV: 466–7.

When the Germans speak of society as it will be reorganized, they imagine it in the form of a *Volksstaat*, a 'people's state'. And we say to them:

> If you establish a new state, a new government, you will by the same token have created a new privileged class, a class of rulers who will dominate the masses, as the bourgeoisie does today the proletariat, and your socialist statesmen will be armed with a power even greater than that which bourgeois governments hold; for they will have control over all the social capital, and the working people, sovereign in name, will in reality be at their mercy. The *Volksstaat* of which you dream will then be a *Klassenstaat*, just like the bourgeois state; and that is why we want none of it.

The conception of the future that we collectivists (that is, anti-authoritarian communists) oppose to the idea of the *Volksstaat* is a free federation of free industrial and agricultural associations, with no artificial frontiers and no government.

41

César de Paepe, *[On the People's State (Volksstaat)]*[54]

[…] The institutions that Guillaume, following Proudhon's ideas in his *General Idea of the Revolution*, considers to be constitutive of any state are therefore in our view only particular powers of the state peculiar to transitory social forms; they are a special aspect of the role of the state considered as the management of social interests. In a society that needs to protect itself against other societies and against that which is below and outside all society, the institution in charge of the general interests – the state – needs to have the means of defence at its disposal (army, clergy, police, judges, jailers, executioners, etc.). In a society that is federated with other societies and in which the old sub-social strata are incorporated into society, the state no longer has to defend society and no longer needs priests, soldiers, jailers, executioners, etc., but that does not mean it would no longer have any powers, or that there would no longer be a need for an institution in charge of managing the general interests – on the contrary. In sum, the real culprit is not the state but society; the state is as the society is, since the state is only a manifestation of society. […]

We believe that, in a society where there are no longer any slaves, any serfs, any proletarians, public services of every kind, as objects of general interest to be administered, will be more numerous than they are today. So the powers of the state, though shorn of the army, the Church, etc., will in reality be more numerous than today.

Besides, despite all kinds of impediments, despite the narrowness of the bourgeois mind and the principles of *chacun pour soi* and *laisser-faire*, the present state is already unable to avoid running certain public services that

---

[54] This text is an excerpt from the synopsis of a long speech by César De Paepe (see note 22) at the same session referred to in note 53. It was published in B1876 and is also found in PI, IV: 471–9.

were completely unknown in any earlier state, and which the future state (or future public administration), in the *reorganized society*, will undoubtedly develop and supplement. So, far from tending towards the abolition of the state (again we add: or public administration, for those who find the word 'state' scary), we think that the powers of the state will be considerably more numerous in the future. [...]

When people speak of the state, they generally forget to distinguish between these two functions: legislation and administration. For the first of these functions, we readily accept that in a more or less distant future the role of the state may and should diminish and eventually die out altogether. Once the all-round development of everyone's faculties, with a complete and equal education for all, has led us to agree on the great natural laws that preside over the organization and life of societies, as scholars are today in agreement over the main laws constituting inorganic matter, we will simply submit to those universally recognized social laws, and there will be no point in artificial laws adopted by legislators of any kind. But we think we are still a long way from that time, and that meanwhile the present state (like the future state, during a more or less lengthy transitional period) should intervene legislatively in a host of cases, even in those where the *laisser faire, laisser passer* of the bourgeois economists today seems to be accepted almost without dispute.

As to the second function, we think that the role of the state, far from diminishing, should tend to increase more and more with the development of civilization. There are two main reasons for this necessary increase in the administrative powers of the state: (1) the growth of needs, the birth of a host of new needs (material and especially moral), whose satisfaction requires the creation of new public services, or at least the expansion and improvement of the existing public services; (2) the transformation of the old individual means of action into means of action based on collective strength; what used to be individual enterprise or household labour has now become collective enterprise and large-scale industry, and has become, or is tending to become, a veritable public service: for example, railways, coalmines, gasworks, metallurgical factories, etc., etc. [...]

To make this easier to understand, let us take some practical examples from the realm of fact. Let us see how what some call the destruction of the state and we call the transformation of the state – that is, suppression of the army, official religion, the police and judiciary, the national bank, etc. – might actually come to pass, while nevertheless maintaining the administration of major public services. [...]

Is the state without a police or official religion still the state, so long as it retains the other powers mentioned above? Is the state without a judiciary or a national bank still the state? Yes, of course. If the state no longer has any of the four aforementioned powers but continues to manage public services and still has an army to defend itself against other states, is it still the state? Yes, of course. And if public services were to grow in number and importance, if the army gradually changed from a war-making institution into a peaceful workers' army engaged in major works of public utility (an *industrial army*, as Fourier put it), we ask when the state would cease to be the state; we ask at which point it would need to be 'debaptised'? For our part, we would see no need to debaptise it; the forms, procedures, methods and powers of the state would have changed, but the state would still be, as before, the social institution managing the interests of society. [...]

It is therefore necessary, at all costs, to ensure the regular continuation of public services, and thus to have an administration that runs all of them harmoniously. With the old state in ruins, it will be necessary to form another state; its powers will not be identical, nor will its way of appointing citizens to be part of it. Yet it will still be the same institution in charge of managing the interests of society. Only, since the interests of society will no longer be mainly the interests of a class but the interests of the whole people, it will no longer be a *Klassenstaat*, a state of one class, but a *Volksstaat*, a people's state.

All this may seem very theoretical, very abstract. I shall try to be even more practical. [...] In the towns, as in country districts where big industry exists (mills, metallurgy, collieries, quarries, etc.), the workers develop through meetings, lectures, special courses, study and propaganda groups, rationalist philosophical societies in which the atheistic, materialist element is dominant; on the other hand, in terms of material interests, they organize into resistance societies or trade unions, start to form countrywide federations of unions in the same trade as well as local federations and cross-trade societies (local chambers of labour). The tendency is to form such organizations in localities and industries where they do not yet exist, and then to form a general federation of all the trade corporations in a country – a federation that is thus the General Chamber of Labour, a kind of parliament of the proletariat. Those are the facts, those are the tendencies. Now, let us suppose that these facts and tendencies are quite well developed, and that one of those events that occur every century in the history of our country, a revolution, then breaks out. If the bourgeoisie was overthrown, what would the proletariat do? Would it have to dissolve the organization it had given itself? We think it would very wary of doing that? We think it would keep its labour parliament up and running; and one of the first tasks of that parliament would be to appoint delegates to the various public services (as happened spontaneously in the Paris Commune), carefully taking into account their particular aptitudes and adding specialists for the very special services (mining and railway engineers, doctors and chemists in the public health service, etc., etc.). And what would this labour parliament be with its various executive commissions for the public services – for health, education, and so forth? What would it be if not a state, with its various ministries? We dare say that for a time it would even be necessary for that state to preserve some of the powers or institutions listed by James Guillaume. The clergy would be abolished, I assume, as religion would become a private matter; the jury would probably replace the present justice system. But if the struggle carried on, might not a militia, a citizens' army, be maintained for a certain time? And how long might the bank be preserved as a central body of circulation, serving as a temporary intermediary for the business that groups of producers in the various industries would have to conduct with one another? These are questions that it is scarcely possible to answer, since they depend on highly variable circumstances.

What would happen if, instead of acting so, the labour parliament – that is, the workers' federation in each country – followed an opposite path? What if, imbued with ultra-anarchist ideas or simply not feeling equal to the situation, it was content to overthrow the bourgeois state and allowed the public services to fall into a state of neglect? The first person to stake a claim, on the pretext of getting us out of the social chaos, would take over public affairs in the name of restoring order and saving society: that is, the people would once again have made a revolution for nothing and find itself back at square one.

To conclude: we would say that the state is a necessary element for society, but one that is eminently modifiable in accordance with the organization of society; the state is as society is. – Of the various social institutions past and present, the state appears to us (irrespective of its form) as an element of socialization and progress, in the sense that it represents the general interest of society vis-à-vis the interests of individuals; whereas other institutions, especially private property, represent the particular interest as opposed to the general interest. At present, we demand of the state that it should remain true to its mission of managing the general interests of society, by intervening wherever the general interest is damaged in the interests of a few individuals. Consequently, we demand that the state, even in its present form, should not abandon public services to private companies but intervene with restrictive laws wherever *laisser faire* is harmful to general interests (e.g., laws on child labour and others relating to factory work, laws on public health and dangerous work, laws on falsification and commercial fraud, etc.). – In the transitional period between bourgeois society and the new society, the workers should take hold of the state and make it serve the emancipation of their class; this would not even deflect the state from its role, which is to safeguard the general interests. […] In the end, without some organization of the state as an administrative body rather than a legislative power, without the existence of a public, general administration, society would not take long to return to barbarism and savagery!

42

Various Authors, *[On Collective Ownership]*[55]

Considering that, in terms of property, the modern mode of production tends towards the accumulation of capital in the hands of a few and increases the exploitation of workers; that it is necessary to change this state of affairs, which is the starting point for all social evils;

Congress considers [it necessary] to bring about collective ownership – that is, that groups of workers should take possession of the social capital. [Congress further declares that a socialist party] truly worthy of the name should include the principle of collective ownership not in a distant ideal, but in its present programmes and its daily manifestations.

---

[55] The text contains one of the resolutions adopted at the Verviers Congress of the 'autonomist' IWMA, which took place from 6 to 8 September 1877. These were published on September 16, in the newspaper *Le Mirabeau*, with the title *Compte rendu du 9e congrès général de l'Association Internationale des Travailleurs*. It may be found in PI, IV: 535.

Part Eight

Education

43

The Bookbinders of Paris, *[On Free Education]*[56]

[...] The International Association wants for all: *justice*; equal rights, not kindness. [...]

Stating at the outset that by *equal rights* we do not mean to imply that we imagine a society in which an equal share of material enjoyment would be distributed to each; no. We want liberty, that first and indispensable condition of well-being, as the foundation, and we categorically rule out any idea of a centralized organization whose object would be the direction of labour and the distribution of general production among citizens.

By *equal rights* we mean that all individuals are entitled to equal means of action in fulfilling their needs. We leave them free, of course, to use as they please the resources placed at their disposal by nature and society, provided that they do not claim more than they have produced.

One of the most powerful means of action, for present as for future society, is and will be education. [...]

Having recognized the necessity of education and agreed upon its mandatory character, it remains to determine who will incur the cost. Two systems are in contention: one which affirms that it is naturally incumbent upon the head of the household; the other which demands that society as a whole take responsibility for it. The latter system is commonly called: *free education*.

Much has been said about free education, but we believe that it has not yet been shown in its true light. Its opponents say: There is no truly free education, free education is nothing but a fiction; while you intend to make the state pay for education, you forget that the state has nothing in itself; its resources are supplied by us; if it pays, it is with taxpayers' money, and in the end it is

---

[56] This text is an excerpt from the *Report Prepared by Parisian Bookbinders* presented at a session of 9 September 1868, of the Brussels Congress, devoted to the issue of education. The author, possibly more than one, of this text is unknown. Published in B1868. The full version is also found in PI, I: 306–9.

always citizens that must pay, as taxpayers if not as heads of households. Thus, there is no sense in pouring our money into the coffers of the state, only then to receive free education back from it in the guise of generosity. It would be preferable to pay teachers ourselves and have them instruct our children to suit our fancy.

Now, all of this reasoning, which, at first, may dazzle the faculties, vanishes into thin air upon closer examination.

There is no such thing as free education, it is always citizens who pay; this is true, *generally speaking*. But when calling for free education, we do not ask not to pay for it, we ask simply for a different distribution, a fairer sharing out of the cost.

If education fees must be borne by the parents, we considerably overburden the responsibility of households and we cannot ensure the equality of education; for, even with the best intentions, those citizens with many children will never be able to spend as much on each of them as those who have only one or two in their care.

Moreover, here we take the case of citizens endowed with equal resources, which does not exist in present society and will never exist, as long as we would like to safeguard individual liberty; for those who are strong, courageous, intelligent, active, will always be able to benefit more from equal means of action than those who are weak, lazy, inept or indolent.

Thus, to the disparity caused by the number of children, must be added the difference in the facility of the parents.

It can, therefore, be said that, with this system, not only will there be an inequality in the education of children, but, in addition, some of them will be deprived of it by the shortcomings of their parents should society fail to intervene in their favour. [...]

It was not necessary to be socialists to focus our attention on the system advocated by bourgeois philanthropists who, accustomed to relying upon inequality, are obliged to constantly bring in charity to mitigate the widest gaps, the worst excesses of their social order.

If we want to rebuild the world, we must base it upon a well-levelled ground in order not to have to rely upon a stop gap to prop up the first piece of our edifice.

With the system of free education, that is of education paid for by the state, or, since it is the same thing, by the taxpayers, the cost is shared among all citizens, no longer according to their number of children, but according to their capacity to contribute. Here all citizens pay, those who have children and those who have not, those whose children are long gone and those whose are still to come, and each according to his wealth (if he has any) or his means.

It is easy to imagine that this burden, a moment ago so heavy for a few, becomes light when shared among all. Furthermore, upon attaining our goal, all children shall be guaranteed to receive an equally complete education, and men, upon entering into the world, shall be able to develop their faculties to the fullest.

It remains to respond to certain objections, of little value, it is true, but which could nevertheless arise. Is it fair to ask society to assume the cost of education, to make those that do not have children pay for the education of those that do? To this, we reply: it is society, not the household, that benefits from education; the more that men are educated, the more they are useful, the more they are helpful to their fellow man: thus it is fair that society pay.

As for those citizens without children, they should not forget that in being born, they have incurred a debt to nature; she created them, they must reimburse her in reproducing themselves, and if they cannot, they should consider themselves fortunate that, in virtue of the solidarity that unites us, others take it upon themselves to discharge them. In paying only for education, they are let off for very little. Moreover, as members of the collectivity, they have an interest in the development of a strong, well-educated and intelligent generation that will be able to provide them with products and services when age will have left them unable to care for themselves: thus it is fair that they contribute to the expenses required by the next generation.

Is it fair that the contribution of citizens be in accordance with the wealth or facility of each? Yes, because the rich, in present society, as in future society, being endowed with greater productive capacity, and having need of a more considerable sum of products and services, must contribute a larger share to the education of producers and traders.

We conclude: public education is in the general interest, the cost must be included in the general expenses of the nation.

44

Karl Marx, [On Education in Modern Society][57]

Citizen Marx said there was a peculiar difficulty connected with this question. On the one hand a change of social circumstances was required to establish a proper system of education, on the other hand a proper system of education was required to bring about a change of social circumstances; we must therefore commence where we were.

The question treated at the congresses was whether education was to be national or private.[58] National education had been looked upon as governmental, but that was not necessarily the case. In Massachusetts every township was bound to provide schools for primary education for all the children. In towns of more than 5,000 inhabitants higher schools for technical education had to be provided, in larger towns still higher. The state contributed something but not much. In Massachusetts one eighth of the local taxes went for education, in New York one-fifth. The school committees who administered the schools were local, they appointed the schoolmasters and selected the books. The fault of the American system was that it was too much localized, the education given depended upon the state of culture prevailing in each district. There was a cry for a central supervision. The taxation for schools was compulsory, but the attendance of children was not. Property had to pay the taxes and the people who paid the taxes wanted that the money was usefully applied.

Education might be national without being governmental. Government might appoint inspectors whose duty it was to see that the laws were obeyed,

---

[57] This text partially reproduces two speeches on the issue of education given by Karl Marx (see note 1) at the GC on 10 August and 17 August 1869. A short summary of the first was released on August 14, in the weekly *The Bee-Hive*. The full versions are in GC, III: 140–1 and GC, III: 146–7.

[58] The question of general education was discussed at the previous congresses of the IWMA, in Geneva (1866), Lausanne (1867) and Brussels (1868).

just as the factory inspectors looked after the observance of the factory acts, without any power of interfering with the course of education itself.

The Congress might without hesitation adopt that education was to be compulsory. [...]

[...] As to Mrs Law's Church budget[59] it would be good policy for the Congress to declare against the Church. [...] Nothing could be introduced either in primary, or higher schools that admitted of party and class interpretation. Only, subjects such as the physical sciences, grammar, etc., were fit matter for schools. The rules of grammar, for instance, could not differ, whether explained by a religious Tory or a free thinker. Subjects that admitted of different conclusions must be excluded and left for the adults to such teachers as Mrs Law, who gave instruction in religion.

---

[59] The proposition that Harriet Law (see note 16) moved at the General Council meeting of 17 August 1869 called for the transfer of the Church's property and income to schools.

45

César De Paepe, [On State Education][60]

[...] We believe that education must be *complete*, that is, at once scientific and industrial, theoretical and practical, and consequently equal for all and common to all. In leaving education to the care of communes, will we not have in one an education that is more profound, more scientific, for example, than in another, if only owing to the advantages, from the point of view of material resources, of that commune over the other? What becomes, then, of *complete* education, if not the privilege of a few, the privilege of the best positioned?

[...] Where education is complete, it provides society with human beings enlightened by science, basing their morals, their actions, and their relations with other human beings exclusively upon scientific truths. We do not need to dwell on this any further. The right of all children to a complete education and society's obligation to provide it are now accepted by all socialist schools; but, in order that it be complete, equal for all and common to all, we believe that education must be considered a public service for which the state is responsible.

---

[60] This is an excerpt from the text by César De Paepe (see note 22) set out in note 52. This part was not included in the volume edited by Daniel Guérin and it is here translated into English for the first time.

Part Nine

The Commune of Paris

46

Karl Marx, *[On the Paris Commune]*[61]

[...] On the dawn of 18 March, Paris arose to the thunderburst of 'Vive la Commune!' What is the Commune, that sphinx so tantalizing to the bourgeois mind?

'The proletarians of Paris,' said the Central Committee in its manifesto of 18 March, 'amidst the failures and treasons of the ruling classes, have understood that the hour has struck for them to save the situation by taking into their own hands the direction of public affairs.... They have understood that it is their imperious duty, and their absolute right, to render themselves masters of their own destinies, by seizing upon the governmental power.'

But the working class cannot simply lay hold of the ready-made state machinery, and wield it for its own purposes.

The centralized state power, with its ubiquitous organs of standing army, police, bureaucracy, clergy, and judicature – organs wrought after the plan of a systematic and hierarchic division of labour – originates from the days of absolute monarchy, serving nascent middle class society as a mighty weapon in its struggle against feudalism. Still, its development remained clogged by all manner of medieval rubbish, seignorial rights, local privileges, municipal and guild monopolies, and provincial constitutions. The gigantic broom of the French Revolution of the eighteenth century swept away all these relics of bygone times, thus clearing simultaneously the social soil of its last hindrances

---

[61] This text consists of excerpts from Parts III and IV of *The Civil War in France*. London: Edward Truelove, 1871. It was written by Karl Marx (see note 1) between mid-April and early June of 1871, approved by the GC at its session of 30 May, and published as a booklet a few days later. It was quickly reprinted twice, and after a year had been translated, in whole or in part, into Danish, German, Flemish, French, Dutch, Italian, Polish, Russian, Serbian-Croatian and Spanish, appearing in newspapers, magazines and brochures in several countries across Europe, and the United States. Never before had a writing of the labour movement been so widely and rapidly translated and disseminated. The complete version is located in the GC, IV: 356–416.

to the superstructure of the modern state edifice raised under the First Empire, itself the offspring of the coalition wars of old semi-feudal Europe against modern France.

During the subsequent regimes, the government, placed under parliamentary control – that is, under the direct control of the propertied classes – became not only a hotbed of huge national debts and crushing taxes; with its irresistible allurements of place, pelf, and patronage, it became not only the bone of contention between the rival factions and adventurers of the ruling classes; but its political character changed simultaneously with the economic changes of society. At the same pace at which the progress of modern industry developed, widened, intensified the class antagonism between capital and labour, the state power assumed more and more the character of the national power of capital over labour, of a public force organized for social enslavement, of an engine of class despotism.

After every revolution marking a progressive phase in the class struggle, the purely repressive character of the state power stands out in bolder and bolder relief. The Revolution of 1830, resulting in the transfer of government from the landlords to the capitalists, transferred it from the more remote to the more direct antagonists of the working men. The bourgeois republicans, who, in the name of the February Revolution, took the state power, used it for the June [1848] massacres, in order to convince the working class that 'social' republic means the republic entrusting their social subjection, and in order to convince the royalist bulk of the bourgeois and landlord class that they might safely leave the cares and emoluments of government to the bourgeois 'republicans.'

However, after their one heroic exploit of June, the bourgeois republicans had, from the front, to fall back to the rear of the 'Party of Order' – a combination formed by all the rival fractions and factions of the appropriating classes. The proper form of their joint-stock government was the parliamentary republic, with Louis Bonaparte for its president. Theirs was a regime of avowed class terrorism and deliberate insult towards the 'vile multitude.'

If the parliamentary republic, as M. Thiers said, 'divided them [the different fractions of the ruling class] least', it opened an abyss between that class and the whole body of society outside their spare ranks. The restraints by which their own divisions had under former regimes still checked the state power, were removed by their union; and in view of the threatening upheaval of the proletariat, they now used that state power mercilessly and ostentatiously as the national war engine of capital against labour.

In their uninterrupted crusade against the producing masses, they were, however, bound not only to invest the executive with continually increased powers of repression, but at the same time to divest their own parliamentary stronghold – the National Assembly – one by one, of all its own means of defence against the Executive. The Executive, in the person of Louis Bonaparte, turned them out. The natural offspring of the 'Party of Order' republic was the Second Empire.

The empire, with the coup d'etat for its birth certificate, universal suffrage for its sanction, and the sword for its sceptre, professed to rest upon the peasantry, the large mass of producers not directly involved in the struggle of capital and labour. It professed to save the working class by breaking down parliamentarism, and, with it, the undisguised subserviency of government to the propertied classes. It professed to save the propertied classes by upholding their economic supremacy over the working class; and, finally, it professed to unite all classes by reviving for all the chimera of national glory.

In reality, it was the only form of government possible at a time when the bourgeoisie had already lost, and the working class had not yet acquired, the faculty of ruling the nation. It was acclaimed throughout the world as the saviour of society. Under its sway, bourgeois society, freed from political cares, attained a development unexpected even by itself. Its industry and commerce expanded to colossal dimensions; financial swindling celebrated cosmopolitan orgies; the misery of the masses was set off by a shameless display of gorgeous, meretricious and debased luxury. The state power, apparently soaring high above society and the very hotbed of all its corruptions. Its own rottenness, and the rottenness of the society it had saved, were laid bare by the bayonet of Prussia, herself eagerly bent upon transferring the supreme seat of that regime from Paris to Berlin. Imperialism is, at the same time, the most prostitute and the ultimate form of the state power which nascent middle class society had commenced to elaborate as a means of its own emancipation from feudalism, and which full-grown bourgeois society had finally transformed into a means for the enslavement of labour by capital.

The direct antithesis to the empire was the Commune. The cry of 'social republic,' with which the February Revolution was ushered in by the Paris proletariat, did but express a vague aspiration after a republic that was not only to supercede the monarchical form of class rule, but class rule itself. The Commune was the positive form of that republic.

Paris, the central seat of the old governmental power, and, at the same time, the social stronghold of the French working class, had risen in arms against the attempt of Thiers and the Rurals to restore and perpetuate that old governmental power bequeathed to them by the empire. Paris could resist only because, in consequence of the siege, it had got rid of the army, and replaced it by a National Guard, the bulk of which consisted of working men. This fact was now to be transformed into an institution. The first decree of the Commune, therefore, was the suppression of the standing army, and the substitution for it of the armed people.

The Commune was formed of the municipal councillors, chosen by universal suffrage in the various wards of the town, responsible and revocable at short terms. The majority of its members were naturally working men, or acknowledged representatives of the working class. The Commune was to be a working, not a parliamentary body, executive and legislative at the same time.

Instead of continuing to be the agent of the Central Government, the police was at once stripped of its political attributes, and turned into the responsible, and at all times revocable, agent of the Commune. So were the officials of all other branches of the administration. From the members of the Commune downwards, the public service had to be done at *workman's wage*. The vested interests and the representation allowances of the high dignitaries of state disappeared along with the high dignitaries themselves. Public functions ceased to be the private property of the tools of the Central Government. Not only municipal administration, but the whole initiative hitherto exercised by the state was laid into the hands of the Commune.

Having once got rid of the standing army and the police – the physical force elements of the old government – the Commune was anxious to break the spiritual force of repression, the 'parson-power', by the disestablishment and disendowment of all churches as proprietary bodies. The priests were sent back to the recesses of private life, there to feed upon the alms of the faithful in imitation of their predecessors, the apostles.

The whole of the educational institutions were opened to the people gratuitously, and at the same time cleared of all interference of church and state. Thus, not only was education made accessible to all, but science itself freed from the fetters which class prejudice and governmental force had imposed upon it.

The judicial functionaries were to be divested of that sham independence which had but served to mask their abject subserviency to all succeeding governments to which, in turn, they had taken, and broken, the oaths of allegiance. Like the rest of public servants, magistrates and judges were to be elective, responsible, and revocable.

The Paris Commune was, of course, to serve as a model to all the great industrial centres of France. The communal regime once established in Paris and the secondary centres, the old centralized government would in the provinces, too, have to give way to the self-government of the producers.

In a rough sketch of national organization, which the Commune had no time to develop, it states clearly that the Commune was to be the political form of even the smallest country hamlet, and that in the rural districts the standing army was to be replaced by a national militia, with an extremely short term of service. The rural communities of every district were to administer their common affairs by an assembly of delegates in the central town, and these district assemblies were again to send deputies to the National Delegation in Paris, each delegate to be at any time revocable and bound by the *mandat imperatif* (formal instructions) of his constituents. The few but important functions which would still remain for a central government were not to be suppressed, as has been intentionally misstated, but were to be discharged by Communal and thereafter responsible agents.

The unity of the nation was not to be broken, but, on the contrary, to be organized by communal constitution, and to become a reality by the destruction of the state power which claimed to be the embodiment of that unity independent of, and superior to, the nation itself, from which it was but a parasitic excrescence.

While the merely repressive organs of the old governmental power were to be amputated, its legitimate functions were to be wrested from an authority usurping pre-eminence over society itself, and restored to the responsible agents of society. Instead of deciding once in 3 or 6 years which member of the ruling class was to misrepresent the people in Parliament, universal suffrage was to serve the people, constituted in communes, as individual suffrage serves every other employer in the search for the workmen and managers in his business. And it is well-known that companies, like individuals, in matters of real business generally know how to put the right man in the right place, and, if they for once make a mistake, to redress it promptly. On the other hand, nothing could be more foreign to the spirit of the Commune than to supersede universal suffrage by hierarchical investiture.

It is generally the fate of completely new historical creations to be mistaken for the counterparts of older, and even defunct, forms of social life, to which they may bear a certain likeness. Thus, this new Commune, which breaks with the modern state power, has been mistaken for a reproduction of the medieval communes, which first preceded, and afterwards became the substratum of, that very state power. The communal constitution has been mistaken for an attempt to break up into the federation of small states, as dreamt of by Montesquieu and the Girondins,[62] that unity of great nations which, if originally brought about by political force, has now become a powerful coefficient of social production. The antagonism of the Commune against the state power has been mistaken for an exaggerated form of the ancient struggle against over-centralization. Peculiar historical circumstances may have prevented the classical development, as in France, of the bourgeois form of government, and may have allowed, as in England, to complete the great central state organs by corrupt vestries, jobbing councillors, and ferocious poor-law guardians in the towns, and virtually hereditary magistrates in the counties.

The communal constitution would have restored to the social body all the forces hitherto absorbed by the state parasite feeding upon, and clogging the free movement of, society. By this one act, it would have initiated the regeneration of France.

---

[62] The moderate bourgeois revolutionaries of the 1789 Revolution.

The provincial French middle class saw in the Commune an attempt to restore the sway their order had held over the country under Louis Philippe, and which, under Louis Napoleon, was supplanted by the pretended rule of the country over the towns. In reality, the communal constitution brought the rural producers under the intellectual lead of the central towns of their districts, and there secured to them, in the working men, the natural trustees of their interests. The very existence of the Commune involved, as a matter of course, local municipal liberty, but no longer as a check upon the now superseded state power. It could only enter into the head of a Bismarck – who, when not engaged on his intrigues of blood and iron, always likes to resume his old trade, so befitting his mental calibre, of contributor to *Kladderadatsch* (the Berlin *Punch*) – it could only enter into such a head to ascribe to the Paris Commune aspirations after the caricature of the old French municipal organization of 1791, the Prussian municipal constitution which degrades the town governments to mere secondary wheels in the police machinery of the Prussian state. The Commune made that catchword of bourgeois revolutions – cheap government – a reality by destroying the two greatest sources of expenditure: the standing army and state functionarism. Its very existence presupposed the non-existence of monarchy, which, in Europe at least, is the normal incumbrance and indispensable cloak of class rule. It supplied the republic with the basis of really democratic institutions. But neither cheap government nor the 'true republic' was its ultimate aim; they were its mere concomitants.

The multiplicity of interpretations to which the Commune has been subjected, and the multiplicity of interests which construed it in their favour, show that it was a thoroughly expansive political form, while all the previous forms of government had been emphatically repressive. Its true secret was this:

It was essentially a working class government, the product of the struggle of the producing against the appropriating class, the political form at last discovered under which to work out the economical emancipation of labour.

Except on this last condition, the communal constitution would have been an impossibility and a delusion. The political rule of the producer cannot co-exist with the perpetuation of his social slavery. The Commune was therefore to serve as a lever for uprooting the economical foundation upon which rests the existence of classes, and therefore of class rule. With labour emancipated, every man becomes a working man, and productive labour ceases to be a class attribute.

It is a strange fact. In spite of all the tall talk and all the immense literature, for the last 60 years, about emancipation of labour, no sooner do the working men anywhere take the subject into their own hands with a will, than uprises at once all the apologetic phraseology of the mouthpieces of present society with its two poles of capital and wage slavery (the landlord now is but the sleeping partner of the capitalist), as if the capitalist society was still in its purest state of virgin innocence, with its antagonisms still undeveloped, with its delusions still unexploded, with its prostitute realities not yet laid bare. The Commune, they exclaim, intends to abolish property, the basis of all civilization.

Yes, gentlemen, the Commune intended to abolish that class property which makes the labour of the many the wealth of the few. It aimed at the expropriation of the expropriators. It wanted to make individual property a truth by transforming the means of production, land, and capital, now chiefly the means of enslaving and exploiting labour, into mere instruments of free and associated labour. But this is communism, 'impossible' communism! Why, those members of the ruling classes who are intelligent enough to perceive the impossibility of continuing the present system – and they are many – have become the obtrusive and full-mouthed apostles of cooperative production. If cooperative production is not to remain a sham and a snare; if it is to supersede the capitalist system; if united cooperative societies are to regulate national production upon common plan, thus taking it under their own control, and putting an end to the constant anarchy and periodical convulsions which are the fatality of capitalist production – what else, gentlemen, would it be but communism, 'possible' communism?

The working class did not expect miracles from the Commune. They have no ready-made utopias to introduce *par décret du peuple*. They know that in order to work out their own emancipation, and along with it that higher form to which present society is irresistibly tending by its own economical agencies, they will have to pass through long struggles, through a series of historic processes, transforming circumstances and men. They have no ideals to realize, but to set free the elements of the new society with which old collapsing bourgeois society itself is pregnant. In the full consciousness of their historic mission, and with the heroic resolve to act up to it, the working class can afford to smile at the coarse invective of the gentlemen's gentlemen with pen and inkhorn, and at the didactic patronage of well-wishing bourgeois-doctrinaires, pouring forth their ignorant platitudes and sectarian crotchets in the oracular tone of scientific infallibility.

When the Paris Commune took the management of the revolution in its own hands; when plain working men for the first time dared to infringe upon the governmental privilege of their 'natural superiors,' and, under circumstances of unexampled difficulty, performed it at salaries the highest of which barely amounted to one-fifth of what, according to high scientific authority,[63] is the minimum required for a secretary to a certain metropolitan school-board – the old world writhed in convulsions of rage at the sight of the Red Flag, the symbol of the Republic of Labour, floating over the Hôtel de Ville.

And yet, this was the first revolution in which the working class was openly acknowledged as the only class capable of social initiative, even by the great bulk of the Paris middle class – shopkeepers, tradesmen, merchants – the wealthy capitalist alone excepted. The Commune had saved them by a sagacious settlement of that ever recurring cause of dispute among the middle class themselves – the debtor and creditor accounts.[64] The same portion of the middle class, after they had assisted in putting down the working men's insurrection of June 1848, had been at once unceremoniously sacrificed to their creditors by the then Constituent Assembly.[65] But this was not their only motive for now rallying around the working class. They felt there was but one alternative – the Commune, or the empire – under whatever name it might reappear. The empire had ruined them economically by the havoc it made of public wealth, by the wholesale financial swindling it fostered, by the props it lent to the artificially accelerated centralization of capital, and the concomitant

---

[63] Professor Huxley [Note written by Karl Marx].
[64] The Commune decreed war debts be repaid over three years, while abolishing interest payments.
[65] Much of the lesser and petty bourgeoisie were ruined in 1848 when the Constituent Assembly decided against deferring debt repayments during the economic crisis following the revolution.

expropriation of their own ranks. It had suppressed them politically, it had shocked them morally by its orgies, it had insulted their Voltairianism by handing over the education of their children to the fréres Ignorantins,[66] it had revolted their national feeling as Frenchmen by precipitating them headlong into a war which left only one equivalent for the ruins it made – the disappearance of the empire. In fact, after the exodus from Paris of the high Bonapartist and capitalist bohème, the true middle class Party of Order came out in the shape of the 'Union Republicaine',[67] enrolling themselves under the colours of the Commune and defending it against the wilful misconstructions of Thiers. Whether the gratitude of this great body of the middle class will stand the present severe trial, time must show.

The Commune was perfectly right in telling the peasants that 'its victory was their only hope.' Of all the lies hatched at Versailles and re-echoed by the glorious European penny-a-liner, one of the most tremendous was that the Rurals represented the French peasantry. Think only of the love of the French peasant for the men to whom, after 1815, he had to pay the milliard indemnity.[68] In the eyes of the French peasant, the very existence of a great landed proprietor is in itself an encroachment on his conquests of 1789. The bourgeois, in 1848, had burdened his plot of land with the additional tax of 45 cents in the franc; but then he did so in the name of the revolution; while now he had fomented a civil war against revolution, to shift on to the peasant's shoulders the chief load of the 5 milliards of indemnity to be paid to the Prussian. The Commune, on the other hand, in one of its first proclamations, declared that the true originators of the war would be made to pay its cost. The Commune would have delivered the peasant of the blood tax – would have given him a cheap government – transformed his present blood-suckers, the notary, advocate, executor, and other judicial vampires, into salaried communal agents, elected by, and responsible to, himself. It would have freed him of the tyranny of the *garde champêtre* [field warden], the gendarme, and

---

[66] Sarcastic reference to the largely religious teaching of a real clerical order, so-nicknamed for their exclusion of theologically trained brothers.
[67] An association of petty bourgeois delegates opposing the Versailles government and supporting the Commune.
[68] Compensation to landowners expropriated during the French Revolution.

the prefect; would have put enlightenment by the schoolmaster in the place of stultification by the priest. And the French peasant is, above all, a man of reckoning. He would find it extremely reasonable that the pay of the priest, instead of being extorted by the tax-gatherer, should only depend upon the spontaneous action of the parishioners' religious instinct. Such were the great immediate boons which the rule of the Commune – and that rule alone – held out to the French peasantry. It is, therefore, quite superfluous here to expatiate upon the more complicated but vital problems which the Commune alone was able, and at the same time compelled, to solve in favour of the peasant – viz., the hypothecary debt, lying like an incubus upon his parcel of soil, the *prolétariat foncier* (the rural proletariat), daily growing upon it, and his expropriation from it enforced, at a more and more rapid rate, by the very development of modern agriculture and the competition of capitalist farming.

The French peasant had elected Louis Bonaparte president of the Republic; but the Party of Order created the empire. What the French peasant really wants he commenced to show in 1849 and 1850, by opposing his *maire* to the government's prefect, his school-master to the government's priest, and himself to the government's gendarme. All the laws made by the Party of Order in January and February 1850 were avowed measures of repression against the peasant. The peasant was a Bonapartist, because the Great Revolution, with all its benefits to him, was, in his eyes, personified in Napoleon. This delusion, rapidly breaking down under the Second Empire (and in its very nature hostile to the Rurals), this prejudice of the past, how could it have withstood the appeal of the Commune to the living interests and urgent wants of the peasantry?

The Rurals – this was, in fact, their chief apprehension – knew that 3 months' free communication of Communal Paris with the provinces would bring about a general rising of the peasants, and hence their anxiety to establish a police blockade around Paris, so as to stop the spread of the rinderpest [cattle plague].

If the Commune was thus the true representative of all the healthy elements of French society, and therefore the truly national government, it was, at the same time, as a working men's government, as the bold champion of the emancipation of labour, emphatically international. Within sight of that Prussian army, that had annexed to Germany two French provinces, the Commune annexed to France the working people all over the world.

The Second Empire had been the jubilee of cosmopolitan blackleggism, the rakes of all countries rushing in at its call for a share in its orgies and in the plunder of the French people. Even at this moment, the right hand of Thiers is Ganessco, the foul Wallachian, and his left hand is Markovsky, the Russian spy. The Commune admitted all foreigners to the honour of dying for an immortal cause. Between the foreign war lost by their treason, and the civil war fomented by their conspiracy with the foreign invader, the bourgeoisie had found the time to display their patriotism by organizing police hunts upon the Germans in France. The Commune made a German working man [Leo Frankel] its Minister of Labour. Thiers, the bourgeoisie, the Second Empire, had continually deluded Poland by loud professions of sympathy, while in reality betraying her to, and doing the dirty work of, Russia. The Commune honoured the heroic sons of Poland [J. Dabrowski and W. Wróblewski] by placing them at the head of the defenders of Paris. And, to broadly mark the new era of history it was conscious of initiating, under the eyes of the conquering Prussians on one side, and the Bonapartist army, led by Bonapartist generals, on the other, the Commune pulled down that colossal symbol of martial glory, the Vendôme Column.[69]

The great social measure of the Commune was its own working existence. Its special measures could but betoken the tendency of a government of the people by the people. Such were the abolition of the nightwork of journeymen bakers; the prohibition, under penalty, of the employers' practice to reduce wages by levying upon their workpeople fines under manifold pretexts – a process in which the employer combines in his own person the parts of legislator, judge, and executor, and filches the money to boot. Another measure of this class was the surrender to associations of workmen, under reserve of compensation, of all closed workshops and factories, no matter whether the respective capitalists had absconded or preferred to strike work. [...] The Commune did not pretend to infallibility, the invariable attribute of all governments of the old stamp. It published its doings and sayings, it initiated

---

[69] Monument to Napoleon Bonaparte's victories, restored after suppression of the Commune.

the public into all its shortcomings. [...] Wonderful, indeed, was the change the Commune had wrought in Paris! No longer any trace of the meretricious Paris of the Second Empire! No longer was Paris the rendezvous of British landlords, Irish absentees, American ex-slaveholders and shoddy men, Russian ex-serfowners, and Wallachian boyards. No more corpses at the morgue, no nocturnal burglaries, scarcely any robberies; in fact, for the first time since the days of February 1848, the streets of Paris were safe, and that without any police of any kind.

'We,' said a member of the Commune, 'hear no longer of assassination, theft, and personal assault; it seems indeed as if the police had dragged along with it to Versailles all its Conservative friends.'

The *cocottes* [prostitutes] had refound the scent of their protectors – the absconding men of family, religion, and, above all, of property. In their stead, the real women of Paris showed again at the surface – heroic, noble, and devoted, like the women of antiquity. Working, thinking, fighting, bleeding Paris – almost forgetful, in its incubation of a new society, of the Cannibals at its gates – radiant in the enthusiasm of its historic initiative! [...]

After Whit-Sunday, 1871, there can be neither peace nor truce possible between the working men of France and the appropriators of their produce. The iron hand of a mercenary soldiery may keep for a time both classes tied down in common oppression. But the battle must break out again and again in ever-growing dimensions, and there can be no doubt as to who will be the victor in the end – the appropriating few, or the immense working majority. And the French working class is only the advanced guard of the modern proletariat. [...]

The police-tinged bourgeois mind naturally figures to itself the International Working Men's Association as acting in the manner of a secret conspiracy, its central body ordering, from time to time, explosions in different countries. Our Association is, in fact, nothing but the international bond between the most advanced working men in the various countries of the civilized world. Wherever, in whatever shape, and under whatever conditions the class struggle obtains any consistency, it is but natural that members of our Association, should stand in the foreground. The soil out of which it grows is modern society itself. It cannot be stamped out by any amount of carnage. To stamp it out, the governments would have to stamp out the despotism of capital over labour – the condition of their own parasitical existence.

Working men's Paris, with its Commune, will be forever celebrated as the glorious harbinger of a new society. Its martyrs are enshrined in the great heart of the working class. Its exterminators history has already nailed to that eternal pillory from which all the prayers of their priest will not avail to redeem them.

Part Ten

Internationalism and Opposition to War

Various Authors, *[International Solidarity]*[70]

[…] The Address and Statutes issued by the Provincial Central Council fully explain the Association's objects and Aspiration, which, however, may be summed up in a few Words. It aims at the protection, advancement, and complete Emancipation, economic and political, of the working classes. As a means to this great end it will promote. The establishment of solidarity between the manifold division of labour in each country, and the cooperation of the working classes of different countries. Its organization, with a Central Medium at London, and numerous affiliated Branches in Europe and America, will assist in uniting the working classes of all countries in a perpetual bond of fraternal cooperation. […]

---

[70] This text is an excerpt from a form sent to the *Operative Bricklayers Society* from the GC, after the decision on 7 February 1865, approving their admission as a section of the IWMA. The full version is in GC, II: 261–2.

48

Eugene Dupont – Johann Georg Eccarius – Peter Fox – Hermann Jung – Karl Marx, *[On the Necessity of an International Organization]*[71]

[…] The power of the human individual has disappeared before the power of capital, in the factory the worker is now nothing but a cog in the machine. In order to recover his individuality, the worker has had to unite together with others and create associations to defend his wages and his life. Until today these associations had remained purely local, while the power of capital, thanks to new industrial inventions, is increasing day by day; furthermore in many cases national associations have become powerless: a study of the struggle waged by the English working class reveals that, in order to oppose their workers, the employers either bring in workers from abroad or else transfer manufacture to countries where there is a cheap labour force. Given this state of affairs, if the working class wishes to continue its struggle with some chance of success, the national organizations must become international. […]

---

[71] From the call of the GC for the Lausanne Congress, adopted at its session of 9 July 1867. Since Karl Marx (see note 1) was busy at the time correcting the proofs for *Capital*, the address was composed by a group of authors. Eugène Dupont [1831–81], a French artisan exiled in London, was a member of the GC from 1864 to 1872 and Corresponding Secretary for France from 1865 to 1871. He participated in all IWMA Congresses (except that of Basel in 1869), and continued his activism in the United States where he immigrated in 1874. For Johann Georg Eccarius, see note 39. Peter Fox [unk.-1869], was a journalist member of the GC from 1864 to 1869, its general secretary for 3 months in 1866 and corresponding secretary for the United States in 1866–67. Hermann Jung [1830–1901], was a member of the GC and corresponding secretary for Switzerland from 1864 to 1872, who took part in all the congresses (except Lausanne 1867 and The Hague 1872) and conferences of the IWMA. This text first appeared in English as a leaflet in mid-July, and then in French, following extensive revisions by Marx, in *Le Courrier International*, 30 July. The full text may be found in GC, II: 285–7.

49

César de Paepe, *[On the True Causes of War]*[72]

I take the floor not to oppose the project as a whole, but to oppose the phrase that states that we want peace in order to arrive more promptly at social reorganization. It seems to me that this phrase expresses a false idea, consecrates a vicious circle, because peace itself can only be the outcome of social reorganization. If I had to express my sentiments to the Geneva [Peace] Congress, I would say: we want peace as much as you do, but we know that so long as there exists what we call the principle of nationalities or patriotism, there will be war; so long as there are distinct classes, there will be war. War is not only the product of a monarch's ambition; for instance, in the [French] Mexican Adventure [of 1862–67], the true cause of war was the interests of some capitalists; war is the result of the lack of equilibrium in the economic world, and the lack of equilibrium in the political world. If the Geneva Congress believes that peace may be secured in the current social context, it is illogical: the ends justify the means.

---

[72] This text corresponds to the synopsis of a speech given by César De Paepe (see note 22) to a session of 4 September 1867, at the Lausanne Congress. It was published in L1867 and is also included in PI, I: 122–3.

50

César De Paepe, [Strike Against War][73]

War is an obvious calamity to us all. Its abolition demands, besides our everlasting protest, that we charge ourselves with the task of intervening in practice.

For this there are two methods: The first is to attack war directly by refusing to perform military service, or, what amounts to the same thing since armies need to consume, by refusing to work. The second, which does not involve direct intervention, aims at achieving the abolition of war through the resolution of the social question itself; such is the method that, through its development, the International is destined to make triumphant.

To rely upon the first method means to constantly repeat it; only the second destroys evil at its source.

Some have sought to attribute the cause of war to individual personalities; this is an error: kings, emperors are merely accidents, instruments. The only true cause of war is to be found in our social institutions. The proof is that states that do not have sovereigns also make war. What was behind the American Civil War if not the question of labour? The bourgeoisie of the South needed their black slaves; the Northern states wanted the abolition of slavery to replace it with modern slavery – harsher perhaps even than the former, since the black slave costs something and the white slave costs nothing – in order, that is, there to substitute the proletariat.

The primary cause of all war is hunger. In the beginning, the savage simply ate his defeated enemy; later, the result, while more complicated in appearance, remains essentially the same: the vanquisher takes from the vanquished his

---

[73] This text corresponds to the synopsis of a speech given by César De Paepe (see note 22) to a session of 7 September 1868, at the Brussels Congress, dedicated to the question of war. It was published in B1868 and may be also found in PI, I: 262.

land, the instruments of labour, and the products of labour, and in doing so, satisfies his needs.

This war in the East[74] that cost so much blood, was it anything other than a battle to seize a source of Oriental products, a real social, commercial struggle?

To sum up: Workers can effectively intervene in the question of war only by continuing their social endeavour, and arriving, through the organization of labour, at the elimination of pauperism, the sole cause of modern anarchy.

---

[74] A reference to the conflicts in the Dutch-occupied East Indies.

51

Louis Henri Tolain, [Against War][75]

The Congress, considering that justice must be the guiding principle of relations between natural groups, peoples, and nations, as much as among citizens;

That war has ever been the right of the strongest and not the sanction of law;

That it is nothing other than a means, employed by the privileged classes or the governments that represent them, to subordinate the people;

That it fortifies despotism, stifles liberty […];

That, in sowing grief and ruin in families, and demoralization at every point where armies are concentrated, it fosters and perpetuates ignorance, misery;

That the gold and blood of the people have only ever served to maintain among them the savage instincts of man in a state of nature;

That, in a society founded upon labour and production, force can only be put into the service of liberty and the rights of each; that it can only be a guarantee and not an oppression, even if it be solely for a single *useful* member of society;

That, in the existing state of Europe, governments do not represent the legitimate interests of workers;

The Congress of the International Working Men's Association, held in Brussels, resolves to protest against the war with the utmost energy.

It invites all sections of the Association, each in their respective countries – as well as workers' societies and groups of workers whoever they may be – to rally around its resolution, to act with the greatest activity and energy to prevent, by the pressure of public opinion, a war of people against people, which today could only be considered a civil war because, waged among producers, it would be nothing less than a battle between brothers and citizens.

---

[75] This text corresponds to the synopsis of a speech given by Louis Henri Tolain (see note 34) in the same session referred to in note 73. It was published in B1868 and is also found in PI, I: 264.

52

Hafner, [The Real Causes of the War][76]

The Congress of the International Working Men's Association, held in Lausanne,

Considering:

That war weighs chiefly on the working class, in that it not only deprives workers of the means of existence, but also compels them to spill their blood;

That armed peace paralyses the productive forces, demands of labour only useless works and intimidates production by placing it under the threat of war;

That peace, the first condition of general welfare, must, in turn, be consolidated by a new order of things in which there will no longer be two classes within society, one which is exploited by the other;

Resolves,

To fully and completely adhere to the Congress of Peace which will be held in Geneva on the 9th of September, to energetically support it and to contribute to all that it might undertake to bring about the abolition of standing armies and the maintenance of peace, with the aim of arriving as swiftly as possible at the emancipation of the working class and its liberation from the power and influence of capital, as well as the formation of a confederation of free states across all of Europe. […]

The Congress,

Considering that the root cause of war is destitution and the lack of economic equilibrium,

---

[76] This text is an address voted by the IWMA and delivered to the Congress of Peace in Geneva, held from 9 September to 12 September 1867. It was presented by journalist Hafner [unk.], delegate of the Working Men's section of Murten (Switzerland) at the Lausanne Congress (1867), and later approved unanimously with an addition proposed by Tolain (see note 34). Published in L1867, it was later printed in PI, I: 235.

That, to put an end to war, it is not enough to do away with armies, but it is further necessary to change the social organization in the direction of an ever more equitable distribution of production,

Makes its agreement conditional upon the acceptance of the above-stated declaration by Congress of the Peace. […]

53

Karl Marx, *[England, Metropolis of Capital]*[77]

[...] Although the revolutionary *initiative* will probably start from France, only England can act as a *lever* in any seriously *economic* revolution. It is the only country where there are no longer any peasants, and where land ownership is concentrated in very few hands. It is the only country where almost all production has been taken over by the *capitalist form,* in other words with work combined on a vast scale under capitalist bosses. It is the only country *where the large majority of the population consists of wage-labourers.* It is the only country where the class struggle and the organization of the working class into *trade unions* have actually reached a considerable degree of maturity and universality. Because of its domination of the world market, it is the only country where any revolution in the economic system will have immediate repercussions on the rest of the world. Though landlordism and capitalism are most traditionally established in this country, on the other hand the *material conditions* for *getting rid of them* are also most ripe here. [...] England can not be considered simply as one country among many others. It must be treated as the metropolis of capital. [...]

---

[77] This is an excerpt from a confidential circular sent by Karl Marx (see note 1) to his friend, and IWMA member, Ludwig Kugelmann, on 28 March 1870, to be forwarded to the Brunswick Committee of the German Social Democratic Workers' Party. The letter included the resolution *The General Council to the Federal Council of Romance Switzerland,* written by Karl Marx and adopted at a meeting of the GC on 1 January 1870. It was published in 1872, in the brochure *Fictitious Splits in the International* (see note 105). The full version may be found in GC, III: 399–407.

54

Karl Marx, [First Address on the Franco-Prussian War][78]

[...] In the *Inaugural Address* of the International Working Men's Association, of November 1864, we said – 'If the emancipation of the working classes requires their fraternal concurrence, how are they to fulfil that great mission with a foreign policy in pursuit of criminal designs, playing upon national prejudices, and squandering in piratical wars the people's blood and treasure?' We defined the foreign policy aimed at by the International in these words: 'Vindicate the simple laws of morals and justice, which ought to govern the relations of private individuals, as the laws paramount of the intercourse of nations.'

No wonder that Louis Bonaparte, who usurped power by exploiting the war of classes in France, and perpetuated it by periodical wars abroad, should, from the first, have treated the International as a dangerous foe. On the eve of the plebiscite[79] he ordered a raid on the members of the Administrative Committee of the International Working Men's Association throughout France, at Paris, Lyons, Rouen, Marseilles, Brest, etc., on the pretext that the International was a secret society dabbling in a *complot* for his assassination, a pretext soon after exposed in its full absurdity by his own judges. What was the real crime of the French branches of the International? They told the French people publicly and emphatically that voting the plebiscite was voting

---

[78] This is an excerpt from *First Address of the General Council of the International Working Men's Association on the Franco-Prussian War* written by Karl Marx (see note 1) between 19 July and 23 July 1870. Approved by the GC on July 26, it was published 2 days later in *The Pall-Mall Gazette*. The text was published in German, French and Russian during the month of August. The full version is in GC, IV: 323–9.

[79] Napoleon III's May 1870 referendum was worded to make it impossible to oppose Second Empire policies without opposing democratic reforms. The sections of the IWMA in France called for members to boycott the vote, leading to charges of conspiring against the Emperor.

despotism at home and war abroad. It has been, in fact, their work that in all the great towns, in all the industrial centres of France, the working class rose like one man to reject the plebiscite. Unfortunately, the balance was turned by the heavy ignorance of the rural districts. The stock exchanges, the cabinets, the ruling classes, and the press of Europe celebrated the plebiscite as a signal victory of the French emperor over the French working class; and it was the signal for the assassination, not of an individual, but of nations. [...]

Meanwhile, the Paris members of the International had again set to work. In the *Reveil* of 12 July, they published their manifesto 'to the Workmen of all Nations,' from which we extract the following few passages:

'Once more,' they say, 'on the pretext of European equilibrium, of national honor, the peace of the world is menaced by political ambitions. French, German, Spanish workmen! Let our voices unite in one cry of reprobation against war! 'War for a question of preponderance or a dynasty can, in the eyes of workmen, be nothing but a criminal absurdity. In answer to the warlike proclamations of those who exempt themselves from the blood tax, and find in public misfortunes a source of fresh speculations, we protest, we who want peace, labour, and liberty! 'Brothers in Germany! Our division would only result in the complete triumph of the despotism on both sides of the Rhine... Workmen of all countries! Whatever may for the present become of our common efforts, we, the members of the International Working Men's Association, who know of no frontiers, we send you, as a pledge of indissoluble solidarity, the good wishes and the salutations of the workmen of France.'

This manifesto of our Paris section was followed by numerous similar French addresses, of which we can here only quote the declaration of Neuilly-sur-Seine, published in the *Marseillaise* of 22 July:

'The war, is it just? No! The war, is it national? No! It is merely dynastic. In the name of humanity, or democracy, and the true interests of France, we adhere completely and energetically to the protestation of the International against the war.' [...]

Whatever may be the incidents of Louis Bonaparte's war with Prussia, the death-knell of the Second Empire has already sounded at Paris. It will end, as it began, by a parody. But let us not forget that it is the governments and the ruling classes of Europe who enabled Louis Bonaparte to play during 18 years the ferocious farce of the Restored Empire.

On the German side, the war is a war of defence; but who put Germany to the necessity of defending herself? Who enabled Louis Bonaparte to wage war upon her? Prussia! It was Bismarck who conspired with that very same Louis Bonaparte for the purpose of crushing popular opposition at home, and annexing Germany to the Hohenzollern dynasty. [...]

If the German working class allows the present war to lose its strictly defensive character and to degenerate into a war against the French people, victory or defeat will prove alike disastrous. [...]

The principles of the International are, however, too widely spread and too firmly rooted amongst the German working class to apprehend such a sad consummation. The voices of the French workmen had re-echoed from Germany. A mass meeting of workmen, held at Brunswick on 16 July, expressed its full concurrence with the Paris manifesto, spurned the idea of national antagonism to France, and wound up its resolutions with these words:

> 'We are the enemies of all wars, but above all of dynastic wars. ... With deep sorrow and grief we are forced to undergo a defensive war as an unavoidable evil; but we call, at the same time, upon the whole German working class to render the recurrence of such an immense social misfortune impossible by vindicating for the peoples themselves the power to decide on peace and war, and making them masters of their own destinies.'

At Chemnitz, a meeting of delegates, representing 50,000 Saxon workmen, adopted unanimously a resolution to this effect:

> 'In the name of German Democracy, and especially of the workmen forming the Democratic Socialist Party, we declare the present war to be exclusively dynastic.... We are happy to grasp the fraternal hand stretched out to us by the workmen of France.... Mindful of the watchword of the International Working Men's Association: Proletarians of all countries, unite, we shall never forget that the workmen of all countries are our friends and the despots of all countries our enemies.'

The Berlin branch of the International has also replied to the Paris manifesto:

> 'We,' they say, 'join with heart and hand your protestation.... Solemnly, we promise that neither the sound of the trumpets, nor the roar of the cannon, neither victory nor defeat, shall divert us from our common work for the union of the children of toil of all countries.'

Be it so! […]

The English working class stretch the hand of fellowship to the French and German working people. They feel deeply convinced that whatever turn the impending horrid war may take, the alliance of the working classes of all countries will ultimately kill war. The very fact that while official France and Germany are rushing into a fratricidal feud, the workmen of France and Germany send each other messages of peace and goodwill; this great fact, unparalleled in the history of the past, opens the vista of a brighter future. It proves that in contrast to old society, with its economical miseries and its political delirium, a new society is springing up, whose International rule will be *Peace*, because its national ruler will be everywhere the same – Labour! The pioneer of that new society is the International Working Men's Association.

55

Karl Marx, [Second Address on the Franco-Prussian War][80]

[...] The war of defence ended, in point of fact, with the surrender of Louis Bonaparte, the Sedan capitulation, and the proclamation of the republic at Paris. [...] The German working class have resolutely supported the war, which it was not in their power to prevent, as a war for German independence and the liberation of France and Europe from that pestilential incubus, the Second Empire. It was the German workmen who, together with the rural labourers, furnished the sinews and muscles of heroic hosts, leaving behind their half-starved families. Decimated by the battles abroad, they will be once more decimated by misery at home. In their turn, they are now coming forward to ask for 'guarantees' – guarantees that their immense sacrifices have not been bought in vain, that they have conquered liberty, that the victory over the imperialist armies will not, as in 1815, be turned into the defeat of the German people; and, as the first of these guarantees, they claim an *honorable peace for France*, and the *recognition of the French republic*.

The Central Committee of the German Social-Democratic Workmen's Party issued, on 5 September, a manifesto, energetically insisting upon these guarantees.

'We,' they say, 'protest against the annexation of Alsace and Lorraine. And we are conscious of speaking in the name of the German working class. In the common interest of France and Germany, in the interest of western civilization

---

[80] This is an excerpt from Karl Marx's (see note 1) *Second Address of the General Council of the International Working Men's Association on the Franco-Prussian War*. It became necessary after the French defeat at Sedan and establishment of the provisional government of the Third Republic. It was written between 6 and 9 September, and approved on the latter date by the GC. It was released in English as a flyer and partially published in *The Pall-Mall Gazette* on the 16th of the same month. Publication in German and French soon followed in several newspapers and magazines of the IWMA. The full version is in GC, IV: 333–42.

against eastern barbarism, the German workmen will not patiently tolerate the annexation of Alsace and Lorraine.... We shall faithfully stand by our fellow workmen in all countries for the common international cause of the proletariat!'

[...] We hail the advent of the republic in France, but at the same time we labour under misgivings which we hope will prove groundless. That republic has not subverted the throne, but only taken its place, become vacant. It has been proclaimed, not as a social conquest, but as a national measure of defence. It is in the hands of a Provisional Government composed partly of notorious Orleanists, partly of middle-class republicans, upon some of whom the insurrection of June 1848 has left its indelible stigma. [...] Some of their acts go far to show that they have inherited from the empire, not only ruins, but also its dread of the working class. [...] The French working class moves, therefore, under circumstances of extreme difficulty. Any attempt at upsetting the new government in the present crisis, when the enemy is almost knocking at the doors of Paris, would be a desperate folly. The French workmen must perform their duties as citizens; but, at the same time, they must not allow themselves to be swayed by the national *souvenirs* of 1792, as the French peasant allowed themselves to be deluded by the national *souvenirs* of the First Empire. They have not to recapitulate the past, but to build up the future. Let them calmly and resolutely improve the opportunities of republican liberty, for the work of their own class organization. It will gift them with fresh herculean powers for the regeneration of France, and our common task – the emancipation of labour. Upon their energies and wisdom hinges the fate of the republic. [...]

Let the sections of the International Working Men's Association in every country stir the working classes to action. If they forsake their duty, if they remain passive, the present tremendous war will be but the harbinger of still deadlier international feuds, and lead in every nation to a renewed triumph over the workman by the lords of the sword, of the soil, and of capital. *Vive la Republique!*

Karl Marx, *[The Novelty of the International]*[81]

Concerning the International, [Marx] said that the great success which had hitherto crowned its efforts was due to circumstances over which the members themselves had no control. The foundation of the International itself was the result of these circumstances, and by no means due to the efforts of the men engaged in it. It was not the work of any set of clever politicians; all the politicians in the world could not have created the situation and circumstances requisite for the success of the International. The International had not put forth any particular creed. Its task was to organize the forces of labour and link the various working men's movements and combine them. The circumstances which had given such a great development to the association were the conditions under which the work-people were more and more oppressed throughout the world, and this was the secret of success. The events of the last few weeks had unmistakably shown that the working class must fight for its emancipation. The persecutions of the governments against the International were like the persecutions of ancient Rome against the primitive Christians. They, too, had been few in numbers at first, but the patricians of Rome had instinctively felt that if the Christians succeeded the Roman empire would be lost. The persecutions of Rome had not saved the empire, and the persecutions of the present day against the International would not save the existing state of things.

What was new in the International was that it was established by the working men themselves and for themselves. Before the foundation of the International all the different organizations had been societies founded

---

[81] This text is the synopsis of a speech made by Karl Marx (see note 1) shortly after the closing of the London Conference in 1871, to celebrate the seventh year of its foundation. It appeared in an article entitle 'The Reds in Session' in the New York newspaper *The World* on 15 October 1871.

by some radicals among the ruling classes for the working classes, but the International was established by the working men for themselves. The Chartist movement in this country had been started with the consent and assistance of middle-class radicals, though if it had been successful it could only have been for the advantage of the working class. England was the only country where the working class was sufficiently developed and organized to turn universal suffrage to its proper account. He then alluded to the revolution of February [1848] as a movement that had been favoured by a portion of the bourgeoisie against the ruling party. The revolution of February had only given promises to the working classes and had replaced one set of men of the ruling class by another. The insurrection of June had been a revolt against the whole ruling class, including the most radical portion. The working men who had lifted the new men into power in 1848 had instinctively felt that they had only exchanged one set of oppressors for another and that they were betrayed.

The last movement was the Commune, the greatest that had yet been made, and there could not be two opinions about it – the Commune was the conquest of the political power of the working classes. There was much misunderstanding about the Commune. The Commune could not found a new form of class government. In destroying the existing conditions of oppression by transferring all the means of labour to the productive labourer, and thereby compelling every able-bodied individual to work for a living, the only base for class rule and oppression would be removed. But before such a change could be effected a proletarian dictature would become necessary, and the first condition of that was a proletarian army. The working classes would have to conquer the right to emancipate themselves on the battlefield. The task of the International was to organize and combine the forces of labour for the coming struggle.

Karl Marx, [On the Importance of Having the International][82]

[...] The difference between a working class without an International, and a working class with an International, becomes most evident if we look back to the period of 1848. Years were required for the working class itself to recognize the Insurrection of June 1848, as the work of its own vanguard. The Paris Commune was at once acclaimed by the universal proletariat.

You, the delegates of the working class, meet to strengthen the militant organization of a society aiming at the emancipation of labour and the extinction of national feuds. Almost at the same moment, there meet at Berlin the crowned dignitaries of the old world in order to forge new chains and to hatch new wars.[83]

Long life to the International Working Men's Association!

---

[82] This text is a short excerpt from the *Report of the General Council To The Fifth Annual Congress Of The International Working Men's Association Held at The Hague*. This writing was approved during a session of the GC in late August (date unknown) and read in German by Karl Marx (see note 1) in a session of this Congress on 5 September. His first printed edition appeared in the biweekly *Der Volksstaat* on 18 September. In October, it was translated into English, Spanish and French. The full version is in GC, V: 453–62.

[83] The emperors of Germany, Austria-Hungary and Russia met in September 1872, attempting to restore the reactionary alliance of these states.

Part Eleven

The Irish Question

58

Eugene Dupont, *[On the Fenian Question]*[84]

[…] What is Fenianism? Is it a sect or a party whose principles are opposed to ours? Certainly not. Fenianism is the vindication by an oppressed people of its right to social and political existence. The Fenian declarations leave no room for doubt in this respect. They affirm the republican form of government, liberty of conscience, no state religion, the produce of labour to the labourer, and the possession of the soil to the people. What people could abjure such principles? Only blindness and bad faith can support the contrary. We hear that those whom the English law is going to strike down for their devotedness to such a cause are exclaiming: 'We are proud to die for our country and for republican principles.' Let us see of what value the reproaches are that are addressed to the Fenians by the English would-be liberators. Fenianism is not altogether wrong, they say, but why not employ the legal means of meetings and demonstrations by the aid of which we have gained our Reform Bill? I avow that it is hardly possible to restrain one's indignation at hearing such arguments. What is the use of talking of legal means to a people reduced to the lowest state of misery from century to century by English oppression – to people who emigrate by thousands, to obtain bread, from all parts of the country? Is not this Irish emigration to America by millions the most eloquent legal protest? Having destroyed all – life and liberty – be not surprised that nothing should be found but hatred to the oppressor. Is it well for the English to talk of legality and justice to those who on the slightest suspicion of Fenianism are arrested and incarcerated, and subjected to physical and mental tortures which leave the cruelties of King Bomba, [Ferdinand II of Naples] of whom

---

[84] This text is an excerpt from the synopsis of a speech by Eugène Dupont (see note 71) to the GC on 19 November 1867, dedicated to Ireland. The speech is reported in GC, II: 175–7.

the would-be liberators talked so much, far behind?[85] [...] Without having right on their side, such conduct is enough to provoke and justify resistance. The English working men who blame the Fenians commit more than a fault, for the cause of both peoples is the same; they have the same enemy to defeat the territorial aristocracy and the capitalists.

---

[85] Irish political prisoners in Britain were treated as common criminals, though Gladstone and the Liberals had criticized Ferdinand II's maltreatment of political prisoners struggling for Italian unification and liberty.

59

Karl Marx, [Ireland and the English Working Class][86]

If England is the bulwark of European landlordism and capitalism, the only point at which one can strike a major blow against official England is *Ireland*.

In the first place, Ireland is the bulwark of English landlordism. If it collapsed in Ireland, it would collapse in England. The whole operation is a hundred times easier in Ireland, because there the economic struggle is concentrated exclusively on landed property, because that struggle is at the same time a national one, and because the people have reached a more revolutionary and exasperated pitch there than in England. Landlordism in Ireland is kept in being solely by the *English army*. If the enforced union between the two countries were to cease, a social revolution would immediately break out in Ireland – even if of a somewhat backward kind. English landlordism would lose not only a major source of its wealth, but also its greatest moral force – the fact of *representing England's domination over Ireland*. On the other hand, by preserving the power of its landlords in Ireland, the English proletariat makes them invulnerable in England itself.

In the second place, in dragging down the working class in England still further by the forced immigration of poor Irish people, the English bourgeoisie has not merely exploited Irish poverty. It has also divided the proletariat into two hostile camps. The fiery rebelliousness of the Celtic worker does not mingle well with the steady slow nature of the Anglo-Saxon; in fact in all *the major industrial centres of England* there is a profound antagonism between the Irish and the English proletarians. The ordinary English worker hates the Irish worker as a competitor who brings down his wages and standard of living.

---

[86] This text is another excerpt from the resolution written by Karl Marx (see note 1) described in note 77.

He also feels national and religious antipathies for him; it is rather the same attitude that the poor whites of the Southern states of North America had for the Negro slaves. This antagonism between the two groups of proletarians within England itself is artificially kept in being and fostered by the bourgeoisie, who know well that this split is the real secret of preserving their own power.

This antagonism is reproduced once again on the other side of the Atlantic. The Irish, driven from their native soil by cattle and sheep, have landed in North America where they form a considerable, and increasing, proportion of the population. Their sole thought, their sole passion, is their hatred for England. The English and American governments (in other words, the classes they represent) nourish that passion so as to keep permanently alive the underground struggle between the United States and England; in that way they can prevent the sincere and worthwhile alliance between the working Classes on the two sides of the Atlantic which would lead to their emancipation.

Furthermore, Ireland is the only excuse the English government has for keeping up a large regular army which can, as we have seen, in case of need attack the English workers after having done its basic training in Ireland.

Finally, what ancient Rome demonstrated on a gigantic scale can be seen – in the England of today. A people which subjugates another people forges its own chains.

Therefore the International Association's attitude to the Irish question is absolutely clear. Its first need is to press on with the social revolution in England, and to that end, the major blow must be struck in Ireland.

The General Council's resolutions on the Irish Amnesty are designed simply to lead into other resolutions which win declare that, quite apart from the demands of international justice, it is an essential precondition for the emancipation of the English working class to transform the present enforced union (in other words, the enslavement of Ireland) into a free and equal confederation, if possible, and into a total separation, if necessary. [...]

Friedrich Engels, *[Relations Between the Irish Sections and the British Federal Council]*[87]

[...] The Irish sections in England were no more under the jurisdiction of the British Federal Council than the French, German or Italian and Polish sections in this country. The Irish formed, to all intents and purposes, a distinct nationality of their own, and the fact that they used the English language could not deprive them of the right, common to all, to have an independent national organization within the International.

[...] There was the fact of seven centuries of English conquest and oppression of Ireland, and so long as that oppression existed, it was an insult to Irish working men to ask them to submit to a British Federal Council. The position of Ireland with regard to England was not that of an equal, it was that of Poland with regard to Russia. What would be said if this Council called upon Polish sections to acknowledge the supremacy of a Russian Federal Council in Petersburg, or upon Prussian Polish, North Schleswig, and Alsatian sections to submit to a Federal Council in Berlin? Yet what it was asked to do with regard to Irish sections was substantially the same thing. If members of a conquering nation called upon the nation they had conquered and continued to hold down to forget their specific nationality and position, to 'sink national differences' and so forth, that was not Internationalism, it was nothing else but preaching to them submission to the yoke, and attempting to justify and to perpetuate the dominion of the conqueror under the cloak of Internationalism. It was sanctioning the belief, only too common among the English working men, that they were superior beings compared to the Irish, and as much an

---

[87] This passage is taken from a manuscript of Friedrich Engels (see note 47) in regard to an intervention he made during the meeting of the GC on 14 May 1872. The full text can be found in GC, V: 297–300.

aristocracy as the mean whites of the Slave States considered themselves to be with regard to the Negroes.

In a case like that of the Irish, true Internationalism must necessarily be based upon a distinctly national organization; the Irish, as well as other oppressed nationalities, could enter the Association only as equals with the members of the conquering nation, and under protest against the conquest. The Irish sections, therefore, not only were justified, but even under the necessity to state in the preamble to their rules that their first and most pressing duty, as Irishmen, was to establish their own national independence. The antagonism between Irish and English working men in England had always been one of the most powerful means by which class rule was upheld in England. [...] Now, for the first time, there was a chance of making English and Irish working men act together in harmony for their common emancipation, a result attained by no previous movement in their country. [...]

If the promoters of this motion were so brimful of the truly International spirits, let them prove it by removing the seat of the British Federal Council to Dublin, and submit to a Council of Irishmen.

[...] If the motion was adopted by the Council, the Council would inform the Irish working men, in so many words, that, after the dominion of the English aristocracy over Ireland, after the dominion of the English middle class over Ireland, they must now look forth to the advent of the dominion of the English working class over Ireland.

Part Twelve

Concerning the United States

61

Karl Marx, *To Abraham Lincoln, President of the United States of America*[88]

We congratulate the American people upon your re-election by a large majority. If resistance to the Slave Power was the reserved watchword of your first election, the triumphant war cry of your re-election is Death to Slavery.

From the commencement of the titanic American strife the workingmen of Europe felt instinctively that the star-spangled banner carried the destiny of their class. The contest for the territories which opened the dire epopee [epic], was it not to decide whether the virgin soil of immense tracts should be wedded to the labour of the emigrant or prostituted by the tramp of the slave driver?

When an oligarchy of 300,000 slaveholders dared to inscribe, for the first time in the annals of the world, 'slavery' on the banner of Armed Revolt, when on the very spots where hardly a century ago the idea of one great Democratic Republic had first sprung up, whence the first Declaration of the Rights of Man was issued, and the first impulse given to the European revolution of the eighteenth century; when on those very spots counterrevolution, with systematic thoroughness, gloried in rescinding 'the ideas entertained at the time of the formation of the old constitution', and maintained slavery to be 'a beneficent institution', indeed, the old solution of the great problem of 'the relation of capital to labour', and cynically proclaimed property in man 'the cornerstone of the new edifice' – then the working classes of Europe understood at once, even before the fanatic partisanship of the upper classes for the Confederate gentry had given its dismal warning, that the slaveholders'

---

[88] This text written by Karl Marx (see note 1), a congratulatory message to Abraham Lincoln upon his re-election as president of the United States of America, was approved by the GC on 29 November 1864, and published on 23 December in *The Daily News*. The American ambassador in London sent it to Lincoln, who replied with a letter also published by *The Times*. It is located in the GC, I: 51–4.

rebellion was to sound the tocsin for a general holy crusade of property against labour, and that for the men of labour, with their hopes for the future, even their past conquests were at stake in that tremendous conflict on the other side of the Atlantic. Everywhere they bore therefore patiently the hardships imposed upon them by the cotton crisis, opposed enthusiastically the proslavery intervention of their betters – and, from most parts of Europe, contributed their quota of blood to the good cause.

While the workingmen, the true political powers of the North, allowed slavery to defile their own republic, while before the Negro, mastered and sold without his concurrence, they boasted it the highest prerogative of the white-skinned labourer to sell himself and choose his own master, they were unable to attain the true freedom of labour, or to support their European brethren in their struggle for emancipation; but this barrier to progress has been swept off by the red sea of civil war.

The workingmen of Europe feel sure that, as the American War of Independence initiated a new era of ascendancy for the middle class, so the American Antislavery War will do for the working classes. They consider it an earnest of the epoch to come that it fell to the lot of Abraham Lincoln, the single-minded son of the working class, to lead his country through the matchless struggle for the rescue of an enchained race and the reconstruction of a social world.

62

Karl Marx, *Address from the International Working Men's Association to President Johnson*[89]

The demon of the 'peculiar institution' [slavery], for the supremacy of which the South rose in arms, would not allow his worshippers to honourably succumb in the open field. What he had begun in treason, he must needs end in infamy. As Philip II's war for the Inquisition bred a Gerard, thus Jefferson Davis's pro-slavery war bred a Booth.

It is not our part to call words of sorrow and horror, while the heart of two worlds heaves with emotion. Even the sycophants who, year after year, and day by day, stick to their Sisyphus work of morally assassinating Abraham Lincoln, and the great Republic he headed, stands now aghast at this universal outburst of popular feeling, and rival with each other to strew rhetorical flowers on his open grave. They have now at last found out that he was a man, neither to be browbeaten by adversity, nor intoxicated by success, inflexibly pressing on to his great goal, never compromising it by blind haste, slowly maturing his steps, never retracing them, carried away by no surge of popular favour, disheartened by no slackening of the popular pulse, tempering stern acts by the gleams of a kind heart, illuminating scenes dark with passion by the smile of humour, doing his titanic work as humbly and homely as Heaven-born rulers do little things with the grandiloquence of pomp and state; in one word, one of the rare men who succeed in becoming great, without ceasing to be good. Such, indeed, was the modesty of this great and good man, that the world only discovered him a hero after he had fallen a martyr.

---

[89] Following the assassination of Abraham Lincoln, the GC decided to send a letter to his successor Andrew Johnson. The text was written by Karl Marx (see note 1), approved at a session on May 9, 1865, and published in *The Bee-Hive* on 20 May. It is located in GC, I: 294–6.

To be singled out by the side of such a chief, the second victim to the infernal gods of slavery, was an honour due to Mr Seward. Had he not, at a time of general hesitation, the sagacity to foresee and the manliness to foretell 'the irrepressible conflict'? Did he not, in the darkest hours of that conflict, prove true to the Roman duty to never despair of the Republic and its stars? We earnestly hope that he and his son will be restored to health, public activity, and well-deserved honours within much less than '90 days'.[90]

After a tremendous civil war, but which, if we consider its vast dimensions, and its broad scope, and compare it to the Old World's 100 years' wars, and 30 years wars, and 23 years' wars, can hardly be said to have lasted 90 days. Yours, Sir, has become the task to uproot by the law what has been felled by the sword, to preside over the arduous work of political reconstruction and social regeneration. A profound sense of your great mission will save you from any compromise with stern duties. You will never forget that to initiate the new era of the emancipation of labour, the American people devolved the responsibilities of leadership upon two men of labour–the one Abraham Lincoln, the other Andrew Johnson.

---

[90] William H. Seward, Lincoln's Secretary of State and a strong opponent of slavery, together with his son, were seriously wounded in an assassination attempt coincident with Booth's shooting of Lincoln. The initial response to the Southern rebellion in 1861 was military mobilization for 90 days.

63

Karl Marx, *Address to the National Labour Union of the United States*[91]

Fellow Workmen: [...] In a congratulatory address to Mr Lincoln on his re-election as president, we expressed our conviction that the American Civil War would prove of as great import to the advancement of the working class as the American War of Independence had proved to that of the middle class. And, in point of fact, the victorious termination of the antislavery war has opened a new epoch in the annals of the working class. In the States themselves, an independent working-class movement, looked upon with an evil eye by your old parties and their professional politicians, has since that date sprung into life. To fructify it wants years of peace. To crush it, a war between the United States and England is wanted.

The next palpable effect of the Civil War was, of course, to deteriorate the position of the American workman. In the United States, as in Europe, the monster incubus of a national debt was shifted from hand to hand, to settle down on the shoulders of the working class. The prices of necessaries, says one of your statesmen, have since 1860 risen 78 per cent, while the wages of unskilled labour rose 50 per cent, those of skilled labour 60 per cent only. 'Pauperism,' he complains, 'grows now in America faster than population.' Moreover, the suffering of the working of the working classes set off as a foil the newfangled luxury of financial aristocrats, shoddy aristocrats, and similar vermin bred by wars. Yet, for all this, the Civil War did compensate by freeing the slave and the consequent moral impetus it gave to your own class movement. A second war, not hallowed by a sublime purpose and a great social necessity, but of the Old World's type, would forge chains for the

---

[91] This text is an excerpt from an address written by Karl Marx (see note 1), and approved by the GC 11 May 1869. It was published 4 days later in *The Bee-Hive*. The full version is in GC, III: 319–21.

free labourer instead of tearing asunder those of the slave.[92] The accumulated misery left in its track would afford your capitalists at once the motive and the means of divorce the working class from its bold and just aspirations by the soulless sword of a standing army.

On you, then, depends the glorious task to prove to the world that now at last the working classes are bestriding the scene of history no longer as servile retainers but as independent actors, conscious of their own responsibility, and able to command peace where their would-be masters shout war.

---

[92] The threat of war with Britain loomed due to American claims for shipping destroyed by the British-built ship *Alabama* under the Confederate flag. Belligerent politicians demanded compensation of as much as $2 billion.

64

Johann Georg Eccarius, [Eliminating Nationalism from the Minds of Working Men][93]

One of our aims is to eliminate whatever may yet remain of national antipathies and, perhaps animosities, from the minds of working men. [...]

The Paris workmen have no such interest to be taken care of on the other side of the Atlantic, against the probable encroachments of the American working men. We consider the interests of the French workmen resident in the United States strictly identical with the interests of all the other working men of the United States. [...]

We cannot admit that either French or Germans have an opposite or special interest from any other workmen, and we always urge them on to take an active part in, and identify themselves with, the movement of the working men of the country, in which they reside, particularly in America. [...]

---

[93] This text is an excerpt of the *Letter from the General Secretary in London*, written on 23 April 1870, by Johann Georg Eccarius (see note 25), in response to the proposal to appoint representatives of the IWMA in the United States based on their nationality. The full version was published in an unknown American newspaper, and entered in the record of the GC meeting of 24 May. It is located in GC, III: 243–5.

Part Thirteen

Political Organization

65

Friedrich Engels – Karl Marx, *General Rules of the International Working Men's Association*[94]

Considering,

That the emancipation of the working classes must be conquered by the working classes themselves, that the struggle for the emancipation of the working classes means not a struggle for class privileges and monopolies, but for equal rights and duties, and the abolition of all class rule;

That the economical subjection of the man of labour to the monopolizer of the means of labour – that is, the source of life – lies at the bottom of servitude in all its forms, of all social misery, mental degradation, and political dependence;

That the economical emancipation of the working classes is therefore the great end to which every political movement ought to be subordinate as a means;

That all efforts aiming at the great end hitherto failed from the want of solidarity between the manifold divisions of labour in each country, and from the absence of a fraternal bond of union between the working classes of different countries;

That the emancipation of labour is neither a local nor a national, but a social problem, embracing all countries in which modern society exists, and

---

[94] The original *Provisional Rules of the Association* was written by Karl Marx (see note 1) in October 1864, and were approved by the GC on 1 November. It was printed in the publication referred to in note 1. Between late September and early October of 1871, Marx and Friedrich Engels (see note 47) prepared this new version that took into consideration the changes within the organization over the years. It was published in November, in the pamphlet *General Rules and Administrative Regulations of the International Working Men's Association*. London: Edward Truelove, 1871. Finally, following approval by the delegates of The Hague Congress (1872) of Resolution IX of the London Conference of 1871 (included in selection 74, below), the text of 1871 was supplemented by Article 7a, drawn from Resolution IX. The 1864 version is located in GC, I: 288–91. The 1871 text, which is the one published here, is included in GC, IV: 451–4; the supplementary Article 7a is in HAGUE: 282.

depending for its solution on the concurrence, practical and theoretical, of the most advanced countries;

That the present revival of the working classes in the most industrious countries of Europe, while it raises a new hope, gives solemn warning against a relapse into the old errors, and calls for the immediate combination of the still disconnected movements;

For these reasons –

The International Working Men's Association has been founded.

It declares:

That all societies and individuals adhering to it will acknowledge truth, justice, and morality as the basis of their conduct towards each other and towards all men, without regard to colour, creed, or nationality;

That it acknowledges *no rights without duties, no duties without rights*;

And, in this spirit, the following Rules have been drawn up.

1. This Association is established to afford a central medium of communication and cooperation between working men's societies existing in different countries and aiming at the same end; viz., the protection, advancement, and complete emancipation of the working classes.
2. The name of the society shall be 'The International Working Men's Association.'
3. There shall annually meet a General Working Men's Congress, consisting of delegates of the branches of the Association. The Congress will have to proclaim the common aspirations of the working class, take the measures required for the successful working of the International Association, and appoint the General Council of the society.
4. Each Congress appoints the time and place of meeting for the next Congress. The delegates assemble at the appointed time and place, without any special invitation. The General Council may, in case of need, change the place, but has no power to postpone the time of the General Council annually. The Congress appoints the seat and elects the members of the General Council annually. The General Council thus elected shall have power to add to the number of its members.

On its annual meetings, the General Congress shall receive a public account of the annual transactions of the General Council. The latter may, in case of emergency, convoke the General Congress before the regular yearly term.

5. The General Council shall consist of workingmen from the different countries represented in the International Association. It shall, from its own members, elect the officers necessary for the transaction of business, such as a treasurer, a general secretary, corresponding secretaries for the different countries, etc.
6. The General Council shall form an international agency between the different and local groups of the Association, so that the workingmen in one country be consistently informed of the movements of their class in every other country; that an inquiry into the social state of the different countries of Europe be made simultaneously, and under a common direction; that the questions of general interest mooted in one society be ventilated by all; and that when immediate practical steps should be needed – as, for instance, in case of international quarrels – the action of the associated societies be simultaneous and uniform. Whenever it seems opportune, the General Council shall take the initiative of proposals to be laid before the different national or local societies. To facilitate the communications, the General Council shall publish periodical reports.
7. Since the success of the workingmen's movement in each country cannot be secured but by the power of union and combination, while, on the other hand, the usefulness of the International General Council must greatly depend on the circumstance whether it has to deal with a few national centres of workingmen's associations, or with a great number of small and disconnected local societies – the members of the International Association shall use their utmost efforts to combine the disconnected workingmen's societies of their respective countries into national bodies, represented by central national organs. It is self-understood, however, that the appliance of this rule will depend upon the peculiar laws of each country, and that, apart from legal obstacles, no independent local society shall be precluded from corresponding directly with the General Council.

Article 7a – In its struggle against the collective power of the propertied classes, the working class cannot act as a class except by constituting itself into a political party, distinct from, and opposed to all old parties formed by the propertied classes.

This constitution of the working class into a political party is indispensable in order to insure the triumph of the social revolution, and of its ultimate end, the abolition of classes.

The combination of forces which the working class has already effected by its economical struggles ought, at the same time, to serve as a lever for its struggles against the political power of landlords and capitalists.

The lords of land and the lords of capital will always use their political privileges for the defence and perpetuation of their economical monopolies, and for the enslavement of labour. The conquest of political power has therefore become the great duty of the working class.

8. Every section has the right to appoint its own secretary corresponding directly with the General Council.
9. Everybody who acknowledges and defends the principles of the International Working Men's Association is eligible to become a member. Every branch is responsible for the integrity of the members it admits.
10. Each member of the International Association, on removing his domicile from one country to another, will receive the fraternal support of the Associated Working Men.
11. While united in a perpetual bond of fraternal cooperation, the workingmen's societies joining the International Association will preserve their existent organizations intact.
12. The present Rules may be revised by each Congress, provided that two-thirds of the delegates present are in favour of such revision.
13. Everything not provided for in the present Rules will be supplied by special Regulations, subject to the revision of every Congress.

66

Johann Georg Eccarius – Karl Kaub – George Odger – George Wheeler – William Worley, *To the Working Men of Great Britain and Ireland*[95]

Fellow Working Men!

It is a fact that amongst the thousands of daily and weekly newspapers existing at the present day, those that advocate the interests of the working class and defend the cause of labour might be counted at your fingers' ends. Nor is this to be wondered at when you bear in mind that, almost without exception, they are the property of capitalists, established for their own use, either for political party purposes or as commercial speculations. Thus, the publicity of matters concerning our political enfranchisement, our social emancipation, or our material well-being as hired wages labourers depends to a great extent on sufferance, and when now and then an editor, in his superior wisdom, takes it into his head to side with us, it is frequently doubtful whether decided opposition would not be preferable to the favour bestowed. This is a very unsatisfactory state of things for a body of men like the working men of this country with high and well-founded aspirations to raise themselves in the political and social scale.

---

[95] This text is an excerpt from the address *To the Working Men of Great Britain and Ireland*, published on 2 September 1865 in *The Miner and Workman's Advocate*. This publication was one of the first acts of the newly-formed shareholders' company *Industrial Newspaper Company*, which bought the newspaper transforming it into one of the official organs of the IWMA. Karl Kaub [unk.] was a German worker who immigrated to London and a member of the GC from 1864 to 1865; George Odger [1820–77] was an English craftsman and leading member of the British labour movement, president of the IWMA from 1864 to 1867, as well as a member GC from its foundation until 1871; George Wheeler [unk.] was a union leader and member of the GC from 1864 to 1867; William Worley [unk.] was an English typographer and member of the GC from 1864 to 1867; while information on Johann Georg Eccarius may be found in note 25. The full version is in GC, I: 299–300.

Benjamin Franklin is reported to have said: If you want a thing done, and well done, do it yourself', and this is precisely what we must do. If your expected elevation is not to prove a delusion and a mockery – we must take the work of our salvation into our own hands, and this can only be done by, acquiring a more prominent position in the press and on the platform than we have hitherto done.

In order that we may guard against deceitful friends, we require a press of our own. To this end we must establish and support as many newspapers and periodicals as we can, wherein we ourselves must advocate and defend our own cause against open antagonists and wily friends. In the press, as well as on the platform, we must qualify ourselves to hold our own against all corners; for then, and not till then, shall we succeed in bettering our condition. [...]

Charles Perron – Pioley – Reymond – Vézinaud – Sameul Treboux, *[On the Deprivation of Political Liberties]*[96]

[…] Is not the deprivation of political liberties an obstacle to the social emancipation of workers and one of the principal causes of social disturbances (unemployment)?

We reply: Yes, the deprivation of political liberties is an obstacle to the social emancipation of workers; yes, the deprivation of these liberties is one of the principal causes of the social disturbances and unemployment of which labourers suffer so cruelly.

The various reports that have been presented to the Congress demonstrate that workers who consent to live deprived of their political liberties are trapped in a vicious circle, one which is fatal to their real interests and must be overcome. […]

To put an end to the fateful status quo, which might otherwise last indefinitely, it is imperative that political emancipation be claimed from the outset and with the same energy that we put into claiming social emancipation.

Consequently, the Commission proposes to the Congress that the assembly adopt the following declaration:

The International Working Men's Congress, held in Lausanne in September 1867, considering:

---

[96] This is an excerpt from the text described in note 10. Probably fruit of a collective effort, the report here reproduced was produced by the committeee on political liberties. His members were: Charles Perron [1837–1909] was a recognized Genevan cartographer; Pioley [unk.] Parisian mechanic, editor of journal *Égalité* and follower of the theories of Mikhail Bakunin. He was a delegate at the Congresses of Lausanne (1867) and Brussels (1868), and later at the 'autonomists' IWMA Congress of Bern (1876); Reymond [unk.], Samuel Treboux [unk.], plasterer of Geneva; and Vézinaud [unk.], shoemaker from Bordeaux. The text may be found in PI, I: 233–4.

That the deprivation of political liberties is an obstacle to the social education of the people and to the emancipation of the proletariat,

Resolves:

1. That the social emancipation of workers is inseparable from their political emancipation;
2. That the establishment of political liberties is a first step of absolute necessity. [...]

68

Karl Marx, *[Against Secret Societies]*[97]

[…] According to the tenor of our Statutes, it is certainly the special mission of all our branches in England, on the Continent, and in the United States, to act not only as centres for the organization of the working class, but also to aid, in their different countries, all political movements tending to the accomplishment of our ultimate end, viz., the *economical emancipation of the working class*. At the same time, these Statutes bind all the sections of our Association to act in open daylight. If our Statutes were not formal on that point, the very nature of an Association which identifies itself with the working classes, would exclude from it every form of secret society. If the working classes, who form the great bulk of all nations, who produce all their wealth, and in the name of whom even the usurping powers always pretend to rule, conspire, they conspire publicly, as the sun conspires against darkness, in the full consciousness that without their pale there exists no legitimate power. [...]

---

[97] This text is part of the synopsis of a speech made by Karl Marx (see note 1) during the session of the GC on 3 May 1870. The full version is in GC, III: 231–2.

69

Friedrich Engels, [*On the Importance of Political Struggle*][98]

[…] As you say, the attention of the people has undoubtedly been attracted to a very large extent by the empty declamations of the old political parties, which have thus greatly obstructed our propaganda. That happened everywhere during the first few years of the proletarian movement. In France, in England and in Germany, the Socialists were compelled, and are still compelled, to combat the influence and activity of the old political parties, whether they be aristocratic or bourgeois, monarchist or even republican. Experience has shown everywhere that the best way to emancipate the workers from this domination of the old parties is to form in each country a proletarian party with a policy of its own, a policy which is manifestly different from that of the other parties, because it must express the conditions necessary for the emancipation of the working class. This policy may vary in details according to the specific circumstances of each country; but as the fundamental relations between labour and capital are the same everywhere and the political domination of the possessing classes over the exploited classes is an existing fact everywhere, the principles and aims of proletarian policy will be identical, at least in all western countries. The possessing classes – the landed aristocracy and the bourgeoisie – keep the working people in servitude not only by the power of their wealth, by the simple exploitation of labour by capital, but also by the power of the state – by the army, the bureaucracy, the courts. To give up fighting our adversaries in the political field would mean to abandon one of the most powerful weapons, particularly in the sphere of organization and

---

[98] This excerpt is from a letter written on 13 February 1871 *To The Spanish Federal Council of the International Working Men's Association*. Reaffirming the importance of battle in the political field, Friedrich Engels (see note 47), Corresponding Secretary for Spain at the time, tried to counter the advance theories on the Iberian Peninsula of Bakunin's. The full version is in GC, IV: 479–82.

propaganda. Universal suffrage provides us with an excellent means of struggle. In Germany, where the workers have a well organized political party, they have succeeded in sending six deputies to the so-called National Assembly; and the opposition which our friends Bebel and Liebknecht have been able to organize there against a war of conquest has worked more powerfully in the interest of our international propaganda than meetings and years of propaganda in the press would have. At present in France too workers' representatives have been elected and will loudly proclaim our principles. At the next elections the same thing will happen in England. […]

70

Édouard Vaillant, [On Working Class Politics][99]

'In the presence of an unbridled and momentarily victorious reaction, which stifles any claims of socialist democracy and intends to maintain by force the distinction between classes, the Conference reminds members of the Association that the political and social questions are indissolubly linked, that they are two sides of the same question meant to be resolved by the International: the abolition of class.

Workers must recognize no less than the economic solidarity that unites them and join their forces, on the political terrain as much as on the economic terrain, for the triumph of their cause'.

[…] Vaillant anticipates two objections to which he responds as follows: one might say that this declaration is imprudent and will draw upon the Association the severity of governments, but have we not always seen governments persecute the Association as a political society? On this matter there is, therefore, no reason to abstain from this affirmation, but, on the contrary, there is to gain from it that, from now on, misunderstanding will no longer have any excuse.

The second objection is this: He heard, from a member of the Conference, that the Association should not be involved in politics. [...]

[...] In the statutes, the principle of its proposition is indicated as a means of achieving the abolition of classes and, from the beginning, this was the spirit

---

[99] This text contains a resolution put forward on 20 September, at the London Conference of 1871, together with an excerpt from the synopsis of a speech made made in support of it. Édouard Vaillant [1840–1915] was one of the principal followers of Louis Auguste Blanqui [1805–81], and one of the most important leaders of the Paris Commune. Following its defeat, he fled to London where he became a member of the GC from 1871 to 1872. He was also a delegate to The Hague Congress (1872) and, in 1901, he was one of the founders of the French socialist party (SFIO). The full version is in PI, II: 191–3.

that inspired the founding of the International, thus, my proposition only energetically affirms an essential principle of the Association. [..]

I shall respond to Citizen Bastelica who said that by the term politics he certainly did not mean that feeble agitation which consists of sending a worker to parliament, since parliaments must also be destroyed.

The politics of the Association must be socialist and have but one objective: the abolition of classes.

Karl Marx, [On the Political Action of the Working Class][100]

[…] In almost every country certain internationalists, basing themselves on the truncated statutes adopted at the Geneva Congress, have said that there is no obligation in the statutes to engage in political action [and] have conducted propaganda in favour of political abstention that the governments have been careful not to interrupt. […]

In America, a recent workers' congress resolved to take charge of the political question and, in selecting men to represent them, decided to replace personalities who make a profession out of being politicians with workers like themselves, responsible for defending the interests of their class.

But political action should be in accordance with the conditions in each country. In England, it is not so easy for a worker to get into Parliament. Since members of Parliament do not receive any compensation, and the worker has to work to support himself, Parliament becomes unattainable for him, and the bourgeoisie knows very well that its stubborn refusal to allow salaries for members of Parliament is a means of preventing the working class from being represented in it. […]

But the tribune is the best instrument of publicity [and] one should never believe that it is of small significance to have workers in Parliament. If one stifles their voices, as in the case of De Potter and Castian, or if one ejects them, as in the case of Manuel – the reprisals and oppressions exercise a deep effect on the people. If, on the other hand, they can speak from the parliamentary tribune, as do Bebel and Liebknecht, the whole world listens to them. In the

---

[100] This text is part of the synopsis of a speech given by Karl Marx (see note 1) during a session of 20 September 1871 of the London Conference, devoted to discussing the political action of the working class. The full version is in PI, II: 202.

one case or the other, great publicity is provided for our principles. To give but one example: when during the [Franco-Prussian] war, which was fought in France, Bebel and Liebknecht undertook to point out the responsibility of the working class in the face of those events, all of Germany was shaken; and even in Munich, the city where revolutions take place only over the price of beer, great demonstrations took place demanding an end to the war – which, in Munich, won many workers to the International Association.

The governments are hostile to us, one must respond to them with all the means at our disposal and launch a general crusade against them. To get workers into Parliament is synonymous with a victory over governments, but one must choose the right men, not Tolains.

[…] The Association has always demanded, and not merely from today, that the workers must occupy themselves with politics.

Karl Marx, [*On the Question of Abstentionism*][101]

He [Marx] explained the history of abstention from politics and said that one should not get worked up over this question. The men who propagated this doctrine were well-meaning utopians, but those who want to take such a road today are not. They reject politics until after a violent struggle, and thereby drive the people into a formal, bourgeois opposition, which we must battle against at the same time we fight against the governments. [...]

Marx shares Vaillant's opinion. We must reply with a challenge to all the governments, also in Switzerland, that are subjecting the International to persecutions. Reaction exists on the whole Continent; it is general and permanent – even in the United States and England – in one form or another.

We must announce to the governments: We know you are the armed power which is directed against the proletarians; we will move against you in peaceful way where it is possible, and with arms if it should become necessary.

---

[101] This text is taken from the synopsis of a speech given by Karl Marx (see note 1) at a session of 21 September, of the London Conference of 1871. The full version is in PI, II: 195–6.

Friedrich Engels, [Apropos of Working-Class Political Action][102]

Complete abstention from political action is impossible. The abstentionist press participates in politics every day. It is only a question of how one does it, and of what politics one engages in. For the rest, to us abstention is impossible. The working-class party functions as a political party in most countries by now, and it is not for us to ruin it by preaching abstention. Living experience, the political oppression of the existing governments compels the workers to occupy themselves with politics whether they like it or not, be it for political or for social goals. To preach abstention to them is to throw them into the embrace of bourgeois politics. The morning after the Paris Commune, which has made proletarian political action an order of the day, abstention is entirely out of the question.

We want the abolition of classes. What is the means of achieving it? The only means is political domination of the proletariat. For all this, now that it is acknowledged by one and all, we are told not to meddle with politics. The abstentionists say they are revolutionaries, even revolutionaries *par excellence*. Yet revolution is a supreme political act and those who want revolution must also want the means of achieving it, that is, political action, which prepares the ground for revolution and provides the workers with the revolutionary training without which they are sure to become the dupes of the Favres and Pyats[103] the morning after the battle. However, our politics must be working-class politics.

---

[102] This text by Friedrich Engels (see note 47) is the handwritten draft for a speech at the session of 21 September of the London Conference of 1871. It was partly included in PI, II: 197–8 and its full version in English can be found in Karl Marx-Friedrich Engels, *Selected Works*, vol. 2: 417–18 (Moscow: Progress, 1986).

[103] Jules Favre and Felix Peyat were leading political figures in France at the time.

The workers' party must never be the tagtail of any bourgeois party; it must be independent and have its goal and its own policy.

The political freedoms, the right of assembly and association, and the freedom of the press – those are our weapons. Are we to sit back and abstain while somebody tries to rob us of them? It is said that a political act on our part implies that we accept the exiting state of affairs. On the contrary, so long as this state of affairs offers us the means of protesting against it, our use of these means does not signify that we recognize the prevailing order.

74

Karl Marx – Friedrich Engels, [*On the Political Action of the Working Class and Other Matters*][104]

[...]

Formation of working women's branches

The Conference recommends the formation of female branches among the working class. It is, however, understood that this resolution does not at all interfere with the existence or formation of branches composed of both sexes.

General statistics of the working class

a. The Conference invites the General Council to enforce art. 5 of the original Rules relating to a general statistics of the working class, and the resolutions of the Geneva Congress, 1866, on the same subject.
b. Every local branch is bound to appoint a special committee of statistics, so as to be always ready, within the limits of its means, to answer any questions which may be addressed to it by the Federal Council or Committee of its country, or by the General Council. It is recommended to all branchesto remunerate the secretaries of the committee of statistics, considering the general benefit the working class will derive from their labour. [...]

---

[104] This text reproduces the main resolutions adopted at the London Conference of 1871. Written by Karl Marx (see note 1) and Friedrich Engels (see note 47), it was published in English in early November (London: International Printing Office, 1871) and in French and German a few days later. The full text may be found in GC, IV: 440–50.

International relations of Trades' Unions

The General Council is invited to assist, as has been done hitherto, the growing tendency of the Trades' Unions of the different countries to enter into relations with the Unions of the same trade in all other countries. The efficiency of its actions as the international agent of communication between the national Trades' societies will essentially depend upon the assistance given by these same societies to the General Labour Statistics pursued by the *International*.

The boards of Trade's Unions of all countries are invited to keep the General Council informed of the directions of their respective offices.

Agricultural producers

The conference invites the General Council and the Federal Councils or Committees to prepare, for the next Congress, reports on the means of securing the adhesion of the agricultural producers to the movement of the industrial proletariat.

Meanwhile, the Federal Council or Committee are invited to send agitators to the rural districts, there to organize publics meetings, to propagate the principles of the International and to found rural branches.

Political action of the working class

Considering the following passage of the preamble to the Rules:

'The economical emancipation of the working classes is the great end to which every political movement ought to be subordinate *as a means*';

That the Inaugural Address of the International Working Men's Association (1864) states:

'The lords of land and the lords of capital will always use their political privileges for the defence and perpetuation of their economical monopolies. So far from promoting, they will continue to lay every possible impediment in the way of the emancipation of labour... To conquer political power has therefore become the great duty of the working classes;'

That the Congress of Lausanne (1867) has passed this resolution:

'The social emancipation of the workmen is inseparable from their political emancipation';

That the declaration of the General Council relative to the pretended plot of the French Internationalists on the eve of the plebiscite (1870) says:

'Certainly by the tenor of our Statutes, all our branches in England, on the Continent, and in America have the special mission not only to serve as centres for the militant organization of the working class, but also to support, in their respective countries, every political movement tending towards the accomplishment of our ultimate end – the economical emancipation of the working class';

That false translations of the original Statutes have given rise to various interpretations which were mischievous to the development and action of the International Working Men's Association;

In presence of an unbridled reaction which violently crushes every effort at emancipation on the part of the working men, and pretends to maintain by brute force the distinction of classes and the political domination of the propertied classes resulting from it;

Considering, that against this collective power of the propertied classes the working class cannot act, as a class, except by constituting itself into a political party, distinct from, and opposed to, all old parties formed by the propertied classes;

That this constitution of the working class into a political party is indispensable in order to ensure the triumph of the social revolution and its ultimate end – the abolition of classes;

That the combination of forces which the working class has already effected by its economical struggles ought at the same time to serve as a lever for its struggles against the political power of landlords and capitalists –

The Conference recalls to the members of the *International*:

That in the militant state of the working class, its economical movement and its political action are indissolubly united.

General resolutions as to the countries where the regular organization of the international is interested with by the governments

In those countries where the regular organization of the international may for the moment have become impracticable in consequence of government interference, the Association, and its local groups, may be reformed under various other names, but all secret societies properly so called are and remain formally excluded.

Karl Marx, Friedrich Engels, *[Against Sectarianism]*[105]

[...] According to Article I of its Statutes, the International Working Men's Association admits 'all working men's societies aiming at the same end, viz., the protection, advancement, and complete emancipation of the working classes'.

Since the various sections of workingmen in the same country, and the working classes in different countries, are placed under different circumstances and have attained to different degrees of development, it seems almost necessary that the theoretical notions which reflect the real movement should also diverge.

The community of action, however, called into life by the International Working Men's Association, the exchange of ideas facilitated by the public organs of different national section, and the direct debates at the General Congresses are sure by and by to engender a common theoretical programme.

Consequently, it belongs not to the function of the General Council to subject the programme of the Alliance to a critical examination. [...] All we have to ask is whether its general tendency does not run against the general tendency of the International Working Men's Association, viz., the complete emancipation of the working class. One phrase in your programme lies open to this objection. It occurs [in] Article 2: 'The Alliance wants above all political, economic, and social equalization of classes.'

---

[105] Extract from a text written by Karl Marx (see note 1) and Friedrich Engels (see note 47) between late January and early March 1872, entitled *Fictitious Splits in the International*. It was published in May as a 39-page brochure in French, with a print run of 2,000, by the Imprimerie coopérative de Genève. It was signed by the whole GC and contained *The General Council of the International Working Men's Association to the International Alliance of Socialist Democracy* (here also reproduced in part), which the GC had adopted at its session of 9 March 1869, and sent to the organization directed by Mikhail Bakunin after it had expressed its willingness to dissolve in order to merge with the IWMA. The full version may be found in GC, V: 356–409.

The 'equalization of classes', literally interpreted, comes to the 'harmony of capital and labour' so persistently preached by the bourgeois socialists. It is not the logically impossible 'equalization of classes', but the historically necessary, superseding 'abolition of classes', this true secret of the proletarian movement, which forms the great aim of the International Working Men's Association. [...]

It suits the principles of the International Working Men's Association to let every section freely shape its own theoretical programme, except the single case of an infringement upon its general tendency. [...]

The first phase of the proletariat's struggle against the bourgeoisie is marked by a sectarian movement. That is logical at a time when the proletariat has not yet developed sufficiently to act as a class. Certain thinkers criticize social antagonisms and suggest fantastic solutions thereof, which the mass of workers is left to accept, preach, and put into practice. The sects formed by these initiators are abstentionist by their very nature – i.e., alien to all real action, politics, strikes, coalitions, or, in a word, to any united movement. The mass of the proletariat always remains indifferent or even hostile to their propaganda. The Paris and Lyon workers did not want the St-Simonists, the Fourierists, the Icarians, any more than the Chartists and the English trade unionists wanted the Owenites. These sects act as levers of the movement in the beginning, but become an obstruction as soon as the movement outgrows them; after which they became reactionary. Witness the sects in France and England, and lately the Lassalleans in Germany, who after having hindered the proletariat's organization for several years ended up becoming simple instruments of the police. To sum up, we have here the infancy of the proletarian movement, just as astrology and alchemy are the infancy of science. If the International were to be founded, it was necessary that the proletariat go through this phase.

Contrary to the sectarian organization, with their vagaries and rivalries, the International is a genuine and militant organization of the proletarian class of all countries, united in their common struggle against the capitalists and the landowners, against their class power organized in the state. The International's Rules, therefore, speak of only simple 'workers' societies', all aiming for the same goal and accepting the same programme, which presents a general outline of the proletarian movement, while having its theoretical elaboration to be guided by the needs of the practical struggle and the exchange of ideas in the sections, unrestrictedly admitting all shades of socialist convictions in their organs and Congresses. [...]

All socialists see anarchy as the following programme: Once the aim of the proletarian movement – i.e., abolition of classes – is attained, the power of the state, which serves to keep the great majority of producers in bondage to a very small exploiter minority, disappears, and the functions of government become simple administrative functions.

The Alliance draws an entirely different picture. It proclaims anarchy in proletarian ranks as the most infallible means of breaking the powerful concentration of social and political forces in the hands of the exploiters. Under this pretext, it asks the International, at a time when the Old World is seeking a way of crushing it, to replace its organization with anarchy. [...]

76

James Guillaume, *[Anarchist politics]*[106]

There is a misunderstanding between us, and I must clarify it, for myself and in the name of my comrades; this misunderstanding had already appeared at Basel [Congress of 1869]. Our point of view is that which Hins had adopted at Brussels [Congress of 1868] when he declared: 'We do not want to participate either in current governments or in parliamentarism, we want to overthrow all governments.' Unfortunately, we have allowed ourselves to be described as abstentionists, a very poor name chosen by Proudhon. We are supporters of a certain politics, of social revolution, of the destruction of bourgeois politics and of the state. [...] We reject the seizure of the political power of the state, but demand, on the contrary, the total destruction of the state as an expression of political power.

---

[106] This text is an excerpt from the synopsis of a speech given by James Guillaume (see note 53) on 5 September 1872 at the Hague Congress. The full synopsis is found in PI, II: 360.

77

Paris Section, [*On the Importance of Having a Central Organization of the Working Class*][107]

Citizens, we do not intend to run after new adventures. Moreover, our ranks have been thinned, out best soldiers exiled or shot. We must not forget it. That is why we come to declare formally and absolutely that we have no interest in any material and violent demonstration until the cadres of the International in Paris have been reformed, until the working class forces have grouped, until each and every member of the International in Paris has become penetrated with social principles.

We reject and repulse at any price all compromise whatever with a purely political party. We do not want to be transformed into a secret society, neither do we want to sink in the bog of purely economic evolution. Because a secret society leads to adventures in which the people is always the victim, because purely economic evolution would lead to the creation of a new class, and this contradicts the spirit of the International.

We consider, claim and declare that we are and will remain the International. [...]

Let us say then that we are thinking of autonomy and concentration. Citizens, The Central Committee and the Commune gave the Paris proletariat a painful but fruitful experience.

Indeed it has experienced all that is disastrous in individual flounder between the centralizing tradition which is, so to speak, in the very marrow

---

[107] This text is an excerpt from the *Declaration of the Paris Sections to the Delegates of the International Association Assembled in Congress*. It was sent by the Ferré section, one of the first branches of the IWMA established after the defeat of the Paris Commune, and was read in one of the sessions of on 7 September at The Hague Congress (1872). Published 8 days later, in the newspaper *La Liberté*, the full text is in HAGUE: 233–6.

of the modern individual's bones and the concept of autonomy which is in his mind in the state of abstraction, of pure theory.

However, citizens, autonomy is the saving principle for modern society. But on the express and absolute condition that its exercise is regulated by consciousness of rights and duties. Otherwise, how could that exercise lead to anything but confusion and ruin when the individuals enjoying it are not conscious of rights and duties when they have to fight enemies disciplined by authority?

We must, we must at all costs, citizens, abandon the regions of pure theory, we must forget ourselves and think that the masses are ignorant, obstinate and inert owing to their mass of prejudices. And it is their education, their transformation, their emancipation, in the final account, that the international association has the mission to accomplish.

Federation derives from autonomy: and autonomy can offer no social and political guarantee unless it is based on the nation of rights and duties. [...]

To succeed in this task requires a central organization which disciplines working class action and distributes it everywhere. The General Council must therefore be an agency for spreading the general principles and the general wills of the proletariat.

We do not want the Council to be a head, a guidance. A thousand time no! That would result necessarily and fatally, in dictatorship. [...]

We want revolution everywhere, and if possible at the same time – because the need is for a general political revolution, the serious guarantee and the only guarantee of a general social revolution.

We have therefore decided not to accomplish a single material political action until our forces have become disciplined, conscious of the aim. The work is difficult and delicate, but it can be accomplished more quickly than is thought – with the method of perseverance, patient and rigorous selection of the combatants.

Mikhail Bakunin – James Guillaume, *[The Destruction of Political Power]*[108]

[...]

Nature of the political action of the proletariat

Considering:

That to want to impose on the proletariat a line of conduct or a uniform political programme as the only path that can lead to its social emancipation is a pretension as absurd as it is reactionary;

That no one has the right to deprive the autonomous federations and sections of the incontestable right to determine for themselves and pursue the line of political conduct that they believe to be best, and that any such effort would inevitably lead to the most revolting dogmatism;

That the aspirations of the proletariat can have no other object than the establishment of an economic organization and federation that is absolutely free, based on the labour and equality of all and absolutely independent of all political government, and that this organization and federation can only be the result of the spontaneous action of the proletariat itself, the various trades, and the autonomous communes;

---

[108] This text, published in English for the first time, corresponds to the third and fourth sections of the resolutions adopted at the International Congress of Saint-Imier (15–16 September 1872), an assembly held soon after The Hague Congress (1872), that constituted the immediate response of the most resolute dissidents. This text was written by Mikhail Bakunin (see note 39) and James Guillaume (see note 53), between 12 September and 13 September, during a preparatory meeting held in Zurich. It was printed with the title *Résolutions du congrès international anti-autoritaire tenu à Saint-Imier 15 septembre 1872*. Neuchâtel: G. Guillaume Fils,1872. Its full version is also found in PI, III: 5–9.

Considering that all political organization can be nothing other than the organization of domination, to the benefit of one class and the detriment of the masses, and that if the proletariat aimed to seize power, it would itself become a dominant and exploiting class;

The Congress meeting in Saint-Imier declares:

1. That the destruction of all political power is the first task of the proletariat;
2. That any organization of so-called provisional and revolutionary political power to bring about such destruction can only be a further deception, and would be as dangerous to the proletariat as all governments existing today;
3. That, rejecting all compromise to reach the fulfilment of social Revolution, the proletarians of all countries must establish, outside of all bourgeois politics, the solidarity of revolutionary action.

Organization of labour resistance – Statistics

Liberty and labour are the basis of morality, strength, life and future wealth. But labour, if it is not freely organized, becomes oppressive and unproductive for the labourer; that is why the organization of work is the indispensable condition for the true and complete emancipation of the worker.

However labour cannot be exercised freely without possession of raw materials and society's capital, and cannot be organized unless the worker, emancipating himself from political and economic tyranny, gains the right to fully develop all his faculties. No state, that is to say no top-down government and administration of the popular masses – necessarily founded upon bureaucracy, military, espionage, clergy – can ever establish a society based on labour and justice, since by the very nature of its organization it is inevitably driven to oppress the former and deny the latter.

In our view, the worker can never free himself from long-standing oppression if he does not replace this debilitating and demoralizing body with the free federation of all groups of producers, founded on solidarity and equality.

Indeed, several efforts have already been made to organize work so as to improve the condition of the proletariat, but any improvement was soon absorbed by the privileged class, which strives continually, without restraint or limit, to exploit the working class. However the advantages of this organization are such that, even in the present state of things, it can not be relinquished. It increasingly brings the proletariat together in a community of interests, develops its collective life, prepares it for the final struggle. Moreover, the free and spontaneous organization of labour, which is what must replace the privileged and authoritarian organization of the political state, will once established be the permanent guarantee of maintaining the economic organism against the political organism.

Consequently, leaving to the experience of the social revolution the details of positive organization, we intend to organize and integrate resistance on a broad scale. We regard the strike as a precious means of struggle, but we have no illusions about its economic results. We accept it as a product of the antagonism between labour and capital, necessarily having the effect of making workers more and more aware of the gulf between the bourgeoisie and the proletariat, of strengthening the organization of workers, and, through the reality of simple economic struggles, of preparing the proletariat for the great and definitive revolutionary struggle that, destroying all privilege and distinction of class, will give the worker the right to enjoy the whole product of his labour, and thus the means to develop collectively all his intellectual, physical and moral strength. [...]

Friedrich Adolph Sorge, [The Struggle With Bourgeois Society][109]

[…] The official report of the General Council of the Hague Congress gives a short account of it, concluding thus: 'You, the delegates of the working class, are at this moment assembled to give a more militant organisation to a society which wants to emancipate labour, and to extinguish national hatreds.'

Workers, if our wounds reopen, when we recall the persecutions we have endured, when we recount this history of the International, of which we ourselves have been the protagonists, we inevitably arrive at the conclusion that there are for us but two alternatives, two paths to choose from.

The alternatives are:

A *submission*, patient, servile and passive to modern society, which assigns us to the position of dispossessed wage-slaves with the absolutely certain prospect of ever-increasing impoverishment and continual deprivations, until the point of famine.

Or else *resistance*, the struggle not only against the few privileged groups of the old society, as in the long-standing, historical struggles between classes, but against the entire organization of this society in the midst of which we live, that is to say against bourgeois society.

One thing is certain, as demonstrated by our own experience:

Modern bourgeois society, though divided into hostile factions, one against the other, and always openly or secretly at war – this society is united and

---

[109] This text is an excerpt from the *Public Address to Members of the IWMA* dated 20 October 1872. It was the first act of the new GC of the 'centralist' IWMA in New York. Friedrich Adolph Sorge [1828–1906] was a German Communist who immigrated to the United States in 1852. Author of various articles on the labour movement, he was among the founders of the overseas IWMA, and was its General Secretary between 1872 and 1874. This text was published on 15 December 1872, in the Belgian magazine *La Science Populaires* and its full version is found in PI, III: 15–17.

unanimous when it comes to maintaining at all costs its political and economic domination over the worker.

It thus vehemently opposes all attempts of the working class to produce an advantageous transformation of the existing social order. […] Given that bourgeois society is possessed of a powerful, centralized organization to oppress us, are we to believe that we can make a single step towards our emancipation through decentralization, division, isolation, disorganization!

When, upon its birth, bourgeois society solemnly proclaimed 'the freedom of the individual,' a new slavery of the working classes resulted from this principle. […]

80

Friedrich Adolph Sorge – Carl Speyer, [*Passing on the Torch*][110]

Comrades,

The general delegate conference in Philadelphia has dissolved the General Council of the International Working Men's Association, and the outward bond of the association has thereby ceased to exist.

'The International is dead', the bourgeoisie of every country will once more cry out, and it will trumpet its scorn and its joy at the decisions of the conference, considering them proof of the defeat of the international workers' movement. Let us not be confused by the shouts of our enemies! Taking into account the political situation in Europe, we have given up the organization of the International, but in its place we see its principles recognized and defended by progressive workers throughout the civilized world.

Let us give our European comrades a little time to gain strength and settle matters in their country, and before long they will undoubtedly be in a position to break down the barriers that separate them from one another and set them apart from workers in other parts of the world.

Comrades! You who with heartfelt love have proclaimed yourselves members of the International will find the means to enlarge the circle of its supporters, even without an organization. You will bring new militants who continue to accomplish the task that our association set itself.

---

[110] This text is an excerpt from the *Report of the General Council Delegates to the Conference of the International Working Men's Association held in Philadelphia* read on 15 July 1876. It marked the end of the 'centralist' IWMA. It was likely co-authored by Friedrich Adolph Sorge (see note 109) and Carl Speyer [1845-unk.], a German carpenter and the last General Secretary of the 'centralist' IWMA. The full version is in PI, IV: 407–12.

The comrades of America promise you that they too will take care to safeguard what has been obtained by members of the International in this country, until more favourable circumstances unite the workers of all countries in joint action, and the call rings out again more strongly:

Workers of the world, unite!

Appendix

Eugène Pottier, *The Internationale*[111]

Arise ye pris'ners of starvation
Arise ye wretched of the earth
For justice thunders condemnation
A better world's in birth!
No more tradition's chains shall bind us
Arise, ye slaves, no more in thrall;
The earth shall rise on new foundations
We have been naught we shall be all.

[Refrain]
'Tis the final conflict
Let each stand firm in place
The International working class
shall be the human race.
'Tis the final conflict
Let each stand firm in place
The International working class
shall be the human race.

We want no condescending saviours
To rule us from their judgment hall
We workers ask not for their favours

---

[111] This text is the slightly modified English translation by Charles H. Kerr [1860–1944] of what can be considered the most famous song of the labour movement. Written by Eugène Pottier [1816–87], in 1871, to celebrate the Paris Commune, it was sung to the tune of the Marseillaise until 1888, when Pierre Degeyter [1848–1932] composed the melody that became famous around the world. Translated into over 100 languages, it was also the national anthem of the Soviet Union until 1944.

Let us consult for all.
To make the thief disgorge his booty
To free the spirit from its cell
We must ourselves decide our duty
We must decide and do it well.

[Refrain]

The law oppresses us and tricks us,
the wage slave system drains our blood;
The rich are free from obligation,
The laws the poor delude.
Too long we've languished in subjection,
Equality has other laws;
'No rights,' says she 'without their duties,
No claims on equals without cause.'

[Refrain]

Behold them seated in their glory
The kings of mine and rail and soil!
What have you read in all their story,
But how they plundered toil?
Fruits of the workers' toil are buried
In strongholds of the idle few
In fighting for their restitution
The workers only claim their due.

[Refrain]

We toilers from all fields united
Join hand in hand with all who work;
The earth belongs to us, the workers,
No room here for the shirk.
How many on our flesh have fattened!

But if the greedy birds of prey
Shall vanish from the sky some morning
The blessed sunlight then will stay.

[Refrain]

Bibliography

Introduction

This bibliography has been divided into three parts. The first section (A) comprises the original editions of all reports of the congresses and conferences of the International Working Men's Association, as published by the organization itself at the time. The second (B) contains printed collections and publications subsequently gathered from the primary source documents; while the third (C) brings together the most significant books and articles written on the subject. To keep the length manageable, the writings of the main protagonists of the organization, as well as biographies written about them, have been omitted. More comprehensive bibliographic information may be obtained by consulting Maximilien Rubel, 'Bibliographie de la Première Internationale', in *Cahiers de l'I.S.E.A., Série S*, n. 8 (1964): 251–75, and Bert Andréas – Miklós Molnár (eds), *La première Internationale*, vol. IV: *Les congrès et les conférences de l'Internationale, 1873-1877*, pp. 745–80.

A Reports of congresses

Congrès ouvrier de l'Association International des Travailleurs tenu à Genève du 3 au 8 septembre 1866. Geneva: J.-C. Ducommun – G. Oettinger.

Procès-verbaux du congrès de l'Association internationale des travailleurs rèuni à Lausanne de 2 au 8 semptember 1867. Le Chaux-de-Fond: Imprimerie de la Voix de l'Avenir.

Troisième Congrès de l'Association Internationale des Travailleurs. Compte rendu officiel. Bruxelles: L. Lemoine.

Association internationale des Travailleurs. Compte rendu du IVe Congrès international tenu à Bâle, en septembre 1869. Bruxelles: Désiré Brismée.

Compte rendu officiel du Sixième Congrès général de l'Association internationale des Travailleurs tenu à Genève du 1er au 6 septembre 1873. [Le] Locle: Courvoisier.

Compte rendu officiel du VII.e Congrès Général de l'Association Internationale des Travailleurs tenu à Bruxelles du 7 au 13 september 1874. Verviers: Emile Counard et Cie.

Association internationale des travailleurs. Compte rendu officiel du VIIIe congrès général tenu à Berne du 26 au 30 october 1876. Berne: Lang.

Compte-rendu du 9e Congrès général de l'Association internationale des travailleurs, tenu à Verviers les 6, 7 et 8 september 1877, in Le Mirabeau, 10, n. 426.

B Primary sources

Institute of Marxism-Leninism of the C.C., C.P.S.U. (ed.) (1962), *The General Council of the First International 1864–1866: Minutes*. Moscow: Foreign Languages Publishing House [2nd ed. 1974].

—(1964), *The General Council of the First International 1866–1868: Minutes*. Moscow: Progress [2nd ed. 1973].

—(1966), *The General Council of the First International 1868–1870: Minutes*. Moscow: Progress [2nd ed. 1974].

—(1967), *The General Council of the First International 1870–1871: Minutes*. Moscow: Progress [2nd ed. 1974].

—(1968), *The General Council of the First International 1871–1872: Minutes*. Moscow: Progress [2nd ed. 1974].

Burgelin, Henri, Knut Langfeldt and Miklós Molnár (eds) (1962a), *La première Internationale*, vol. I [1866–1868]. Geneva: Droz.

—(1962b), *La première Internationale*, vol. II [1869–1872]. Geneva: Droz.

Andréas, Bert and Miklós Molnár (eds) (1971a), *La première Internationale*, vol. III: *Les conflits au sein de l'Internationale, 1872–1873*. Geneva: Institut Universitaire de Hautes Études Internationales.

—(1971b), *La première Internationale*, vol. VI: *Les congrès et les conférences de l'Internationale, 1873–1877*. Geneva: Institut Universitaire de Hautes Études Internationales.

Gerth, Hans (ed.) (1958), *The First International: Minutes of the Hague Congress of 1872*. Madison: University of Wisconsin Press.

Institute of Marxism-Leninism of the C.C., C.P.S.U. (ed.) (1976), *The Hague Congress of the First International*, vol. 1: *Minutes and Documents*. Moscow: Progress.

—(1978), *The Hague Congress of the First International*, vol. 2: *Reports and Letters*. Moscow: Progress.

Bernstein, Samuel (ed.) (1961), 'Papers of the General Council of the International Workingmen's Association. New York: 1872–1876.' *Annali dell'Istituto Giangiacomo Feltrinelli* IV: 401–549.

C Secondary literature

Archer, Julian P. W. (1997), *The First International in France, 1864–1872: Its Origins, Theories, and Impact*. Lanham/New York/Oxford: University Press of America.
Bernstein, Samuel (1962), *The First International in America*. New York: A.M. Kelley.
Bourgin, Georges (1938), 'La lutte du Gouvernement Français Contre la Première Internationale; Contribution à l'Histoire de l'Après-Commune'. *International Review for Social History* 4: 39–138.
Braunthal, Julius (1966 [1961]), *History of the International*. New York: Nelson (trans. from the German ed.).
Bravo, Gian Mario (ed.) (1978), *La Prima Internazionale*. Rome: Editori Riuniti.
—(1979), *Marx e La Prima Internazionale*. Rome/Bari: Laterza.
Centre national de la recherche scientifique (1968), *La Premiere Internationale, l'institute, l'implantation, le rayonnement*. Paris: Editions du Centre national de la recherche scientifique.
Collins, Henry and Chimen Abramsky (1965), *Karl Marx and the British Labour Movement: Years of the First International*. London: Macmillan.
Colloque International sur La première Internationale, 1964: Paris (1968), *La première Internationale: l'institution, l'implantation, le rayonnement, Paris, 16–18 novembre 1964*. Paris: Centre National de la Recherche Scientifique.
Del Bo, Giuseppe (ed.) (1958–63), *Répertorie international des sources pour l'étude des mouvement sociaux aux XIXe et Xxe siècles. La Première Internationale*, vol. I: *Périodiques 1864–1877* (1958); vol. II: *Imprimés 1864–1876* (1961); vol. III: *Imprimés 1864–1876* (1963). Paris: Armand Colin.
Dlubek, Rolf, Evgenija Stepanova, Irene Bach, et al. (eds) (1964), *Die 1. Internationale in Deutschland (1864–1872) Dokumente Und Materialien*. Berlin: Dietz.
Drachkovitch, Milorad M. (ed.) (1966), *The Revolutionary Internationals, 1864–1943*. Stanford: Stanford University Press.
Engberg, Jens (ed.) (1985; 1992), *Den Internationale Arbejderforening for Danmark*, (2 vols). Copenhagen: Selskabet til forskning i arbejderbevaegelsens historie.
Fernbach, David (2010 [1974]), 'Introduction', in Karl Marx (ed.), *The First International and After: Political Writings (vol. 3)*. London: Verso, pp. 9–71.
Freymond, Jacques (ed.) (1964), *Etudes et Documents sur la Première Internationale en Suisse*. Geneva: Droz.
Giele, Jacques (1973), *De Eerste Internationale in Nederland. Een onderzoek naar het ontstaan van de Nederlandse arbeidersbeweging van 1868 tot 1876*. Nijmegen: SUN.

Guillaume, James (1969 [1905–10]), *L'Internationale, Documents et Souvenirs (1864–1878)* (4 vols). New York: Burt Franklin (trans. from the French ed.).

Haupt, Georges (1978), *L'internazionale Socialista dalla Comune a Lenin*. Turin: Einaudi.

Lehning, Arthur (1965), 'Introduction', in A. Lehning, A. J. C. Rüter, P. Scheibert (eds), *Bakunin – Archiv*, vol. II: *Michel Bakounine et les Conflits dans l'Internationale*. Leiden: Brill, pp. ix–lxvi.

—(1977), 'Introduction', in Arthur Lehning (ed.), *Bakunin – Archiv*, vol. VI: *Michel Bakounine sur la Guerre Franco-Allemande et la Révolution Sociale en France (1870–1871)*. Leiden: Brill, pp. xi–cxvii.

Léonard, Mathieu (2011), *L'émancipation des travailleurs. Une histoire de la Première Internationale*. Paris: La Fabrique.

Masini, Pier Carlo (1963), *La Federazione italiana dell'Associazione Internazionale dei Lavoratori*. Milano: Avanti!.

McClellan, Woodford (1979), *Revolutionary Exiles: The Russians in the First International and the Paris Commune*. London/Totowa, NJ: Frank Cass.

Mins, L. E. (1937), *Founding of the First International: A Documentary Record*. New York: International Publishers.

Molnar, Miklos (1963), *Le declin de la Premiere Internationale*. Genève: Droz.

Morgan, Roger (1965), *The German Social Democrats and the First International, 1864–1872*. New York: Cambridge University Press.

Nettlau, Max (1969), *La Premiere Internationale en Espagne (1868–1888)*. Dordrecht: D. Reidel.

Rjazanov, David (1926), 'Zur Geschichte der Ersten Internationale. I. Die Entstehung der Internationalen Arbeiter-Association'. *Marx-Engels Archiv* I: 119–202.

Rosselli, Nello (1967 [1927]), *Mazzini E Bakunin*. Turin: Einaudi.

Rougerie, Jacques (1972), 'L'A.I.T. et le mouvement ouvrier a Paris pendant les evenements de 1870-1871'. *International Review of Social History* 17(1): 3–102.

Rubel, Maximilien (1964–5), 'Karl Marx et la Premiere Internationale. Une chronologie. (I: 1864-1869; II: 1870-1876)'. *Cahiers de l'I.S.E.A.*, Série S, n. 8: 9–82; and n. 9: 5–70.

—(1965), 'La Charte De La Premiere Internationale'. *Le Mouvement Social* 51: 3–22.

Schrupp, Antje (1999), *Nicht Marxistin und auch nicht Anarchistin. Frauen in der ersten Internationale*. Königstein/Taunus: Ulrike Helmer.

Serrano, Carlos Secco (ed.) (1969), *Actas de los consejos y commission federal de la region espanola (1870-1874)* (2 vols). Barcellona: Universidad de Barcelona.

Stekloff, G. M. (1928), *History of the First International* (trans. from the third Russian ed.). London: Dorrit.

Verdes, Jeannine (1964), 'Les delegues francais aux Congres et Conferences de l'A.I.T.' *Cahiers de l' I.S.E.A.*, Série S, n. 8: 83–176.

Index

abolition of classes   24, 47, 268, 276–7, 281, 285, 288–9
American Civil War   73, 230, 256, 258, 259
anarchism   xvi, 27, 37, 56, 61, 61n. 155, 62, 63, 135n. 26, 183, 183n. 50, 185–6, 187, 192, 197, 289
Applegarth, Robert   17, 136n. 27
Aubry, Emile Hector   180n. 46
authoritarian   40, 55, 105, 183, 185, 187, 190, 192–3, 295
autonomists   11, 42, 51–4, 57, 57n. 145, 59–60, 60n. 150, 61, 61n. 155, 63, 66, 67

Bakunin, Mikhail   xvi, 8, 23–4, 27–8, 31, 37–41, 42, 47, 49–50, 51–3, 53n. 132, 53n. 134, 54, 55, 55n. 138, 55n. 140, 56–7, 58, 60, 110n. 14, 161, 161n. 39, 173, 176, 182–3, 183n. 50, 184–6, 287n. 105
Basel Congress (1869)   23–4, 25, 28, 67, 132n. 25, 135n. 26, 136n. 27, 159n. 38, 161n. 39, 163n. 40, 175n. 43, 176n. 44, 178n. 45, 290
Bebel, August   30, 275, 278, 279
Becker, Johann Philipp   12, 22, 27, 28n. 65, 58, 59, 143, 143n. 30
Bee-Hive, The   1, 12, 73n. 1, 89n. 7, 124n. 21, 130n. 24, 206n. 57, 257n. 89, 259n. 91
Berne Congress (1876–'Autonomist')   62, 67, 192n. 53
Blanqui, Louis Auguste   21n. 44, 26, 276n. 99
Blanquism   32, 37, 38, 41, 42, 48
Bote vom Niederrheim, Der   122n. 19
bourgeoisie   20, 52, 58, 64, 147, 150, 180, 193, 197, 213, 222, 230, 243, 249–50, 274, 278, 288, 295, 298
bourgeois revolution   217

bourgeois society   14, 34, 213–14, 219, 296–7
Brussels Congress (1868)   xiii, 2, 21–3, 26, 67, 89n. 7, 105n. 13, 113n. 15, 154n. 36, 170n. 42, 203n. 56, 206n. 58, 230n. 73, 232, 290
Brussels Congress (1874–'Autonomist')   62, 67, 187n. 52
Büchner, Ludwig   148, 148n. 32
bureaucracy   56, 183, 211, 274, 294

capitalism   3, 53, 235, 249
centralists   11, 48, 53, 57–9, 61, 66, 67
Chartist movement   76, 243, 288
children   84, 99, 102, 103–4, 160, 162, 198, 204, 206, 208, 220
church   2, 182, 183, 207, 207n. 59, 215
class struggle   37, 45, 55, 212, 223, 235
collective ownership   156, 161, 171–2, 174, 176, 199
collectivism   11, 19, 22n. 46, 23, 61n. 155, 89n. 7, 161, 193
  anarcho-   24, 44, 60
cooperative   16, 19, 20, 26, 85, 147, 149, 154, 156, 218
  association   90, 153, 155, 156
  banks   147
  labour   78, 85, 152
  movement   18, 77, 85, 148, 151
  system   3, 78, 85
Courrier Français, Le   12
Courrier International, Le   12, 83n. 3, 228n. 71
crisis   xv, 10, 25, 41, 42, 50, 76, 106, 107, 219n. 65, 241, 256

Daily News, The   255n. 88
de Beaumont, Jean Henri   99, 99n. 10
debt   164, 180, 183, 205, 212, 219n. 64, 219n. 65, 259
Degeyter, Pierre   300n. 111

de Paepe, Cesar   18, 19n. 38, 21, 22, 42, 60, 62, 63–4, 101n. 11, 126, 126n. 22, 147, 148, 170, 178, 187, 194, 208, 229, 230
dictatorship   52, 56, 183, 292
Dupleix, François   99, 99n. 10
Dupont, Eugene   21n. 44, 36n. 87, 58, 228, 228n. 71, 247

Eccarius, Johann Georg   5, 25, 40, 41, 58, 60, 62, 152, 152n. 34, 161, 163n. 40, 228, 261, 269
education   64, 85, 90, 129, 137, 153n. 35, 155, 169, 178, 190, 195, 203–5, 206, 206n. 58, 207, 208, 215, 272
Emancipación, La   35
emancipation   xii, 14, 62, 64, 65, 78–9, 83, 87, 89, 97, 102, 109, 114, 116, 116n. 16, 139, 147, 148, 156, 198, 213, 221, 218, 227, 233, 236, 241, 242, 244, 250, 252, 258, 265–6, 272, 274, 287, 292, 294, 297
  economic(al)   19, 56, 217, 265, 273, 284, 285
  political   271–2, 285
  self-   38, 55
  social   165, 269, 271–2, 285, 293
  women's   3, 19, 101, 101n. 11
Engels, Friedrich   2n. 3, 9n. 23, 28, 42, 45, 47–8, 54, 58, 182, 182n. 47, 251, 265, 265n. 94, 274n. 98, 281, 281n. 102, 283, 287
environment   22
Eslens, P.   101, 101n. 11

Fanelli, Giuseppe   27, 28
feudalism   211, 213
Fluse, Pierre   110, 110n. 14
Fox, Peter   228, 228n. 71
fraternity   1, 2, 79, 112, 143, 227, 236, 238, 265, 268
free trade   74, 76, 129
French Revolution   211, 220n. 68

Garbe, R. L.   148, 148n. 32
Garibaldi, Giuseppe   35
Gazzettino Rosa, Il   35

General Association of German Workers   4, 7, 12, 28, 30n. 69, 44, 61, 62
General Council   xvi, 5, 5n. 9, 6n. 11, 9, 9n. 23, 10, 10n. 24, 11–13, 17–18, 20, 22–4, 25–7, 29, 31–2, 35, 36, 37–41, 42–6, 46n. 112, 47–9, 50–1, 57–61, 116, 131, 141, 143, 250, 266–8, 283–5, 287, 292, 298
Geneva Congress (1866)   10, 13, 14, 38, 67, 83, 83n. 3, 92, 97n. 8, 206n. 58, 278, 283
Geneva Congress (1873–'Autonomist')   61–2, 67, 135n. 26, 143n. 30
Geneva Congress (1873–'Centralist')   59, 67
Geneva Peace Congress   18, 23, 229, 233–4, 233n. 76, 234
Grinand, Aimé   154, 154n. 36
Guillaume, James   27, 39, 41, 47, 52–3, 58, 60, 60n. 150, 62–3, 192, 192n. 53, 194, 197, 290, 293

Hafner   233, 233n. 76
Hague Congress (1872)   xiv, 9n. 23, 18n. 37, 38n. 92, 42, 43, 46, 46n. 112, 49, 52–3, 57–8, 60–1, 66, 67, 126n. 22, 293n. 108, 180n. 46, 242n. 82, 290n. 106, 291n. 107, 293n. 108, 296
Hamann, Johann   15n. 31
Herman, Alfred   141, 141n. 29
Hins, Eugène   101, 101n. 11, 135, 156, 290
House of Commons   74, 78
House of Lords   73, 159

imperialism   213
industry   21, 73, 75, 77, 84, 101, 105–7, 120, 122, 132, 134, 135, 136, 139, 152, 171, 188, 190, 195–6, 212–13
inheritance   161n. 39, 163–5
  abolition of the right of   159–60, 161, 164
  right of   24, 160, 161–2, 163–5
International Alliance for Socialist Democracy   23–4, 27–8, 47, 51, 159, 183–6, 287, 289

Ireland   36, 58, 247n. 84, 249–50, 251–2, 269

Johnson, Andrew   257n. 89, 258
Journal de l'Association Internationale des Travailleurs   12, 26n. 58, 199n. 55
Jung, Hermann   58, 228, 228n. 71
Jura Federation   27, 39, 60–2

Kaub, Karl   269, 269n. 95
Kerr, Charles H.   300n. 111
Klassenstaat   192–3, 196
Kugelmann, Ludwig   235n. 77

Lafargue, Paul   10n. 24, 42, 47, 182n. 47
laisser faire   194–5, 198
landowner(ship)   19, 162, 170, 172, 178, 178n. 45, 220n. 68, 235, 288
Lassalle, Ferdinand   4, 12, 14, 14n. 29, 53n. 134
Lausanne Congress (1867)   5, 18, 19, 67, 99, 124n. 21, 206n. 58, 228n. 71, 229n. 72, 233, 271, 285
Law, Harriet   116n. 16, 207, 207n. 59
L'Égalité   35, 271n. 96
Lessner, Friedrich   58, 122n. 19
Liberté, La   51, 52n. 128, 101n. 11, 291n. 107
Liebknecht, Wilhelm   12, 23, 28, 30, 63, 275, 278–9
Lincoln, Abraham   255n. 88, 256, 257, 257n. 89, 258, 258n. 90, 259
London Conference (1865)   11, 19, 67
London Delegate Conference (1871)   xvi, 26n. 59, 36, 38, 38n. 92, 39, 41, 43, 45–6, 50, 53, 61, 67, 242n. 81, 265n. 94, 276n. 99, 278n. 100, 280n. 101, 281n. 102, 283n. 104
Lucraft, Chartist Benjamin   34
'lumpenproletariat'   54

machine   57, 99, 100, 102, 104, 105, 114, 155, 185, 190
machinery   76, 90–1, 99, 100, 103–4, 105, 105n. 13, 106–8, 110–12, 114, 188, 190, 211, 217

Marly, Jean   99, 99n. 10
Marseillaise   237
Marx, Karl   xii, xv, 4–6, 7n. 16, 10, 13–14, 15n. 31, 18, 18n. 37, 20, 22, 24–5, 29, 31–3, 36–8, 38n. 92, 39, 41, 42, 45, 46n. 112, 47–50, 51, 54–5, 55n. 138, 56, 61, 64–5, 73, 73n. 1, 74n. 2, 83, 97, 103, 119, 122, 122n. 19, 130, 159, 163, 175, 182, 206, 211, 228, 228n. 71, 235, 236, 240, 242, 244, 249, 255, 257, 259, 265, 265n. 94, 273, 278, 280, 283, 287
Mazzini, Giuseppe   4, 34, 39
middle class   34, 45, 77, 85, 86, 147, 160, 176, 211, 213, 217, 219–20, 241, 243, 256, 259
Miner, The   12, 269n. 95
Mirabeau, La   199n. 55
motherhood   102
Müller, Louis   148, 148n. 32
Murat, André   148, 148n. 32
mutual credit   90, 99, 148
mutualism   3, 11, 13–14, 18–19, 20–1, 23–4, 25, 43, 52, 89n. 7, 148n. 32, 148n. 33, 150, 152

negative politics   52

Odger, George   1, 34, 269, 269n. 95
Owen, Robert   14, 78, 103

Pall-Mall Gazette, The   236n. 78, 240n. 80
Paris Commune   6, 10, 31–2, 32n. 72, 34, 38, 42, 49–50, 152n. 34, 181, 197, 211, 214–24, 243, 244, 276n. 99, 281, 291, 291n. 107, 300n. 111
  bloody week   33
pauperism   73, 106, 154, 231, 259
Pellicer, Rafael Farga   28
People's State   53, 60, 62, 193, 196
Perron, Charles   271, 271n. 96
petty bourgeoisie   219n. 65
Peuple Belge, Le   xvii
Philadelphia Delegate Conference (1876–'Centralist')   59, 67, 298, 298n. 110
Pindy, Jean Louis   32, 132, 132n. 25

political abstentionism 45, 51, 278, 280, 281, 288, 290
political party 38, 38n. 92, 46, 53, 53n. 132, 58, 64–5, 76, 78, 199, 268, 269, 274, 275, 281–2, 285, 291
positive politics 52–3
Pottier, Eugène xvii, 300, 300n. 111
poverty 73–4, 76, 126, 138, 169, 178, 249
proletariat 8, 39, 45–6, 48, 52–5, 55n. 138, 56, 64, 138–9, 149, 150, 152, 176, 178–9, 180–1, 186, 197, 213–14, 221, 223, 230, 244, 249, 281, 284, 288, 292, 293–5
property
  landed 21, 23, 129, 170–2, 174, 178–9, 249
  private 159, 163–5, 176, 183, 198, 214
protectionism 107, 129
Proudhon, Pierre-Joseph 3, 14, 21, 28, 52, 148n. 33, 170, 187, 194, 290
Proudhonism 18, 19–20, 23, 24, 26, 175
public health 74–5, 197–8

Quinet, Ferdinand 99, 99n. 10

Reclus, Elisée 175n. 43
Réforme Sociale, La 35
Reform League 11, 17
republican 4n. 5, 30, 32, 85, 212, 241, 247
resistance funds 128, 133, 139, 140
resistance societies 26, 64, 127, 127n. 23, 128–9, 132–3, 135, 136–7, 140, 143, 178, 196
revolution
  economic 235
  social 55, 55n. 138, 61, 138, 159–60, 164, 249–50, 268, 285, 290, 292, 294–5
Reymond 271
Robin, Paul 101, 101n. 11
Romande Federation 27, 58

Saint-Imier Congress xvi, 53, 59, 60, 293n. 108, 294
St Martin's Hall 1–2, 5, 50, 79
Schettel, Adrien 99

Schwitzguébel, Adhemar 47, 138, 138n. 28
Science Populaires, La 296n. 109
secret societies 4n. 5, 38, 55, 185, 286, 291
self-government 88, 215
Seward, William H. 258, 258n. 90
slavery 79, 119, 122, 163, 217, 230, 255–6, 257–8, 258n. 90, 297
  modern 180, 230
  wage 85, 86, 218, 296, 301
Social Democratic Workers' Party of Germany 7, 23, 28, 30, 35, 44, 58, 68, 235n. 77, 238, 240
socialism xv, 4, 4n. 5, 15n. 31, 21, 22, 32, 35, 46, 54–7, 62–5, 148n. 33, 171, 187, 193, 199, 204, 208, 276–7, 288–9
Socialist Congress 63–4
Socialisten 35
solidarity 2, 8, 15–16, 24, 34, 52–3, 59, 76–7, 93, 112, 114, 139, 142, 143, 153, 171, 205, 276, 294
  international 51–2, 114, 129, 132–3, 227, 265
Sorge, Friedrich Adolph 40, 59, 296, 296n. 109, 298, 298n. 110
Speyer, Carl 298, 298n. 110
spontaneous movement 10, 16, 85, 86, 187, 188, 197, 293, 295
standing army 88, 92, 211, 214–15, 217
state 13, 14n. 29, 21, 53, 53n. 132, 54, 56–7, 91, 178–9, 183, 187–91, 192–3, 194–8, 205, 208, 211–13, 274, 294–5
  abolition of 56, 176, 183–4, 186, 187, 192, 195, 290
  (non-) Authoritarian 185, 190
  bourgeois 178, 193, 197
  central(ized) 53n. 134, 173, 211
  ownership 19, 169
Steens, Eugène 105, 105n. 13
strike 3, 12, 15–18, 20, 26, 44, 57, 64, 89, 92, 97, 100, 116, 124, 126–7, 127n. 23, 128, 130–1, 133–4, 139–40, 141, 295
  general strike 22, 61, 135n. 26
suffrage 169, 213–14, 216, 243, 275

Tartaret, Eugène   113, 113n. 15
taxation   75, 83n. 3, 87–8, 113, 160, 174, 175–8, 179, 203–5, 206, 220–1, 237
Times, The   2, 7, 18, 255n. 88
Tinayre, V.   116, 116n. 16
Tolain, Henri Louis   13, 19, 23, 25–6, 152, 152n. 34, 232, 233, 279
trades' union   1–4, 9, 13–14, 15n. 31, 17, 25, 34, 38, 44, 45, 58, 66, 86, 119n. 17, 137, 138, 143, 147, 178, 188, 196, 235, 284
transitional period   52, 56, 105, 164, 179, 195, 198
Tribune du Peuple, Le   12, 105n. 13

unemployment   114, 128, 271
unification of Germany   44
Utin, Nikolai   27

Vaillant, Édouard   32, 37, 48, 276, 276n. 99, 280
Varlin, Eugène   23, 25, 32
Vasseur, Jean   169, 169n. 41
Verviers Congress (1877–'Autonomist')   63, 67, 199n. 55
Vézinaud   271, 271n. 96

Volksstaat, Der   15n. 31, 35, 143n. 30, 244n. 82
von Bernhardi, Friedrich   9n. 22
von Bismarck, Otto   12, 30, 53n. 134, 217, 238
von Schweitzer, Johann Baptist   xii, 12, 28
Vorbote, Der   12, 143n. 30

wage   1–2, 14n. 29, 18, 76, 86, 101, 104, 105–8, 110–11, 113, 119, 119n. 17, 120–1, 126–7, 127n. 23, 128, 131, 133, 149, 222, 228, 249, 259
  abolition of   15, 90, 100, 121, 128, 133–4, 135
war   18, 19, 19n. 38, 22, 30, 31, 42, 52, 92, 93, 181, 184, 196, 220, 222, 229, 230–1, 232, 233–4, 237
  Franco-Prussian   29, 31, 236–9, 240–1, 279
Wheeler, George   269, 269n. 95
working hours   13, 24, 64, 77, 83, 90, 103, 109, 112, 113–15, 133, 136, 141, 155
Workman's Advocate, The   12, 269n. 95
World, The   242n. 81
Worley, William   269, 269n. 95

www.ingramcontent.com/pod-product-compliance
Ingram Content Group UK Ltd.
Pitfield, Milton Keynes, MK11 3LW, UK
UKHW021903220326
469204UK00008B/152